# CHRISTMAS WORLDWIDE

# CHRISTMAS WORLDWIDE

## A Guide to Customs and Traditions

Cathy C. Tucker

3282-TUCK

| Library of Congress Number: | | 00-192314 |
|---|---|---|
| ISBN #: | Hardcover | 0-7388-4037-8 |
| | Softcover | 0-7388-4038-6 |



This book was printed in the United States of America.

**To order additional copies of this book, contact:**
Xlibris Corporation
1-888-7-XLIBRIS
www.Xlibris.com
Orders@Xlibris.com

# CONTENTS



2-TUCK

3282-TUCK

# DEDICATION

---

To Ted, Edward Charles, Ellen and Ian

# Introduction

I am writing this book out of sheer necessity. During my thirty-four years as a media specialist, especially during my time in elementary and middle schools, each year in November or early December, I would receive requests for information from teachers doing units on Christmas customs around the world. The information available was very scanty, and the countries covered were invariably the same ones: Germany, the United States, France, or Italy. Another reason that I wish to author such as book is that the world is getting smaller each year with the media and the Internet; thus, peoples' customs are becoming very similar. Soon, indigenous Christmas celebrations will become fewer and fewer.

When I decided to go forward with my project, I thought that it would be a piece of cake. I could look for scattered sources and bring them together, much the way one writes a term paper. Was I wrong! I had to use many more primary sources than I had anticipated. I wrote to literally hundreds of embassies, churches, cathedrals, museums, and individuals such as anthropologists and teachers. I owe a deep gratitude to many missionaries out in the fields of some very remote places on this globe. I spent a year at the University of Cambridge researching and made several, extended visits to the Library of Congress in Washington, D.C. My correspondents range from His Eminence Cardinal Sin of the Philippines to a Catholic priest on a remote island of the Pacific that receives mail once every couple of months to an assistant from the Opinions Department at the China Daily News to many people in differing positions at embassies. I wrote to a priest who was assassinated during an uprising in Africa, and my letter was answered by his replacement. I have learned more about the Christians of this world and their practices in celebrating their Lord's birth; I have shed tears at some of the letters I received from some Third World countries; I even learned a lot of geography.

I include with each country the Merry Christmas greeting used plus the customs practiced from the beginning of the annual celebration through the close of the holiday season. I have also included legends and superstitions that are well known in each country and therefore an important part of the celebration.

I received much more information than I have been able to use; at times, I received interesting information, but simply, not enough to justify including the country. The countries included are diverse, and often, their inclusion is a result of materials I could find. If this book proves helpful, I hope to write another one to supplement this study by including countries not yet included.

# Antigua & Barbuda

Merry Christmas!

The British colonized the Caribbean islands making up the nation of Antigua & Barbuda over 300 years ago. They only recently became an independent country; therefore, the holiday traditions tend to reflect this English heritage. The geographical closeness to the United States has also had an influence on Christmas celebrations.

Fifty years ago, Christmas traditions were much different than today's. In those days, from Christmas Day to New Year's Day, groups of people in colorful costumes would cavort in the streets, with the bells and glass trinkets on their costumes glittering and tinkling as they danced madly about. There were tall and short ghosts in white sheets with lanterns in their hands. The tall ghosts walked on six, eight, or even ten-foot tall stilts. As these ghosts strutted around town, they would peer into upstairs windows to frighten people.

Masqueraders, costumed and masked, wandered in groups, striking fear into the hearts of the young. Some dressed as Highlanders in kilts, representing the large Scottish population in Antigua. The most famous masquerading figure was John Bull, a terrifying creature dressed in burlap and dried banana leaves with bull's horns mounted on his head. He would charge into the crowd from time to time, but he was usually a gentle bull, concentrating mainly on gathering coins tossed his way. Often, busloads of people would come from the countryside to the city of St. John to take part in these celebrations, especially on New Year's Day.

Santa Claus or Father Christmas appears today at the many

pre-Christmas parties organized for children by civic groups. Schools have Nativity pageants and lots of caroling.

Church decorations are usually limited to a manger scene and a star. In the stores and homes, artificial or real Christmas trees imported from North America glow with typically American-European decorations of lights, tinsel, and snow.

December 25 and 26 are public holidays as is New Year's Day. On December 24, most business places give their employees time off to shop, and most stores remain open until very late. People crowd the streets making last minute purchases. Swarms of children can be seen making demands upon their parents, even those who no longer believe that Santa brings gifts.

Some churches have midnight mass on Christmas Eve, while others have only Christmas Day services.

## Christmas Day

Christmas Day is a family day, and often those living alone join a family for the day. Santa visits the children, and gifts are exchanged. Christmas dinner results from lots of serious cooking and baking the previous day. Cakes, pies, puddings, ham, turkey, pork, rice, john cakes, sweet potatoes, yams, beans, salads, and above all, sorrel are served. Sorrel is a drink made from the pods of a member of the euphorbia plant family, and with its bright red color and distinctive flavor, it plays a very popular role in celebrating Christmas in the Caribbean. Many families, having filled themselves with Christmas dinner, settle down to some carols or to spinning tales. Some people receive New Year's cards and presents also.

# Australia

Merry Christmas!

The "down under" Australians celebrate Christmas in a variety of ways, reflecting the population's many ethnic groups. People of British background represent a large proportion of the population; thus, British traditions dominate the Australian Christmas. Many Australians struggle to keep alive the Christmas of their ancestors from many countries in spite of the diverse life styles of this country.

People often spend the holiday outdoors, since December 25 falls at midsummer when a lot of people enjoy their summer vacations at beaches, camping, swimming, surfing, flying kites, and playing cricket on the sand.

Father Christmas, or Santa Claus, according to where you live in Australia, delivers gifts on Christmas morning, and people exchange presents then also. In spite of the summer heat, he still wears the hot, red, fur-trimmed suit and heavy boots. He has been known to come roaring down the Nerang River on water skies, white-bearded and wearing swimming trunks. Father Christmas often delivers gifts such as beach balls, surfboards, sun hats, beach towels, and cricket sets.

For many Australians, after the exchange of gifts at breakfast, there are Christmas church services to attend. Then people often struggle in the warm weather to cook the traditional British Christmas dinner of turkey and Christmas pudding. When the weather becomes especially hot, dinner may be prepared in a camp oven, or dinner may turn into a picnic of cold turkey, ham, salad, and a cold plum pudding with ice cream.

After dinner, playing or watching sports, heading for the beach,



3282-TUCK

and sleeping are favorite pastimes. Sports traditionally play an important part of people's lives during the holiday season, especially tennis and cricket.

Christmas trees usually come from pine or gum; a gum tree belongs to the evergreen eucalyptus family. Tree decorations reflect European and American influences, mainly brightly colored ornaments, tinsel, and bright lights. Two popular decorative Christmas plants are the Christmas bush and the Christmas bell. The Christmas bush grows abundantly with multiples of tiny, white flowers tinged delicately with pink or blue and grows in soft, hazy clusters. The bright green leaves of the Christmas bell plant contrast beautifully with its red, bell-shaped flowers fringed with orange or yellow. Front doors often display beautiful arrangements of large ferns or palm leaves.

Popular Christmas cards depict not only Australia's white, sandy beaches, blue water, and spreading gum trees, but also often show scenes of snow-capped roofs, holly and ivy, and warmly-dressed people from far away, much colder climates.

A very lovely, universal Christmas tradition started in Australia, that of gathering in public places to sing Christmas carols. The most famous of these "carols by candlelight" began on Christmas Eve, 1937, in Melbourne. It continues today and is imitated in many places in Australia as well as broadcast by radio to many parts of the world. Some 300,000 people gather in the riverside Alexandra Gardens, with candles in hand, to sing the traditional Christmas carols and some particularly Australian songs. At midnight the people join hands and sing "Auld Lang Syne" as the bells welcome Christmas. Special candles are sold for the celebration, with the profits going to charity.

In 1943, Norman Banks, the man who started the Melbourne singing, wrote the first truly Australian Christmas carol, "Melbourne Carol."

> "Yuletide in Melbourne means mass jubilation
> And carols by candlelight on Christmas Eve.
> Thousands assemble in glad dedication
> To hail Him with joy, and the vow—I believe."

## Christmas in the Bush

Sixty-five percent of Australia's land consists of the "bush," a vast, nearly uninhabited area where people live very far apart in isolated families or in tiny towns, farming and mining.

Christmas in remote areas of the bush country often reflects a season of worry. Little rain during this time results in very dry conditions, often causing huge bush fires; in other parts of the bush this marks the time of the great rains called "Big Wet" that quickly flood roads and isolate families and whole towns from the outside world for weeks at a time.

Isolated bush people receive meals and gifts flown in. On Christmas afternoon the inter-farm radio network, operated in order to keep these isolated people in touch with the outside world in emergencies and to help the "flying doctor" who serves these people, helps pass on Christmas greetings from station to station.

Holiday decorations in the bush often consist of vases of gum leaves on the table and green bushes tied to verandah or patio posts.

The traditional dinner of roast turkey or mutton is served, often on the verandah. In earlier days, when the supplies didn't always make it to the remote areas in time for Christmas, dinner was often roast kangaroo, parrot pie, or stewed cockatoo.

After dinner, some may take a nap or indulge in a bush custom called "yarning." People in the bush country have little or no contact with other people for very long periods of time during the year; therefore, they use this time to exchange old stories over a pot of tea.



2-TUCK

# Austria

*Fröliche Wehnachten!*

Beautiful, musical Austria, deep in the heart of Europe, has many strong religious traditions, celebrations, and holidays, but none more filled with interesting customs than Christmas.

The festive season begins four Sundays before Christmas, a time called the Advent season. Families hang up the Advent wreath or *Advent-kranz* made of fir or spruce and decorated with four candles that are lit successively on the four Sundays before Christmas Day.

Advent customs include the daily opening of the Advent calendar, *Advent-kalendar*, a colorful calendar with the first twenty-four days of December printed on it. Little windows or flaps display each date, and every day in Advent, the children open that day's window to discover a religious scene, a comic scene, an old-fashioned Christmas scene, or a fairy tale scene, a saying, or sometimes even a treat such as a piece of candy or a miniature toy.

During Advent season many Austrian towns have their own *Christkindlmarkt* or Christmas market. Christmas decorations, wares, and sweets are sold. One such charming outdoor Christmas fair is held in front of Salzburg's Cathedral and Residenz, its origins dating back to the seventeenth century. Dozens of little, wooden stalls protected from the elements by brightly colored, overhead umbrellas and strung with garlands are lined up in the square. Peasant women dressed in layers of sweaters and wearing enormous rubber boots man the stalls stocked with every imaginable Christmas treat: candied apples, honey cake, fruit-nut bread, hot jelly doughnuts, popcorn, and pink and white cotton candy. Breads and rolls of many shapes and textures hang from ribbons. One finds hand-painted tree decorations of glass, long and mournful faces carved out of wood, dried flower arrangements, holiday candles, hand puppets, and much, much more. There are the tantalizing aromas of incense, wax, mulled wine, and roasted chestnuts. During the evenings, the air fills with Christmas music, and countless tiny lights framing the stalls twinkle.

Beginning with St. Nicholas Day on December 6, children make Christmas tree decorations. They change fancy, colored paper into long chains, paint nuts silver and gold, and create baskets, paper stars, and other delightful decorations.

The holy family's search for shelter before Jesus' birth plays an important part in the Austrian Christmas celebration, and Nativity plays are very popular all over Austria. In small villages, groups dressed as Mary, Joseph, and the shepherds walk or ride on horseback through the snowy streets, singing carols and ringing bells. Knocking at each door, they are received inside and given donations for local charities as well as food and a glass of schnapps, a beer-like beverage. One might also meet groups of caroling, alms-seeking choir boys or men dressed as the Three Wise Men and holding long poles atop which are candle-lit stars.

Several seasonal customs strongly linked with prophecy or seeing into the future take place. On December 4, St. Barbara's Day, a young, unmarried woman may place a cherry twig in water. If it blooms by Christmas Eve, she will marry the following year. On St. Thomas Day, December 21, each single girl in the village of Flachgau says a specific rhyme before bedtime. Later, in her dreams, she will see the face of her future husband. She should also pay attention to the barking of the dogs that night, for her intended will come from whatever direction the barking is heard.

In a number of villages, the women carry out one of the most solemn and quiet celebrations of the holy season. A small statue or picture of the Virgin Mary is brought to a family that has signed its name on a list, and for a full day or two, that replica serves as the subject of adoration and prayer and then is taken to the next house on the list.

In some small villages, the custom called "Showing the Christ Child" is observed. Villagers carry a manger scene from house to house while carolers sing along the way. In some mountain villages, the family living the farthest from the church starts out with torches and goes caroling toward the next neighbor's house. Family after family joins until they gather on the church steps. After they have sung and acted out most of "Through the Darkness Gleams the Light," the whole village sings the final chorus.

Other customs, reflecting pagan origins, have as their purpose the expelling of evil spirits. In the mountain valleys around Salzburg during so-called "Rough Nights," certain ugly and demonic creatures are supposedly exorcized when men disguised as women don heavily decorated face masks and heavy, elaborate headdresses and parade around, wearing these costumes for as long as ten hours.

## St. Nicholas Day

As people do in many other European countries, the Austrians observe the special St. Nicholas Day on December 6. The third century saint, St. Nicholas, comes down from heaven to visit, bringing well-behaved children fruits, nuts, and other goodies. Dressed in his bishop's vestments of red with a bishop's mitre on his head and bearing a lantern, tall staff, and the Golden Book, the tall, dignified figure offers a quiet contrast to jolly, fat Santa Claus. Accompanying St. Nicholas is Krampus, an ugly, dark, devil-figure with horns. He threatens to carry bad children off in a sack. St. Nicholas, of course, never allows this, but he does let Krampus leave his switch as a warning.

While the visit of St. Nicholas and Krampus is staged often in villages, city children sometimes have to settle for leaving their shoes out overnight to be filled with goodies. In Salzburg, a special treat presents itself. "When is Krampus coming to Getreidegasse?" (a narrow, shopping street) is a question asked in a tone mingled with fear and anticipation. On December 5 and sometimes on the sixth, not one Krampus, but many of them, wind their ways through the old part of town, carrying whips in hands, looking for tender behinds to swat. They lumber along in their heavy, awkward costumes while adults scream and the children perch on their fathers' shoulders for protection. Although usually a lot of fun, it can get out of hand, so police are on hand to assist. To appear as a Krampus, a person must have a special license. The Krampus costumes are very old and always grotesque, consisting of heavy, long animal coats and misshapen masks representing sheep, deer, or other beasts. Wicked looking horns, red, bulging eyes (sometimes battery-run ones that blink on and off), sneering lips, and long fangs are standard. They wear chain belts, and cowbells hang behind as tails. With such awkward costumes, the Krampus figures are barely able to see, hear, run, or bend and cannot chase people very well, so sometimes a helper guides the way.

## Christmas Decorations

The custom of having Christmas trees came to Austria in 1826 when a German linen-draper and lace merchant who moved to Austria and opened a shop on the old market in Salzburg introduced the trees. The idea was slow to catch on, but Christmas trees of spruce and pine are now an important part of the Austrian Christmas. Each town has its own huge tree on the main square and frequently an extra one adorned with breadcrumbs for the birds. Trees stand decorated traditionally with apples, animals made of marzipan, gingerbread kings, painted walnuts, straw stars, and tiny, wooden angels. Often real wax candles are put on the trees, and special sparklers are added at the last moment. Many Austrians leave their trees up until Epiphany on January 6, or some even leave them up until Candlemas on February 2.

A favorite addition to the table is a candle centerpiece featuring angels, manger scenes, or windmills. These rotate with the heat put off from the flickering of the candles, tinkling as they turn.

Another traditional decoration uses the tip of a spruce or fir tree decorated with colored paper, nuts, and apples and then hung upside down in a corner of a room; this is called "the Lord's corner."

## Christmas Eve and Christmas Day

On Christmas Eve, the previously locked living room door is opened to the sound of a bell, revealing the tree with its dozens of live candles, sparklers, silver ornaments, and candy. Everyone surrounds the tree and sings carols.

Each household member has a small table or area assigned to him, covered with wrapped gifts and plates filled with apples, nuts, and every imaginable sweet. After the presentation of the gifts or *bescherung*, many families gather to eat the traditional meal of carp. Roast goose, turkey, or white sausage is often served too. Other favored foods are *mehlspeise*, a round, hot tart and the famous *linzertorte*, a tart filled with raisins and nuts and flavored with almond and rose oil. Some people create a pastry in the shape of a man and call it the "Father of the House." Its consumption on Christmas Eve brings health and happiness.

After Christmas dinner, the father often reads the story of *Kriskindl*, the Christ Child, to family and guests. Later in the evening, the older children and grownups go to the traditional midnight mass or *mette*. In earlier days, special Christmas plays were performed during mass; these were the *Christi-Geburtsspiele*.

Each church displays the *krippen* or Nativity scene, and the Carolina Augusteum Museum exhibits some particularly beautiful ones each year. Many are made of wood, china, paper, and terracotta, with some even mechanically run with moving parts. Characters may be clad in fine wool, velvet, and silk or in the more traditional clothing. Tyrolean innkeepers, dirndl-clad virgins, and even characters from Wagnerian opera are often featured.

## Christmas Music

Austria, known for its beautiful music, exhibits this especially during the holiday season. Regular Sunday masses and special Advent services ring with beautiful music, but the highlight is the midnight mass on Christmas Eve. Many places of worship are not heated; thus, warm clothes must be worn. On a snowy Christmas Eve, as worshippers wend their way, candles in hand, to their incense-scented churches, the scene looks much as it did centuries ago.

Austria's most important contribution to the worldwide celebration of Christmas must be the beautiful, most popular Christmas carol of all time *"Stille Nicht, Heilige Nacht"* or "Silent Night, Holy Night." In December of 1818, Franz Gruber, who was the village schoolmaster of Amsdorf and the church organist, corroborated with Joseph Mohr, an assistant priest in the same village, to write the song. Gruber composed the music, and Mohr wrote the words. First performed on Christmas Eve, December 24, 1818, in St. Nicholas Church at Obendorf during midnight mass, the song was created, as the legend goes, because a mouse had chewed a hole in the organ bellows, making the organ inoperable. The song was quickly written and accompanied by a guitar. A man sent to repair the organ later heard the carol and asked for a copy which was passed on to a family who sang it on Christmas Eve of 1819 for Emperor Francis I of Austria and in 1822 for Czar Alexander I of Russia.

The many Salzburg musical events are fine examples of the rich, holiday musical heritage of Austria. Beginning the first Sunday of Advent and continuing each of the next three Sundays, an unusual half-hour concert is staged in the Old Town area with instrumental groups answering each other from different buildings. A French horn on a balcony, trombones on a tower, and trumpets near the cathedral all answer each other musically. On Christmas Eve at 5:00 P.M., trumpets herald the celebration, playing carols from the rocks above St. Peter's in Salzburg as candles are placed by the graves and in the windows of the catacombs.

Chamber music afternoons and evenings are featured in Salzburg's Mirabell Palace Marble Room, decorated in greenery and flowers. The Salzburg Marionette Theater has holiday programs, with the high point a New Year's Eve performance of the operetta *"Die Fledermaus."*

In 1945, Tobi Reiser and Karl Heinrich Waggerl started another important musical event in Salzburg, the Advent singing or *Adventsingen.* Originally a modest, homespun event, it has become so popular that it now has as many as twelve sold-out performances presented to a total audience of 25,000. Along with carols, people listen to poetry recitations, watch dances, and listen to instrumental solos and choral selections by many groups.

The highlight of the Christmas musical season in Salzburg must be the presentation of Johann Sebastian Bach's "Christmas Oratorio" performed by many outstanding groups. Women wear gowns, and men wear dinner jackets to the performance which is so lengthy that there is one very long intermission during which people may dine at nearby restaurants. In recent years, one-half of the composition is performed one year and the other half the following year due to the length of the work.

## New Year's Eve

On New Year's Eve, Austrians partake of their dinner of *krenfleisch* or pig's head, belly, and shoulder flavored with horseradish. A feast of pork brings luck for the coming year. At midnight, fireworks are set off. Those too cold to venture out stay home with family and friends drinking wine or champagne and perhaps indulging in a popular entertainment called *bleigiessen* in which they put small balls of lead in ladles and melt them over a candle or in a fireplace and then pour the melted lead into a pan or bowl of cold water. The resulting shapes are used to tell the future.

On a snowy New Year's Day, one might watch on television the Vienna Philharmonic in its annual medley of waltzes, or one might engage in some cross-country skiing.

## Epiphany

On January 6 called Epiphany or Twelfth Night, all over Austria the procession of the Three Kings takes place. Often the "kings" are accompanied by heralds with fanfares, pages, and shepherds.

Sometimes boys in oriental costumes move from house to house singing their traditional songs and receiving small gifts.

In Salzburg, a Twelfth Night procession of young men known as Bell Runners or *Glockerlaufen* winds in and out of the snowy squares of town in a figure eight formation. They dress in white with cowbells tied to their waists and wear heavy, handmade headdresses which are wooden structures covered with opaque paper. Various ornaments, symbols, figures, and landscapes are cut into it and are then covered with colored tissue paper. They are lighted from within and look like stained glass windows.

On Epiphany, Frau Perchia and her demon crowd appear, trying to wreak havoc. Epiphany is the last and most dangerous night of the twelve nights of Christmas. Many people write in chalk the initials of the Three Wise Men, C for Caspar, M for Melchior, and B for Balthasar, on their doors to protect themselves from evil spirits.

# Belgium

*Vrolyk Kerstfeest!* (Dutch)
*Joyeux Noël!* (French)

Belgium is a country carved out of parts of the Netherlands and France. Fifty-six percent of the population speaks Dutch, and 32 percent speaks French, thus the two ways of saying Merry Christmas.

## Feast of St. Nicholas

The first of the seasonal celebrations of Belgium, the Feast of St. Nicholas, takes place on December 6 and reflects a family celebration and a social occasion for the children. St. Nicholas wears his bishop's robes, a mitre or bishop's hat, white gloves, and an enormous bishop's ring on his left hand. He rides a white horse or a donkey and is accompanied by Père Fouettard also known as The Bogeyman, *Zwarte Piet*, or Black Peter. Weeks before, the children write letters to the saint, letting him know what they want; they give the letters to their fathers to mail since fathers know how to get in touch with St. Nicholas. The saint walks around the shops, supermarkets, and shopping centers and visits hospitals, day care nurseries, and children's homes. He parades through towns escorted by bands. The large department stores set up a "throne room" where the saint receives the children, and a photographer is on hand to record it.

St. Nicholas rides over the rooftops on the night of December 5 and drops presents for good children down the chimney and into the children's shoes left on the hearth. Along with the shoes, children put carrots, turnips, or anything else that St. Nicholas' horse or donkey might like to eat. In the morning, the food will be gone, and some treats appear in its place.

Among the traditional gifts left by St. Nicholas are *speculaus*, cookies made of flour, butter, brown sugar, and cinnamon and shaped into figures. There might also be little marzipan pigs, chocolate figures, oranges, or other gifts.

Schools arrange children's parties for the youngest pupils, and during the parties, St. Nicholas appears to distribute sweets. During the first two weeks of December, employers, sports clubs, cultural associations, and other groups arrange parties for the children of their staffs or members.

## St. Thomas Day

St. Thomas Day on December 21 brings out the mischievousness of the children. In earlier days, schoolboys would set fire to paper roosters placed in front of the school door. Students would tie a hen and a rooster together by the legs and allow them to escape and then scramble after them to catch them. The boy who caught the rooster was declared king and the girl who caught the hen, the queen. Today school children still play tricks on their teachers. The chief trick is coaxing the teacher to the door of a little room and locking him or her in there until the teacher agrees to give in to the children's wishes.

All over Belgium, crèches, or manger scenes, are set up both indoors and outdoors. Christmas trees adorn the main squares of Belgian cities and towns. Both the cities of Antwerp and Brussels receive a huge Christmas tree as a gift from the country of Norway. The trees are magnificently decorated and are the focal point for outdoor carol singing organized by a group called "Community Christmas" which also encourages the custom of leaving gifts near the outdoor crèche displays.

Throughout December, Brussels and other cities have elaborate



3282-TUCK

light displays in the streets and parks. Gala entertainments abound, with operas, ballet, and theater all popular.

## Christmas Eve

On Christmas Eve, midnight church services take place. If the children have been good and said their prayers faithfully throughout the year, the Archangel Gabriel or, in some places, the Child Jesus will bring them an *engelskoek*, an angel's cake or kind of bun under their pillows on this night.

## Christmas Day

Belgians celebrate Christmas Day as a religious time. The children form processions on the way to church. As they march, they carry religious figures or display little shrines and crucifixes decorated with ribbons and streamers. Often, a boy appears as St. John the Baptist, leading a white lamb and carrying a crucifix. Church bells ring as the children, accompanied by the clergy, make their way to church.

## Holy Innocents Day

Holy Innocents Day on December 28 commemorates the time when King Herod had all of the male babies in Bethlehem put to death in fear of the new king, Jesus. This story has an impact on Belgians, for it is said that the bodies of two of the innocents were buried at the Convent of St. Gerard in the Belgian province of Namur. Children in some parts of Belgium used to dress up like their parents, using their parents' clothes and adopting the air of very raucous, rowdy adults on this day.

In the area of Belgium called Flanders, Nativity plays represent an important part of the Christmas season. The people casting the roles of the characters take their job very seriously. Local school children are usually chosen to be a choir of angels. The Nativity play undergoes some unique changes and includes some most unusual characters. For example, in some of the border towns where smuggling is sometimes quite common, the cast of characters might include a poacher or a smuggler who brings his gift to the Christ Child. These Nativity plays require that each character participating must resemble a character from a painting of the famous, sixteenth-century, Belgian painter Brueghel. This limits the use of costumes to those that were worn by ordinary townspeople back in the sixteenth century when Brueghel did his painting. This also encourages the type of acting found during that time.

Another Christmas custom from Flanders is the appointment of three men who have the privilege of walking among the streets dressed as the Magi or Wise Men. In order to receive this honor, each man must have shown outstanding character and virtue during the last year. Dressed in their robes, they make their rounds from door to door and sing two songs at each home. One song describes the journey of the Three Wise Men. The other is a Flemish version of "*O Tannenbaum.*" After singing the two songs, people invite the Magi in for a cup of tea and perhaps some pancakes. These men would certainly have to be very hardy to keep this up for very long.

Belgians love good food and wine. Many areas have their Christmas specialties.

In Andenne near Namur, *cougnous* or small oblong loaves must be won in a game of cards. The city of Liege has won fame for its *bouquettres,* a sort of pancake. Turkey has pretty much replaced the hare or rabbit for the main course at Christmas dinner.

## New Year's Day

On *Nieuwjaarsdar* or New Year's Day, people visit and exchange greetings with family and friends. For weeks before this, children save their francs to buy elaborately decorated papers on which to inscribe

New Year's wishes to parents and grandparents. Often these papers are decorated with roses, ribbons, golden cherubs, and angels. Children practice these letters in school until they make the final copies, having no erasures or errors. The messages are then hidden away. On the morning of January 1, each boy and girl reads aloud his or her composition before the family. Not only are wishes for a Happy New Year expressed, but also promises are made for improved behavior during the next year.

The holiday season ends on January 6 or Twelfth Night when children dress up as the Three Wise Men and go caroling in the streets.

# Bethlehem

Merry Christmas!

Bethlehem, located in a part of the country of Jordan, has been in Israeli-occupied territory since 1967. The city lies five miles south of Jerusalem and serves as a religious shrine shared by the Eastern Orthodox Church, the Roman Catholic Church, and various Protestant churches.

Bethlehem is considered to be the birthplace of Jesus Christ, the Son of God, the long-awaited Messiah, the son of Joseph and Mary of Nazareth, the founder of the Christian faith, whose birthday is the foundation for the celebration of Christmas.

Modern Bethlehem reflects the historical unrest of the Middle East. Armed troops march everywhere. Commercialism runs rampant, with noisy vendors selling a myriad of trinkets and souvenirs, even on Christmas Eve and Christmas Day. Life proves hectic, loud, and crowded.

Western and Eastern Christians celebrate Christmas at different times. Western Christians including the Roman Catholics, Anglicans, and many other Protestant religious celebrate Christmas December 25, while Eastern Christians including Greek and Syrian Orthodox, Egyptian Coptics, and others celebrate the event on January 6. Thus, Bethlehem continues to be a busy place throughout this period.

The eastern churches control many of the holy places in Bethlehem. The most holy places are the Church of the Nativity and below the church, the Grotto of the Manger that has been identified as the actual birthplace of Jesus. This was identified as His birthplace by St. Helena, the mother of Constantine, the first Christian emperor of Rome.



3282-TUCK

Constantine built a church over the grotto in 325 A.D. Some of the original structure still stands but was built upon by Emperor Justinian in 560 A.D. The exterior of the Church of the Nativity looks much like a medieval fortress. Within the compound, there are churches and buildings of other faiths besides the Eastern Orthodox, such as St. Catherine's Roman Catholic Church and an Armenian monastery. The Orthodox, the Roman Catholics, and the Armenians share rights to the Grotto of the Manger. This actual spot of Christ's birth is marked with a fourteen point, inlaid, silver star with the inscription *"Huc de virgine maria, Jesus christus natus est"* or "Here Jesus Christ was born of the Virgin Mary." Above the star is the altar of the birth of Jesus.

On Christmas Eve, the Roman Catholic Patriarch of Jerusalem leads a motorcade procession from Jerusalem, five miles away over the hills, to St. Catherine's Roman Catholic Church and the Grotto of the Manger for devotions and prayer. As the procession moves along, people stand and cheer, bells ring, and children run after the Patriarch's car. The procession arrives through the narrow streets of Bethlehem to Manger Square, a scene with a bazaar-like atmosphere including the smells of Middle Eastern food being sold and the excitement of the throngs of people. The procession moves to the eastern end of the square to the Church of the Nativity compound. Choirs sing, and other religious ceremonies take place. The Patriarch of Jerusalem leads the mass at St. Catherine's Church that is a beautiful mixture of the exquisite vestments, the aromatic incense, the beautiful music, and the many, adoring pilgrims come in search of the birthplace of their Lord. After midnight, a procession journeys from St. Catherine's through the courtyards to the Grotto of the Manger beneath the Church of the Nativity. The Patriarch lays a statue of the Baby Jesus upon the exact spot where it is believed He was born. The procession then returns to St. Catherine's Church.

Shepherds still tend their flocks on the outskirts of Bethlehem, and many pilgrims journey to the eastern outskirts to pay respect to the shepherds who were the first to hear of Christ's birth. This field is maintained by the Y.M.C.A., and thousands journey there, particularly Protestants. A large, walled-in enclosure where a choir leads in the singing of familiar carols is the focal point of the field. The beauty of the night, the peacefulness of the setting, and the hushed atmosphere recall for many the scene of the original shepherds. This place's authenticity is in question, and the Eastern Orthodox and the Roman Catholic churches have their own shepherds' fields close by.

Christian homes in Bethlehem are marked by a cross painted over their doors, and each home displays a homemade manger scene.

Those who make a pilgrimage to Christ's birthplace at Christmas must look beyond the hustle and bustle, the commercialism, and the unrest to the event for which the holiday is celebrated.

# Brazil

*Boas Festas!* or *Feliz Natal!*

December in the South American country of Brazil means summertime with its vacation from school, a season for boating, picnics, and swimming. Portuguese settlers brought many of the Christmas traditions. Brazil has the largest per capita Roman Catholic population in the world, and much of the celebrating reflects that fact. Brazil, physically a very large and diverse country with a very diverse population, has 150 million people.

The celebration of Christmas in Brazil has certainly been helped along by a law enacted in the early 1960s called the 'Thirteenth Salary" which states that every worker should receive an extra month's pay at Christmas.

## Advent Season

Advent season, beginning the fourth Sunday before Christmas, acts as a vital prelude to Christmas. During this time, people hurry about preparing the *presepe* or manger scene. This may be a very simple display of the crib with the figures of Mary, Joseph, the shepherds, and the Magi standing around, or the display may reflect a very elaborate scene and fill an entire room or even more than one room. The *presepe* often shows a delightful hodgepodge with, perhaps, a quiet manger scene alongside the latest space age developments. There may be an electric train, sailboats, or airplanes next to the shepherds quietly tending their flocks in the fields. A display of all the many achievements linked to mankind is shown to the Infant Jesus. The *presepe* is usually left on show through January 6 called "King's Day" or "Little Christmas." The Baby Jesus figure is not placed in His crib until Christmas Eve, and the Three Wise Men make their way slowly to the manger, arriving on January 6.

The Santa Claus figure called Papai Noel, though the weather is very hot, wears the traditional red suit and has a sleigh with reindeer. He enters the home through the front door, not the chimney. Brazilian children hang stockings, but they put out their shoes as well, usually placing them in the kitchen near the stove. Some place their shoes on the roof for the convenience of Papai Noel. Sometimes the sly old gentleman hides gifts all over the house for the children to find.

In the city of Rio de Janeiro, Papai Noel arrives by helicopter in mid-December and lands in the city's Maracanã Stadium and distributes gifts such as water pistols, balloons, whistles, and other small toys and trinkets. In São Paulo where the European and United States' influences are felt the most, store windows are decorated beautifully, with prizes being awarded for the best displays. Papai Noel and his many helpers wander the streets of São Paulo giving out small toys to the children.

Christmas cards are sent, many times not until after Christmas, and often show the same wintry scenes as European or North American cards. Changing slowly, cards are beginning to depict a "Brazilian" Christmas.

The Christmas tree, popular now, is first seen on Christmas Eve, gaily decorated and lighted with candles. Many parents in southern Brazil decorate the tree themselves, locking themselves in the parlor and decorating the tree with candles and ornaments like metallic balls, figurines, and poinsettia blossoms. Other popular decorations include arrangements of eucalyptus leaves and many different kinds of red flowers such as poinsettias.

Some Protestant churches in Brazil have the tradition of the "white gift" at Christmas when all of the people bring gifts of white food such as rice or potatoes to help make a Christmas dinner for the poor. People often invite those less fortunate to spend Christmas with them.



3282-TUCK

## *Auto de Natal*

A tradition of over twenty-five years, the *Auto de Natal* or *Act of Christmas*, an outdoor Christmas play, is held in Rio de Janeiro. This free play attracts many viewers and usually has the role of poor people living in Brazil as its theme. There are also other local holiday plays and pageants scattered throughout the country.

## Christmas Eve

On Christmas Eve, adults may sing, dance, and talk in the gentle summer breezes while the children amuse themselves with pastimes such as singing *roda,* old, traditional songs, in which the children join hands in a circle and do various gestures as they sing. Christmas Eve serves as a time for family gatherings with several generations joining in the celebration.

A very important part of the Christmas celebration in Brazil is attending the *Missa do Galo* Or Mass of the Cock at midnight on Christmas Eve. Carol singing follows, after which people return home to eat the *ceia de Natal* or Christmas dinner. The many traditional dishes served usually include turkey that is usually stuffed with *farofa* made of toasted manioc flour, onions, garlic, turkey livers and gizzards, olives, hard-boiled eggs, and bacon. Another popular dish is dried cod. In the interior parts of the country one might dine on roast pig, African couscous, a steamed fish pie made with corn meal, cassava flour, sardines, shrimp and seasonings, or fried shrimp, and of course, champagne. Years ago, the Portuguese ate the traditional, dried cod for Christmas dinner, and some people still do. A favorite dessert is *rabanada,* a dish similar to French toast. Happy chatter, laughter, bells, and firecrackers fill the air.

Recently a new tradition has caught on called *Amigo Secreto* or Secret Friend. A group of friends, co-workers, children, or family members write their names on pieces of paper and draw a name in confidence. When gifts are opened, the Secret Friend is revealed. These are often fun, gag gifts, all in good fun.

## New Year's Eve and Day

New Year's Eve or *Reveillon* reflects a very social time in Brazil. Some celebrations continue all night. There are formal balls, dinner parties, and beach parties. In São Paulo, an international running marathon is held; in Rio de Janeiro, an all day and all night festival in honor of the African goddess of the sea, Lemanja takes place. People often eat lentils for good luck on *Reveillon.*

On New Year's Day, a boat parade called *Nossa Senhora dos Navegantes,* Our Lady of Sailors, takes place in many parts of the country. This day also marks the beginning of the month long, religious festival held in some rural areas in central Brazil, *Folia Des Reis* or Festival of the Kings. *Congada* is an end-of-the-year festival held in many cities.

## The Day of the Kings

The Day of the Kings, January 6, for the most part, marks the end of the Christmas season and commemorates the visit to the Christ Child by the Three Wise Men from the East. They arrived on camels, so Brazilian children put out some corn for the poor, tired animals when the Wise Men pay them a visit bringing toys and other gifts. In some areas, poetry contests involving verses accompanied by guitar are held on this day. The month long *Folia Des Reis* does continue after this day. Religious groups called *Reisados* parade through the streets playing instruments and singing.

# British Virgin Islands

Merry Christmas!

In the Caribbean British Virgin Islands, the three big celebrations of the year are Easter, August Festival, and Christmas. Like many other countries which have a strong tourist trade and are located near the United States, the Virgin Islands is losing its older, more traditional ways of celebrating Christmas and reflects more the traditions of the United States.

When school closes for the Christmas holidays, the country bustles with activity. People usually repair, paint, and redecorate their homes at this time of year, and this requires, for those living in rural areas, a special shopping trip to town by sailboat, horse, or foot. Shops become cluttered with curtain and cushion materials, paint, toys, and bags of flour. Shopkeepers put up bright, colorful, tissue holiday decorations.

Young people at the church youth clubs practice carols for their annual serenading. School students prepare for the school's annual Christmas concert. Father Christmas appears at the concerts, strutting to this song:

"I'm Father Christmas with my toys
I visit all good girls and boys. . . ."

Community bands perform special programs at the towns' bandstands.

One tradition still popular is the drinking of a liqueur made from guavaberry, a much-craved for, but scarce fruit in the Caribbean, drunk only during the holiday season and in small amounts. Serenaders sing at each house and are expected to drink some guavaberry at each stop. Children help pick blydens to make the other special holiday drink called mixed blyden.

## Christmas Eve

Everyone gets up early on Christmas Eve. The baking is done first. Children used to play with their shock-shock toys, a type of rattle, as the baking was being done. Then they would go to cut down a Christmas tree, usually an indigo tree. It must be tall enough to stand straight in an empty paint can.

Children hang pillowcases and go to bed to wait for Father Christmas to come. While the children lie asleep, serenaders go around and sing traditional songs like "Silent Night, Holy Night" or "O, Come All Ye Faithful." As midnight comes, they attend Fore Day Prayers in the churches to greet Christmas. Just before daybreak, they may sing to the rhythm of a Fungi Band:

"Morning, Good Morning
And how are you this morning?
Morning, Good Morning
And how are you this morning/

Morning, Good Morning, I come fay may Guavaberry
Good morning, good morning, put it on de table
Morning, I wish you a Merry Christmas
Morning, and how are you this morning?
Morning to the Mistress
And how are you this morning?
If you have any Guavaberry put it on de table."

When they stop singing, the leader comes forward, takes the mistress's hand, and wishes the family a Merry Christmas, long lives, and the blessings of life. Everyone makes merry as the serenaders wish well, sing, dance, eat some pudding, tart, and boyah, and drink guavaberry.



3282-TUCK

## Christmas Day

Children awaken in the morning to pillowcases bulging with presents. Soon it's time to kill the goat, for its meat has to be cooked into a stew in an open pot. Church bells ring as the special Christmas Day services begin. Christmas means open house; therefore, throughout the day friends, relatives, and serenaders come and go. They bring Christmas cards, drink guavaberry, eat, dance, and sing all the popular Christmas carols. Boxing Day on December 26 is a day of merry-making, and at night a concert takes place at which a special guest will sing a solo or do a recitation.

## New Year's Eve

Tradition says a clean house on New Year's Day makes a clean house all year; therefore, everything receives a thorough cleaning on Old Year's Day or New Year's Eve. People go to church to hear the local preacher count the last seconds of the year and bring in the first of the New Year with:

"Come let us anew
Our Journey pursue
Roll round with the years
Roll round with the years . . ."

When church services end, people sing the annual Virgin Island greeting:

"A Happy New Year, Happy New Year,
A Happy New Year, Happy New Year,
Happy New Year, Happy New Year,
A Happy New Year to you all!"

# Bulgaria

*Tchestita Koleda!* or *Vessela Koleda!*

As in many European settings, in the Eastern European country of Bulgaria, the celebration of the Christmas season begins on December 6, St. Nicholas Day or *Nikulden*, celebrated for the saint who delivers people from perils. He is honored with a warm, family celebration. Traditional food prepared includes *sharan*, a special kind of fish served with rice, and a bread made for St. Nicholas. A priest often visits the home and sanctifies the meal with prayers and a blessing.

Christmas trees enjoy popularity in Bulgaria, and garlands hang all around the houses as well as in busy shops and on bustling streets.

On December 23, people shop for their food for the holiday as well as the Christmas tree. The food is then put in the refrigerator or left out on the balcony since the temperatures are so cold. The family gathers in the living room, and Christmas carols are played on the CD while they decorate the tree. They then sit down to watch television. The next day is spent cleaning, cooking, and doing last minute shopping.

## Christmas Eve

*Budnivecher* or Christmas Eve officially begins with the appearance of the first star in the sky. The strict, two-week fast observed before this evening is joyfully broken. The chief food on this day, *kravat*, a large, round loaf decorated by the eldest daughter with figures of a bird, a flower, and a cross, is placed in the center of the table with a lighted candle and surrounded by festive foods. After burning incense and offering prayers, the father and mother raise the loaf over their heads, saying, "May our wheat grow as high as this." Everyone breaks a piece from the loaf, for the saying goes that good luck will follow the one getting the largest portion.

## Christmas Day

A quaint ceremony begins *Koleda Rozhdestvo Kristovo* or Christmas Day. Before breakfast, some corn is placed in a stocking, and the head of the house sprinkles a portion of it on the doorstep saying, "Christ is born" to which the family responds, "He is born indeed." The man approaches the fireplace and strikes the blazing log, and with each blow, he utters a wish of good health to the stock and to the land and makes a wish for a bountiful harvest. Then the ashes of the log are carefully gathered, and pieces of the log's ends are placed in trees to assure a good crop.

A long church service is held. Children receive their gifts from Grandpa Koleda who looks exactly like Santa Claus and comes from the mountains on Christmas Day and walks through the door carrying a bag full of presents. The children wrote to him earlier to tell him what gifts they would like to receive.

Traditional Christmas dinner includes roast pig and *kravaitza* or blood sausage.

## New Year's Day

For days before *Nova Godina* or New Year's Day, housewives have been baking *kolach*, tasty little round cakes with holes in the centers. *Novogodishna Vecher* or New Year's Eve is a great occasion for all kinds of fortune telling. The favorite method of looking into the future occurs with a leaf being dropped into water and remaining there overnight. A fresh leaf in the morning means sound health throughout the year.

On New Year's Eve, shortly after the village clock strikes midnight, groups of boys shouldering red switches decorated with gaudy paper flowers steal through the silent streets and rap smartly at doors. As they knock, the boys sing the traditional greeting for good luck and a plentiful harvest:

"Happy, happy New Year,
Till next year, till eternity,
Corn on the cornstalk,
Grapes in the vineyard,
Yellow grain in the bin,
Red apples in the garden,
Silkworms in the house,
Happiness and health
Until next year."

With a last tremendous rap, the door flies open, and the boys rush into the kitchen where the entire household awaits them. Lads gently switch good wishes into every family member, beginning with the oldest and on to the youngest. In reward, the boys receive money and dozens of crisp *kolach*, the tiny white cakes prepared by the women. The boys slip the *kolach* over the decorated rods that they are carrying.



3282-TUCK

# Canada

Merry Christmas!
*Joyeux Noël!* (French)

In the North American country of Canada, the English background of 45 percent of the population influences the celebration of Christmas. One-fourth of the people, with their French heritage, try to maintain the French traditions. Like the United States, her northern neighbor is a melting pot of cultures, and Christmas celebrations reflect this fact.

Since 1986, Canadians of all backgrounds unite in a celebration called Christmas Lights Across Canada that occurs on the first Thursday in December. In Ottawa, the capital city, the Governor General of Canada flips a switch at 6:55 P.M., and over 150,000 lights illuminate the parliament buildings and nearly fifty other important national institutions along Confederation Boulevard. These lights remain lit at night all though the Christmas season. Video messages from provincial and territorial leaders are shown.

At the exact time the lights turn on in Ottawa, a government leader in each provincial and territorial capital across the country also switches on Christmas lights. The ceremonies unite the country's different areas, yet each brings its own distinct character to its ceremony.

In Charlottetown, capital of tiny Prince Edward Island, lights shine from Province House, considered to be the birthplace of Canada. The town crier announces the arrival of dignitaries, and many townspeople dressed in Victorian costumes and carrying candles listen to the choir's carols and partake of refreshments.

In Fredericton, the capital of New Brunswick, a tree lighting ceremony is held in front of the Legislative Assembly Building, and Santa arrives to distribute "barley toys" and "chicken bones," traditional, hard candy suckers. Another tree is lit in front of city hall where hot apple cider is served, and Santa Claus passes out candy canes.

In Regina, Saskatchewan's capital, people join the Christmas Lights Across Canada celebration in front of the Saskatchewan Legislative Building with carols, candles or lights, and shouts of welcome to the Christmas season. Hot apple cider and candy canes are served, and a live Nativity scene is displayed inside the building. A contest called Regina Sparkles takes place during the holidays to choose the best light displays.

In the frigid Yukon capital of Whitehorse, people celebrate inside the warm Yukon Government Administration Building that has five decorated trees inside as well as one outside. Children's choirs and bands perform, and children receive a bag of goodies.

Like the United States, Canada has a strong tradition of church attendance. Primarily Anglican from its English roots and Roman Catholic, all churches offer a variety of special Christmas services.

In 1905 Toronto had the first of its annual Santa Claus parades sponsored by Eaton's Department Store. The parade features Santa Claus' arrival plus floats, marching bands, and clowns. Many other parades are held all over the country. Eaton's offered its first Christmas catalog in 1896, and it rapidly expanded. Many families all over Canada purchase from this annual catalog and depend on it for Christmas gifts.

## British Canada

The Sunday before Advent begins, or the fifth Sunday before Christmas Eve is referred to as "Stir Up Sunday." (For a better understanding of the day's origins, see England).

Filled with caroling parties, visiting, decorations, trees, beautiful lights, candles and lots of delicious food on Christmas Day, Canadians gather around the television to watch the English monarch Queen Elizabeth II's, Christmas message to the British Commonwealth.

In the maritime province of Prince Edward Island, the season reflects a peaceful, religious time with the family at the center. The season's activities revolve around the churches. The traditional school Christmas concert is an important event, and people on the small island province gather to hear the children sing, watch a play, buy delicious fudge candy or Christmas crafts, and feast grandly.

The first British settlers did not use Christmas trees; in fact, a lot of the traditions that they had observed before, they could not in their new home of Canada because the surroundings did not provide the needed resources. Canada, a frigid place in the winter, has no holly or ivy. There were wintergreen, hemlock, cedar, and spruce that they used for boughs and wreaths. Instead of Christmas trees, they had kissing boughs also called kissing bunches or kissing balls which were hung in hallways or doorways. Anyone caught under the kissing bough received a kiss.

In Victorian times, Christmas in Canada became much like that in England and the United States. There were fancy dinners, parties, dances, christenings, engagement parties, and weddings. Ornately decorated trees replaced the kissing boughs. Christmas cards became popular when, in 1876, J.T. Henderson of Montreal offered for sale Christmas cards showing traditional holiday themes such as people riding in sleighs, ice-skating, Santa Claus, plum puddings, and Canadian scenes.

An interesting menu of the "grooming board" or fully-laden Christmas table is given for a household in Toronto in 1855 in Phillip Snyder's *December 25*; this was a typical Christmas feast for a middle class family of parents, two grandparents, a bachelor son, two daughters and their husbands, and seven grandchildren. Breakfast was lamb chops, toast, pork pies, deviled kidneys, porridge, and coffee. Dinner was four kinds of soup: oyster, chicken, gumbo, and mutton broth; eleven roasts consisting of beef, pork, mutton, turkey, and venison; three chickens and three geese. Add to that, potatoes, carrots, turnips, parsley, and onions. Desserts were trifles, suet puddings, a huge plum pudding, four kinds of fruitcake, and three kinds of wine. For those still hungry, there were lozenges, fruit drops, sugared almonds, licorice sticks, and barley sugar rings. Supper in the evening was ham, veal, pork, beef, chicken, tongue, turkey, brawn headcheese, seven kinds of fruit jelly (Jello), and a dozen pies and cakes.

Early Irish settlers had very religious celebrations of Christmas with but a few simple, homemade decorations such as a handmade Nativity scene and some candles in the windows.

Scottish settlers celebrated Christmas as a very religious day and, as in Scotland, saved their celebrating for Hogmanay on New Year's. (For a more extensive explanation of Hogmanay, see Scotland.) To prepare for Hogmanay, people cleaned, wound clocks, changed bedding, mended clothes, and polished brass. They paid their debts and returned anything borrowed. A grand Hogmanay party was held on New Year's Eve. This holiday is filled with superstitious customs such as the "first-footer," the first person to enter a house after midnight. This figure determines a family's luck during the coming year. A dark-haired man would bring good luck. All visitors carried in bread, salt, and coal that symbolized life, hospitality, and warmth.

Music serves as an important part of a Canadian Christmas. Caroling and performances for the season are everywhere. Charity also is particularly remembered at this time when many help the needy.

Most Canadians bring the season to a close on January 6 at Epiphany, Twelfth Night, or Little Christmas. Often a special Twelfth Night cake is eaten which contains a bean and a pea baked into it. The finders determine the king and queen for the evening.

## French Canada

In the province of Quebec, about 80 percent of the people are of French background. Proud of their heritage, they attempt to preserve it closely.

In the city of Montreal, the church called St. Joseph's Oratory has a collection of Nativity scenes from around the world. At Notre Dame



3282-TUCK

Basilica they listen to Christmas carols and hymns on the 5,772 pipe organ.

Before midnight mass, some people take a sleigh ride or go cross-country skiing or ice-skating in places like Montreal's Mount Royal Park with its many snow trails and small mountains.

For the French Canadians, midnight mass is observed, followed by *le réveillon,* the very elaborate midnight dinner at which some of the main foods are traditional pig's knuckles called *le ragoût de patte* and meat pies called *les tourtièrres.* The feasting goes on into the early hours of the morning.

In earlier times, French children received gifts on New Year's Day. Today many French Canadian children have presents under the tree after *le réveillon* or on Christmas morning as well as on New Year's Day.

French Canadian young couples have traditionally announced their engagements on Christmas Eve.

In French Canadian celebrating, carolers perform in public a few days before Christmas and on New Year's Eve; young people dressed in old style, country costumes gather to perform and go from house to house singing and collecting gifts of food and clothing for the poor. Many businesses, churches, and charitable organizations solicit for the poor during the season.

New Year's Day has always been very special to French Canadians. Children must seek the blessing of the head of the family. Many grown children who have left home return during this special time. Turkey dinner is served, and all welcome the New Year.

In the maritime province of New Brunswick, 35 percent of the population is a French-speaking group called Acadians. They begin their celebrations with Advent, the season covering the first four Sundays before Christmas Eve. Advent wreaths in the shape of crosses are placed at the foot of church altars. The first Sunday one candle is lit; the second Sunday two candles are lit, and so on.

After midnight mass, Acadians have the *le réveillon* or Christmas meal, but theirs includes "Pot A" or rabbit pie and *la pâté à la rapture,* a ragpie dish made from potatoes, meat, onions, bacon, salt, and pepper. The crèche or manger scene serves as the most important Acadian Christmas decoration. They appear everywhere in homes and churches. Acadian children prepare a special gift for their parents, *Le Bouquet Spirituel.* These are little cards decorated with colorful drawings and dried flowers. On these, children mark each prayer that they have said in the weeks before Christmas.

New Year's is an important celebration for Acadians. They greet friends and family with, "Happy New Year and Heaven at the end of your days." They also place importance on the first visitor of the New Year, much as the Scots do. Young boys at the door bring good luck, so many young boys used to go around being first visitors and receiving treats in return.

For Epiphany on January 6, Acadians prepare a special cake called *le gâteau des rois* or "cake of the kings" in which a ring and a piece of silver are baked along with a bean and a pea. The bean and pea determine the king and queen for the celebration, while the ring reveals the first woman to marry, and the silver foretells the one who will attain wealth.

## German Canadians

Many Germans fled the United States during the Revolutionary War. They were loyalists who wanted to remain under the English monarchy. Many also preferred to go to the partially settled Canadian lands rather than to the unknown perils of the American West. They brought with them their own customs, and today people of German descent represent about 10 percent of the Canadian population and are found mainly in Ontario, British Columbia, the Prairie Provinces, and Nova Scotia.

They introduced Advent wreaths and calendars, gingerbread houses, and Christmas trees. Germans introduced the Christmas tree to Canada as they did to the entire world. Trees are decorated with German glass balls and gold and silver cardboard ornaments that are die-stamped and hand-painted. These hollow "Dresdens" are often filled with surprise treats. From Germany to Canada via the Germans also came foil icicles and angel hair.

The Advent season, beginning the fourth Sunday before Christmas Eve is celebrated with the Advent wreath. Early German settlers hung the wreath from the ceiling. Today they appear in homes and churches. The wreath has four candles on it; the first Sunday one candle is lit, the second Sunday two candles, etc. Advent calendars are popular also. Such a calendar represents the first twenty-four days of December, and each date has a little flap or door behind which might be a picture, a symbol, a saying, a scripture verse, or even, sometimes a prize.

As in Germany today, many German Canadians receive gifts from St. Nicholas on his day, December 6. He collects their letters they send to *Christkindl* or the Christ Child who delivers gifts on Christmas Eve. In Nova Scotia "bellsnicklers" dress up in wild costumes, hiding their identities, and drop in on people to act wild, stomp, sing loudly, play instruments, dance, and perform ridiculous skits. The people in each house try to guess the identity of the "bellsnicklers." When all are guessed, there are snacks and drinks.

On Christmas Eve, *Christkindl,* Kris Kringle, or *Weihnachtsmann,* the ancient man of the woods who wears dark, fur-trimmed robes and carries an evergreen tree, delivers presents. A sumptuous meal is served of turkey or roast goose, dumplings, red cabbage, and hot coleslaw. Carrot pudding and *lebkuchen* or spicy cakes are served. Fruit-filled breads called *stolen* and lots of different Christmas cookies are eaten, including gingerbread men and hearts. Traditional carols are sung, and people attend church.

## First Nations People

In Canada, the name First Nations People or aboriginal people is preferred to Native Americans or American Indians. There are 598 aboriginal bands or groups in Canada today.

From the late 1600s to the mid-1700s, French Jesuit missionaries brought Christianity to many First Nations People, and they brought

Christmas. European and aboriginal cultures intermixed, and many aboriginals became Christians.

Cree children make the rounds of relatives' homes on Christmas Eve; at each home, a cloth bag is hung for each child. On Christmas morning, the children return to find filled bags.

In a Tingit village, the celebrations center on a large, community party in the village hall or a local school gym. On Christmas Day, everyone gathers before the village tree for speeches, storytelling, and Christmas hymns and carols sung in their native language. There is an abundance of food and an appearance from Santa Claus.

Micmac Christians decorate their homes with spruce boughs, sing Christmas carols in their native language, and whisper special prayers each night of the Advent season. On Cape Breton, the Micmacs combine their own unique traditions with Christian ones. There is a processional mass at the Catholic Church on Christmas Eve, ending with a traditional Micmac dance.

"Twas in the Moon of Wintertime," a Huron Christmas carol, is believed to be the first Canadian carol, and it was originally written in the Huron language in 1640 and set to a French tune by a Jesuit priest, Jean de Brebeuf. The Huron in Ontario sang this until 1649 when the Iroquois killed Father Brebeuf, wiped out the Jesuit mission, and drove the Huron from their homes. In Quebec, to which many of the Huron escaped, the song re-emerged and was translated into English and French. The song, still sung today, is considered a national treasure. In recent years, it has appeared on a set of Canadian postage stamps.

The Metis, descendants of aboriginal women and colonial fur traders, celebrate with a huge family reunion on Christmas Eve. Metis fire their guns into the air to begin the celebration. Everyone wears his finest, and there are the exchange of gifts, dancing to fiddle music, singing, and playing traditional games.



3282-TUCK

## Inuit

Most Inuit or Eskimos are now Christian, primarily Anglican, Roman Catholic, or Evangelical. They are devout and celebrate Christmas joyously. Carols are sung in both English and Inuktitut at school concerts. A massive feast consisting of caribou, seal, and char, a raw, frozen trout, share the table with turkey as the focal point of the holiday celebration. Santa gives toys to the children. Many tests of skill are performed such as harpoon throwing, whip cracking, wrestling, and igloo building. Many games are played: One-Hand Reach, The Eagle, and One-Foot-High Kick. In the traditional Drum Dance, performed by a single person or a group, a story is told through song and dance.

On Boxing Day, December 26, or on New Year's Eve, the Inuit take part in a *pallaq*. A family with something special to celebrate shares its good fortune with neighbors. Standing on top of the house, one or more family members throw gifts, clothing, blankets, and handfuls of candy to those below.

To celebrate the New Year, the Inuit have created a new tradition of the snowmobile parade. Hundreds of lighted snowmobiles follow a trail in the darkness with joyous shouts and many rifle shots.

In an article by Frank S. Gonda called "Christmas in the Big Igloo," he describes Christmas at Pelly Bay where he taught for a while. The traditional snow house or *kaget* is built for Christmas. The big igloo is erected over three smaller igloos, and these three snow houses are built for families who must come over twenty miles for these annual festivities.

On Christmas Eve, over 100 brightly dressed people assemble in the big igloo for three nights and two days of games, contests, feasting, and prayers. Ancient Eskimo games and target shooting are the highlights. They open their presents, such items as chess sets, cloth, and knives.

Midnight mass takes place, and those who are close enough to go home, leave to return for Christmas dinner at 3:00 P.M. Christmas Day. The first course is sliced Arctic char, caribou stew that has been cooking all night, and hot tea. After dinner, more games and contests such as an archery contest and foot races are held. The Drum Dance follows, and some elder ladies perform ancient chants. At 10:00 P.M. people return to their homes.

On Baffin Island near Iqaluit in the eastern Arctic about 600 km above the tree line, stands the little village of Apex and its 200 residents. The average daylight for the entire day at the time of Christmas is four hours, and the temperature stays at–20 degrees centigrade with frequent dips to–45 degrees. The area, known for its killer blizzards and wind speeds rising to 190 km per hour, has wind chills as low as–60 degrees.

The Christmas season begins with the Nanook School concert and feast held on the last Friday evening before the holidays. Each household receives a hand-delivered invitation, and everyone who is able attends. Many people travel hours by snowmobile along the sea ice from outpost camps. The school gym becomes a banquet hall with festive holiday decorations of paper chains, tin foil stars, and paper bells. Recitals and caroling provide the entertainment, and then everyone eats. A raw, frozen fish called char is popular as are caribou, seal, and turkey.

Santa Claus arrives with a sack full of presents, and the children's names are called one by one. Mothers have been busy working with the two teachers buying and wrapping gifts for each child from the older children past sixth grade who attend school in Iqaluit to the preschoolers. As people walk home, the colorful northern lights ripple and dance on the snow.

The church tree is trimmed with iced, gingerbread ornaments and ribbon bows. Services are held in the Inuktitut language. During church services, children are allowed to play; some sit quietly and listen while others wander forward to sit on the laps of relatives in the choir. After church, the congregation heads for tea and breakfast at the home of that week's volunteer. Usually variations on bannock cakes, yeast breads, and sometimes maybe caribou stew, char, or a whole meal are served.

The annual women's gift exchange takes place in the *qammaq,* a sod hut built on the beach of scrap materials as a meeting place for women in the winter to congregate for sewing to support the church, to help the needy, and to donate to charities. Soapstone dish lamps light the *qammaq*. For the *qammaq* party, men are invited. Tests of skill are performed in which families cheer for mothers and grandmothers in such events as the four-strand braiding contest. Some of the older women engage in throat-singing, a game of skill in which two women stand face-to-face and throw sound into each other's open mouth, creating a sing-song rhythm that is unlike any other human sound. The first to laugh or break the rhythm loses. Games go on into the night interspersed with the exchange of gifts and the arrival of Santa Claus with his sack.

In the larger town of Iqaluit, there is a bilingual Christmas Eve carol service at St. Jude's Cathedral, and people visit after church. Christmas Day passes quietly with the family, and by afternoon children are out showing off their new sealskin boots, parkas, and bicycles.

In Labrador, Christmas celebrations extend into early January, the final event being *Nalujuk's* Night or Jannie's Night celebrated on the sixth. *Nalujuk* is an Inuit word meaning "the one who is ignorant or uninformed." The origin of the English equivalent word, Jannie, is unknown.

Christmas in far, northern Labrador is generally religious. A lot of preparation for Christmas such as cleaning, washing, and sewing takes place. People chop wood for home and church, and the church receives painting and decorating too. Caribou and seal meat are distributed to those who cannot afford to or are unable to get their own. Church services occur daily before Christmas; church bells ring, and a brass band plays hymns throughout the town and sometimes goes to the roof of the church to play.

A "love feast" at the church has the church elders serving tea and cookies while people sing hymns and carols.

As Christmas Eve gets closer, children go to bed earlier so mother may sew and make surprises and father may make wooden toys. Large, woolen stockings are hung on a nail behind the stove, on a windowsill, or on a doorknob. They will be filled with apples, raisins, apricots, prunes, candy, and some item of clothing such as a new pair of skin boots or mitts.

On Christmas Day, a candlelight service takes place for the children. They are given a bun, an apple, or something else into which a lighted candle is stuck.

Midnight church services occur on New Year's Eve.

In the evening of January 5, children go from house to house hanging up stockings. Early the next morning, they return to collect the stockings filled with gifts.

On January 6 or *Nalujuk* at a church service, all information about what has happened during the past year is announced.

During this day years ago, six or seven men used to leave the village unnoticed. They dressed in fur clothing and wore ugly masks. Each of the *Naliyuk* carried a weapon such as a whip, a harpoon, a stick, or a piece of chain. Each had a large bag hanging in front from a string around his neck. As these men walked around, if anyone was caught outdoors, he was chased indoors after receiving a whack on the bottom with a whip or stick. Older boys and men gathered outside to entice the *Naliyuk* to chase them. These *Naliyuk* visited all the homes, especially where children had been good. If bad, the children got a firm smack and were told not to be bad again. They were told to listen and to respect older people, especially their mothers and fathers. Each child had to sing a song or recite a poem, and if he or she refused, the child was smacked and not left alone until he or she cried. If the child sang or recited, there was a reward of goodies, anything from candy to homemade toys or clothing.

In the isolated coastal villages of Newfoundland, for the twelve nights of Christmas from December 25 to January 6, men and women "janney up" dressed in costumes that totally conceal their identities and go mumming door to door. They sometimes go alone or in pairs, but usually in groups. They knock loudly on the kitchen door and call, "Mummer allowed in?" in unidentifiable ingression (breathing-in speech.) Men often dress as women and women as men, or both may be fishermen or be masked with the head of a sheep. Faces are concealed with masks, veils, or paint. In small communities where small details are known, gloves hide hands. Posture and the way one walks are both altered. Some even disguise their size by stuffing their costumes or by putting lifts in their shoes.

The masked mummers stomp into a house and tease, prod, and jostle. As they perform, they are questioned, pinched, and prodded back until bit-by-bit, one-by-one, they make themselves known. The people of the house are invited to come around to drink later or invited to join the mummers on their rounds. This ends with a final party. Mumming dates back to the early 1800s. In the early part of the twentieth century, it was present in almost all of the fishing villages, but today it is rapidly disappearing.

In Newfoundland during Christmas week, it is also customary for people to "fish for the church." They bring their catches to be sold for the local parish.

## Christmas in the Early Canadian West

These reminiscences are too good to leave out in a discussion of Christmas in Canada. Christmas came to the West with the first fur traders, but the church didn't become institutionalized until the arrival of missionaries in the first half of the nineteenth century. In the pre-railway times, the fur-trading frontier celebrated Christmas in its own way.

The Hudson's Bay Company in 1843 was an oasis for Christmas. Lonely fur trappers came by dogsled to celebrate. Every man, woman, and child for miles came, including the aboriginals, for the hardy celebration which included shooting partridges, a ball in the Bachelor's Hall, and a grand dinner in the winter mess hall. Wild goose, roast beef, partridges, salt pork, and plenty of drinks were the main staples. The trappers and traders in their Sunday best and Indian women in printed calico gowns with huge, balloon-shaped sleeves and scanty skirts with colored handkerchiefs on their heads and decorated moccasins on their feet made a colorful group of celebrators at the ball. An aboriginal provided the music with a homemade fiddle along with a boy playing a kettledrum as they all danced Scottish reels. Tables at the dance were spread with cold venison, bread and butter, sweets, and tea.

From Christmas in Fort Edmonton in 1847, comes a particularly delicious recipe for moose nose. You remove the nose from the moose and place it in the coals of a hot fire until the hair is burned off, including the hair in the nostrils. The nose will be pure white after the hair comes off. Scrape the hard stuff away, and boil the meat, adding spices and onions or other vegetables to taste. Cook quickly. Some people like to let it hang for a few days before cooking to make it tender, while others put it in a smokehouse for a day or two to give it a smoked flavor. On the same menu were a dish of boiled buffalo hump and boiled buffalo calf taken by Caesarean. Other rare delicacies were "mouffle" or dried moose nose, buffalo tongue, beavers' tails, white fish browned in buffalo marrow, roast wild goose, potatoes, turnips, and bread.

Another interesting recipe is for baked beaver tail. Remove the tail from the beaver's body. Dip it into boiling water to remove the outer skin, exposing the meat. To cook in a stone oven, place the meat on a rack over a drip pan and bake one-half hour in a moderate oven. To cook over an open fire, skewer the tail on a green stick and cook slowly over the coals. This meat is very fat and rich and must be allowed to drip. Save the drippings to use over potatoes baked in their skins in an oven or a campfire.

As one can see, it is impossible in Canada, as in other countries that have a multitude of ethnic backgrounds represented in their populations, to speak of a "typical" Canadian Christmas.

# Cayman Islands

Merry Christmas!

The Cayman Islands lie about fifty miles south of Cuba in the Western Caribbean. The Caymans have around 24,000 people, and Grand Cayman is the largest of the islands with seventy-six of the total one hundred square miles and the largest population. Cayman Brac has about 1,300 residents, and Little Cayman has approximately twenty natives.

Christmas in the Caymans has become a celebration very much like that in America. Church services are held on Christmas Eve as well as at different times during the day on Christmas Day. Both Christmas and Boxing Day, December 26, are legal holidays. If Christmas should fall on a Sunday, then the following Monday and Tuesday are holidays.

Santa Claus has recently been arriving by boat, and he travels the islands in a decorated car or bus, distributing gifts to the children who have written letters to Santa Claus. Many of these are published in the newspaper. Children also hang their stockings, and Santa delivers their gifts on Christmas Eve. People exchange Christmas cards and presents with neighbors, friends, and family.

An important tradition is that of painting and brightening homes for Christmas, so interior design and decorating stores do a booming business during the season. Stores decorate extensively with tinsel, lights, toys, posters, and Nativity scenes.

Homes display numerous strings of Christmas lights for decoration as well as fresh or artificial plants, tinsel, floral garlands, strings of Christmas cards, and Nativity scenes. Many people decorate an

Australian pine tree cut from the wilds of the islands, but purchasing an imported tree, natural or artificial, seems to be increasingly popular. These trees are decorated with lights, balloons, tinsel balls, figurines, and other items similar to those used in other western nations.

Marching bands were once a very important part of the holiday celebration, but these are fading from the scene. Serenading continues in some areas where groups of carolers travel from house to house and sing Christmas carols at night about two weeks before Christmas. This culminates in the singing on Christmas Day beginning at 4:00 A.M. and continuing until sunrise, heralding Christmas Day.

Concerts are popular during the Christmas season. Many of them feature children and take place on Christmas Eve. The Cayman Drama Society presents a pantomime like those in England. A pantomime is part drama, part song and dance, and all comedy. The story line comes from a famous fairy tale or children's story. The lead character is called "Dame" and is portrayed by a man. The audience cheers the heroes and heroines and boos the villains. Schools and churches also put on their own Christmas programs.

## Christmas Eve

Young people celebrate Christmas with all-night dances, beach picnics, parties, or boat rides, but a typical Christmas Eve for families is spent doing last-minute shopping and last-minute chores like mowing and raking the lawn, last-minute house cleaning, preparing food, wrapping presents, and ironing clothes to be worn the next day.

## Christmas Day

A typical Christmas Day consists of families having morning devotions, opening Christmas gifts, exchanging Christmas greetings by visits or telephone, and attending church services. Many first, second,



3282-TUCK

and third generation family reunions take place. Late in the evening, people attend concerts in their churches.

Christmas dinner is often a baked beef and pork dish served with "bammie," a heavy, round cake made from fruits and vegetables like cassava or yam or roast plantains.

The people of Cayman Brac have some interesting traditions. The Christmas season is greeted with many intricately designed kites. Ideal winds usually occur at this time of year, and children compete to see who can create the biggest, most beautiful, and highest-flying kites.

"Backing sand" is another tradition. Many, many baskets full of clean, white sand are brought up from the beaches and spread around peoples' yards. Each housewife wants to make sure that her yard presents the most sparkling appearance of all the yards. People carrying the sand carry it with long straps holding the baskets, the straps firmly fixed across their foreheads. While the women take care of the sand, the men are busy painting the houses, for everyone wants his house to look brand new for Christmas.

The Caymans celebrate New Year's much as others around the world, by partying, dancing, and reveling.

# Chile

*Feliz Navidad!*

Christmas traditions in the South American country of Chile reflect very much those in North America. Christmas comes at a hot time of year, at the beginning of the summer vacation period.

Downtown streets and stores are decorated, and people sing and play traditional Christmas carols. Christmas trees appear everywhere and are decorated much the same as in the United States. Children write letters to Santa Claus or *Viejo Pascuero.* He comes down the chimney or through a window and puts the presents either under the Christmas tree or at the foot of the bed.

As in most predominately Roman Catholic countries, midnight mass, or, in this case, *Misa del Gallo* , Mass of the Cock, occurs. Christmas dinner usually follows with turkey as the main course. A drink called *cola de mono* similar to eggnog is served during the celebrations.

Thousands of pilgrims annually visit the small Chilean community of Andacollo. Legend claims that an Indian woodcutter named Collo had a vision in which a celestial figure spoke to him saying, "Go, Collo, to the hills where wealth and happiness await you." Obedient to the vision, he went, and as he was hacking his way through the undergrowth, his machete struck a half-buried object. He dug it out and found that it was a statue of the Virgin May. He made an altar for it in his hut. The villagers started to venerate the figure, and Collo was established as its guardian. Soon increasing numbers came to see the statue of the Virgin Mary. In the festive season, numerous dancers perform, dressed in red, blue, and green costumes, and the statue is displayed, surrounded by a carved wooden frame of roses. The statue's golden crown contains emeralds and other precious stones. A white robe edged with gold is placed on her. She is known as the *Virgin del Rosario.* On the streets around the statue, vendors sell dolls, trinkets, handkerchiefs, and hot meat pies.

Christmas is a popular time for fairs where racehorses are the main attraction, and there are booths displaying beautiful, Indian-made rugs, blankets, and jewelry.

# China

*Gun Tso Sun Tan'Gung Haw Sun!* (Cantonese) or *Kung His Hsin Nien bing Chu Shen Tan!* (Mandarin)

Christians make up only about 1 percent of the largest country in the world, China; thus, the ordinary Chinese person does not usually celebrate Christmas. The holiday has been known in China for over 400 years, but most Christian churches are isolated, and the general public does not know many of their celebrations. Church attendance at Christmas is very high. Many non-Christians attend out of curiosity

Like Japan, China has witnessed a large growth of commercial Christmas. Places like luxury hotels where foreign visitors stay often have the traditional trimmings of Christmas. Christmas trees with colored lights and traditional Christmas food and music are featured. Stores have men dressed as Santa Claus giving out candies, and waiters and waitresses don Santa hats.

The Chinese call Christmas *Sheng Dan Jieh* or Holy Birth Festival. The Christmas tree is called The Tree of Light. Because of their love of color, the Chinese greatly enjoy western Christmas decorations, and they make extensive use of their own colorful paper lanterns for holiday decorating. Evergreens are used also as are brightly colored paper chains, paper flowers, and posters carrying messages of peace and joy.

Children hang muslin stockings, and they expect *Shengdan Laoren* (Father Christmas) or *Dun Che Lao Ren* (Christmas Old Man) to fill them. In giving gifts, people stick to their traditional way of giving choice, costly presents only to family members, while giving lesser ones for remembrance to friends and distant family members.

Fireworks are sometimes used to usher in Christmas. Christmas cards are sent, and they often show the holy family with Chinese features and the manger scene is in a Chinese setting.

# Colombia

*Feliz Navidad!*

In the South American country of Colombia, Christmas occurs in the summertime. People have Christmas trees and use pine branches, Spanish moss, and flowers to decorate. A manger scene or *pesebre* is displayed in a prominent place in the house; it may be simple or elaborate, according to the family's wishes and means. A backdrop for the scene, often made of fine, blue muslin strewn with silver stars is arranged first. Sometimes the manger figures are imported or made by native craftsmen from Raquira or other villages. Shimmering candles and small, colored lanterns surround the *pesebre.* Children gather round the scene, singing *villancicos* or old Christmas carols to the accompaniment of guitars and other stringed instruments.

## Christmas Eve

Christmas Eve in Colombia has a tradition not found elsewhere. At about 9:00 P.M. Christmas Eve in Bogota, Papayan, and other towns in the Departments of Cauca and Tolima, one sees happy, laughing groups of people coming out of houses, dressed in masquerade costumes. This is the night of *aguinaldos* or presents when everyone disguises himself with fancy dress and mask and goes out into the streets for merrymaking. Everyone tries to recognize his friends, and when someone's identity is discovered, the person recognizing him claims an *aguinaldo* or gift from the one recognized. This tradition has great popularity among the young and especially sweethearts. As midnight approaches, the masqueraders disappear from the streets, and stillness descends.

Church bells peal for midnight mass. Families gather for Christmas dinner after mass. The meal usually includes tamales, chicken, turkey, or roast pig. There are *bunuelos* served with golden honey for dessert. Feasting and fun continue among the grownups until the early morning hours, but children go to bed after placing their shoes on their windowsills or in the corridors. While they sleep, the Christ Child and the Three Kings will fill the shoes with toys and candy.

In the northwestern state of Antioquia, Christmas customs center largely on people's country homes. Beginning December 15 and ending January 6, there is one *marrano asado* or barbecue after another with plenty of food and drink and lots of music. Musicians often play folk music on the *bambuco,* a *conjunto* or guitar, and maracas. Plenty of singing and dancing occur, and the main course is usually roast pig served with *arepas* that are flat, cornmeal cakes. *Bunuelos,* Colombian doughnuts, are served also.

Another traditional Christmas custom found only in Antioqula is the sending up of the *globo,* a huge balloon made of colored paper. With the whole family assisting, the brightly colored paper is cut into sixteen triangles and glued together into a global shape which stands four or five feet high. At the base is a ring of wire to which are fastened rags dipped into gasoline. It takes eight children to hold out the sides of the balloon so that air can inflate it. The father sets fire to the rags, turning around three times. He releases the balloon that drifts off, ablaze. The launching of *globos* is illegal throughout Colombia, but so ingrained is the tradition that the law often turns a blind eye.

# Cuba

*Feliz Navidad!*

Christmas returns to Cuba at last! Communist Cuba officially became an atheist country three years after the 1959 revolution that brought Fidel Castro to power. Christmas as a government-sanctioned holiday disappeared in 1969. President Castro suspended all Christmas celebrations then, arguing that they would hinder a 1970 sugar harvest that he expected to hit a record ten million tons, but the harvest fell disastrously short. For the next two decades, the Communist Party's official atheism and government animosity toward religion was enough to dissuade most Cubans from openly celebrating Christmas. The collapse of Communism in 1989 forced changes in Cuba, ranging from the legalization of the use of United States currency to a revival of the Roman Catholic Church and attendance at mass and baptism.

In January of 1998, Pope John Paul II visited Cuba. As a favor to the Pope before his visit, the Cuban government announced that Christmas, 1997, would be a one-day national holiday. The Pope's visit caused a great warming of relations between Fidel Castro's government and the Church. In late fall of 1998, the Cuban government declared that Christmas Day would become an official, permanent holiday. Cuba granted the Roman Catholic Church the authority to send a national holiday greeting over government-controlled radio. Cardinal Jaime Ortega, Cuba's top Catholic leader, received permission to read the message of Christmas in the afternoon over the music station called Radio Musical Nacional.

Cubans have embraced the idea of having another day off, but the Christmas celebrations remain mainly secular. For many people, the holiday times bring nostalgia and a longing to see friends and relatives who have fled to other countries, especially the United States.

Difficult economic times have caused a severe shortage of goods needed for the celebration such as food, toys, and new clothes. Some say that goods are even less available than in earlier days. People line up at the dollar stores that sell imported goods and usually hold end-of-the-year sales. Although prices have dropped somewhat, it is still so expensive that often families must pool their money to buy the basic ingredients of a holiday dinner.

Christmas trees and decorations sell out weeks before Christmas. Bright decorations are found on trees and lights throughout the streets. Even during the government's ban of Christmas, state-run hotels like the five-star Melia Cohiba Hotel displayed fancy Christmas trees in their lobbies and had a bell-ringing Santa Claus for the diplomatic corps.

Despite bad economic conditions, the people do find money for pork, apple cider, and other treats. Most families, especially in the capital, decorate a small artificial tree in their homes and share quiet holidays meals.

As in 1997 when Christmas was again declared a national holiday, people crowd the churches for midnight mass. This tradition continues to grow each year.

# Cyprus

*Kala Christougenna!*

On the Mediterranean island of Cyprus, Greeks represent 80 percent of the population and occupy the southern two-thirds of the island. In 1974 the Turks invaded the north, and now these predominately Muslim people dominate the northern one-third of the island. Christmas celebrations reflect the dominant Christian church, the Church of Cyprus, which adheres to the Greek Orthodox traditions. The celebration reflects a mixture of Cypriotic and European traditions and is not as commercialized as in Europe and America, being a more religious occasion, with gift giving taking place on New Year's Eve.

Window decorations and other signs of Christmas begin to appear in mid-December. Many people fast the week before Christmas. Seasonal concerts and plays are performed, and groups of children go around to houses singing carols, some collecting money for charity. Customarily, people offer these children cakes or other sweets.

## Christmas Day

On Christmas Day, the churches of all denominations are crowded. Christmas breakfast follows church. For a Cypriot family this can be an ordinary breakfast or the traditional soup called *mayiritsa* made of rice, eggs, and lemon juice. In the villages, housewives still make *Christopsoma* or the bread of Christ that is shared among family members.

Finishing breakfast, people go around to visit relatives and friends to wish them the season's greetings. Christmas lunch features a magnificent display of beautifully prepared dishes, a mixture of Cypriotic and European delicacies. In most villages, the ancient tradition of killing a pig is still observed, the meat used to prepare dishes such as sausages, smoked pork fillet, smoked leg of pork, and brawn.

## New Year's Day

New Year's Day coincides with St. Basil's Day. The saint, an old man with white hair and beard, dresses in a red outfit with black boots and brings good luck to households and presents to children. The equivalent of Santa Claus, he brings presents on New Year's Day rather than at Christmas.

This day centers on the family, but this is beginning to change as more people spend a night celebrating in a hotel, restaurant, or nightclub. A lot of drinking, eating, and merrymaking take place on New Year's Eve. After the exchange of wishes and kisses for the New Year, the *vassilopitta,* the traditional St. Basil's cake, is cut. The cutting of the cake follows a strict order according to tradition. The head of the family first cuts a piece of cake for Christ, then for the Virgin Mary, then for the poor. Next he cuts his own piece, his wife's, and then those for absent family members. Finally, everyone gets a piece. The cake contains a coin, and whoever finds it will be lucky throughout the coming year. The legend goes that Caesaria was being threatened with an attack by the Cappadocians, and St. Basil made an appeal to his people to contribute to the defense of their country. The people offered money and jewelry. The Cappadocians gave up their plans of attack, and St. Basil wanted to return the contributions of the people, but he didn't know who gave what. He made loaves of bread in which he hid the gifts and gave these to the people. On New Year's Eve also, some children or adults dressed as St. Basil go round to homes singing popular songs about St. Basil or New Year's.

## Epiphany

Epiphany or *Kalanda* on January 6, commemorating the baptism of Christ, is celebrated with religious fervor in Cyprus. A special church service is held in the morning, and a baptism ceremony takes place. In seaside towns, this service is conducted in the sea. The priest throws a cross in the water, and swimmers dive in to retrieve it. At the moment when the priest casts the cross into the sea, white doves are released, symbolizing the Holy Ghost. In other places, the baptism ceremony takes place in streams, rivers, or ponds.

The common name for Epiphany in Cyprus is *Phota* meaning lights. It is believed that the Holy Trinity present at the baptism gives the Christmas season its light. On leaving church, people try to bring back to their homes the flame of the candles that have been blessed. This flame is used to light the oil lamp before the *iconostasis* or arrangement of religious icons or figures. People also receive bottles of holy water on this day. They sprinkle all parts of their house, garden, and yard. They also drink some of it and keep the rest to use in the event of sickness or misfortune.

Epiphany, according to superstition, is the last day when the evil spirits or werewolves called *kalikanjdari* stay on earth. They represent the souls of children who died unbaptized. The *kalikanjdari* leave the underworld to spend the twelve days of Christmas among the living. During this time, they cause trouble and mischief among unsuspecting persons. In order to protect oneself from them, one makes *xcotiana* or pancakes the day before Epiphany, and together with the sausages and other food, they are thrown on the roof for the *kalikanjdari* to eat. The only thing these spirits fear is Christianity, and seeing the sign of the cross, they run away to hide, and the priest sprinkles holy water on the houses to keep them away.



3282-TUCK

# Czech Republic

*Vesele Vanoce!*

The highlight of the most celebrated holiday in the European Czech Republic is Christmas Eve. Preparation starts well before then, about ten days before Christmas. Market stalls sell carp that are kept in the bathtub until prepared for the special Christmas feast. Christmas trees appear everywhere. Department stores are busy places as people hurry to buy Christmas tree candles, chocolate figures, glass ornaments, sparklers, and twinkling stars. Almonds and raisins must be purchased for the traditional Christmas cake. Presents must be bought for family and friends, presents that are practical, funny, special, or plain luxurious.

Children behave very well, learn Christmas carols and poems, and offer to help at home. Very lucky at Christmas, children get presents from their grandparents, at school, from the places where their parents work, and at home.

At about 5:00 P.M. on Christmas Eve, dinner begins. The fragrances of coffee, ginger, vanilla, frying carp, and fish soup fill the air. Everyone takes his place at the table that is decorated with fir and mistletoe. Often candlesticks made from apples decorate the table.

Years ago, there was a tradition of placing a chain all around the table to ensure that nothing in the household got lost and that no household member would die in the coming year. The table then was laden with plenty of everything including a lot of meat. In the nineteenth century this changed, and today the main courses are fish soup usually made of carp, potato salad, and carp again, either fried or baked with a sauce. *Calta,* a plaited white bread baked to a golden crisp, is often served with *masica* or fruit stew made of dried pears, apples, prunes, nuts, and raisins.

When the tradition of eating a sumptuous meal with a lot of meat ceased, some regions got around this. In one area they celebrated Christmas twice; they had a feast with meat on December 23 to ensure prosperity, and on December 24, they had a Christmas dinner without meat.

Wafers with honey were popular at Christmas years ago. Wafer making was a special trade, and they were made with special utensils resembling long, metal tongs with flat or square jaws and having an engraved or smooth surface. After honey was spread on the wafers, they were decorated with rose hips, garlic, or special herbs, not merely for decoration, but also to protect the health of household members and domestic animals.

Until a short time ago, special pancakes were grilled from "exact dough" made from flour of the first or last harvested ears and ground at home. These pancakes were believed to have magical powers, but only if they had been made in a very ritualistic way. Besides special requirements for the flour, the water had to come from different springs, wells, or brooks. Magical herbs had to be boiled in the water, and only then could the dough be made. The pancakes had to be taken out of the house before dawn of Christmas Day, and one had to walk with them around the altar in the church. Only after all this did they have magical powers that were used all year. Pancakes were grated and added to the food of people who took ill; crumbs were added to animal food and children's bath water, and they were burned as incense.

Gingerbread was and still is a holiday favorite. The oldest record of gingerbread is from a part of the Czech Republic called Turnov in North Bohemia where it was sold at Christmas in the fourteenth century. Today's recipe is almost identical to the original. Gingerbread making has become very sophisticated. Cardboard patterns are created for shapes such as figures of people, stars, houses, birds, fish, baskets, or manger scenes. These are placed on the rolled-out dough and cut with a sharp knife. After having baked, they are glazed with egg white and decorated with a white icing. Many of these decorate the trees.

There is a custom of cutting an apple and guessing the length of one's lifetime from the shape of the core. Apples since very early days have been carriers of news of happiness and health. Another tradition requires cutting a branch from a cherry tree and putting it in water indoors to bloom. If the bloom opens in time for Christmas, one will have good luck; it's also a sign that winter may be short.

After finishing dinner, the whole family goes to the room where the Christmas tree stands. It was decorated on the twenty-third or the morning of the twenty-fourth with small red apples, nuts, gingerbreads, miniature animals made from dough, baubles, tinsel, stars, chains, and chocolate candies. The top of the tree usually displays a star, often made from straw. The Czech St. Nicholas, *Svaty Mikalas,* climbs down a golden rope from heaven along with his companions, an angel and a whip-carrying devil, to deliver presents.

Manger scenes or "Bethlehems" are often placed under the trees. They may be hand-carved of wood or sculpted from bread dough that is painted. In addition to the regular crib setting, there are peasants and tradesmen from the area such as bakers, butchers, night watchmen, miners, and shepherds.

Late at night, the little ones are put to bed, and the others continue to sit around with a warm feeling of celebration while some go to midnight mass. The sounds of Bach, Ja Jakub Ryba, and old Czech carols resound in the night.

# Denmark

*Glaedig Jul!*

It's not surprising that the lovely, European country of Denmark, the home of a writer such as Hans Christian Andersen, would take the many happy traditions of the Christmas season so to heart.

As early as October, Danish newspapers begin to insert notices about sending Christmas mail to far-off countries, and the Copenhagen theater, *Folketeatret,* announces its annual Christmas program which has taken place each year since 1888. The year's Christmas stamp, the idea first invented by a Danish postmaster in 1904 and sold annually to raise money for charity, is published. Soon there is a story in the papers about a ninety foot tall fir tree being cut down in Grib Forest in the area of North Zealand; the new tree will stand in the square facing the town hall in the capital city of Copenhagen.

The Danes observe the four Sundays of Advent before Christmas. A common scene has the father struggling through the cold, snowy dark heading homewards from the baker's shop with a very special Christmas cake, the recipe known only to the baker. The family gathers around the coffee table to enjoy the special cake, to light the candles on the Advent wreath, and to listen to old Christmas songs. Advent wreaths are made of spruce or fir and decorated with four candles that are lit successively on the four Sundays of Advent.

In mid-December the Great Baking Day occurs when the housewife mixes the dough for the *brune kager* or brown cookies. The mixing is often done two or three weeks before the baking so that the dough might ripen and the flavors blend. They make three to four hundred cookies since every visitor during the holidays must be fed, lest he or she take the Yule spirit from the home.

By mid-December, thousands of letters begin to pour into Denmark. They are mostly from American and English children and addressed to "Santa Claus, Greenland." Since Greenland is a Danish possession, the letters turn up at the Tourist Association in Copenhagen. Ladies write letters around the clock answering these letters. Danish children never write to Santa Claus, or in their case, *Julemand*, for they know that it is their fathers who are really Santa Claus or *Julemand*. They also do not hang stockings by the chimney.

The Danes love to decorate for Christmas. The shops fill their windows with displays and frame them with garlands of fir. The windows are often filled with paper hearts, Christmas stars, a little, white village church, toy electric trains, and dozens of tobogganing *nisser*, small gnomes or sprites. Fir garlands are often strung in the streets from lamppost to lamppost, and large papier-mâché Christmas bells and stars are hung.

A long-standing tradition occurs the evening the family prepares its tree decorations, the unofficial start of the Yuletide season in Denmark. In his story "The Christmas Tree," written in 1845, Hans Christian Andersen describes the excitement of choosing the tree in the forest, bringing it home, and decorating it. " . . . on one branch there were finely made nets, cut from coloured paper; each net filled with sweets and other goodies; gilded apples and walnuts hung as if they had grown there, and more than a hundred red, blue, and white candles were carefully stuck among the branches . . . and right at the top was placed a star of gold tinsel; it was a magnificent scene, quite unforgettably magnificent."

Most Danish homes have one or two large, mysterious, cardboard boxes that are brought out once a year. These contain the Christmas tree decorations. The dining table is covered with protective paper, and lots of colored paper, paste, scissors, tapes, ribbons, a staple machine, and odds and ends are placed on the table. The family gathers to set to work to add to its collection of handmade, Christmas decorations. They inspect the older decorations: multicolored paper cones and hearts, baskets in the shapes of woodland animals, silver bells, golden stars, angels, tinsel, tiny ships made of walnut shells, tiny animals of fir cones and scraps of wood, and delicate decorations made of glass, paper, and straw. They create new masterpieces, munch on cookies, and sing Christmas songs.

A well-known decoration, the Danish interwoven heart, was first created in Denmark, and it is believed that Hans Christian Andersen invented it. These paper hearts are traditionally made of red and white paper, the colors of the Danish flag. Andersen was quite handy with scissors, cutting out silhouettes and folding and snipping many delightful miniatures. He was also an expert at making paper cones and baskets with silky paper edging.

Small Danish flags are often used as decorations. Stalls in towns sell gingerbread cookies in the shapes of peasant men and women or hearts, and these are placed on the trees as decorations also. Stalls also sell Swedish *julebukke* or billy goats made of plaited straw. These range from very tiny ones for the tree to huge ones that will hold several loads of hay.

The first known, illuminated tree in Denmark was in 1802, at the Holsteinborg estate. The custom came from Germany. There weren't many paper decorations on the early trees; paper decorations didn't become popular until the Victorian age, for by then, paper had become common and inexpensive.

## Little Christmas

On December 23, known as Little Christmas, it is often customary to make enough apple fritters on this day to last over the next three days.

## Christmas Eve

Christmas Eve or *Juleaften* marks the biggest family event of the Danish year. All work stops in the afternoon, and at 4:00 P.M. church bells throughout the country begin to chime, summoning people to candlelit churches decorated with fir garlands and Christmas trees before the altars.

The traditional Christmas dinner of roast goose or duck stuffed with apples and prunes or a pork roast is served, usually with red cabbage, pickled gherkins, cowberry jam, and small, sugar-glazed potatoes. A rice pudding called *ris a l'amonde* made of rice cooked in milk and mixed with whipped cream and chopped almonds is served with the meal. One almond in the pudding is not chopped, but left whole, and whoever finds it wins a small prize, usually a baby pig made of marzipan.

After dinner, the Christmas tree candles are lit, and everyone joins hands and walks around the tree singing old Christmas hymns like "*Glade Jul, Dejilige Jul*" or "Silent Night, Holy Night." Brightly wrapped gifts are then exchanged. While all of this takes place, the father or some other family member slips mysteriously from the room, and there is a sudden knock at the door. Who should appear but *Julemand,* a very close relative of Santa Claus, who looks quite similar to Santa. He wishes everyone *Glaedig Jul* as he enters the house and asks if the children have been good. They answer "Yes, *Julemand.*" Then he asks if they will promise to obey Mummy and Daddy always. The children often lose their patience with this and tell their father to stop kidding and get on with the presents. After all of the excitement of the evening, beverages and cookies of all sorts and shapes are served.

On Christmas Eve, the Danes forget no living creature. A sheaf of rye or corn is placed outside for the birds to eat. Horses and cattle are given extra food and care, and even the *Julenisse,* a Christmas gnome or sprite, is remembered with some of the rice pudding or a saucer of milk. A candle is placed in the windows of homes to offer food and shelter to travelers.

## Christmas Day

In some parts of Denmark, there is a custom called "blowing in the Yule." At sunrise, musicians climb to the church belfry and play four hymns, one to each point of the compass. The church bells begin to ring, and the peace of Christmas is ushered in.

Christmas Day or *Juledag* is often spent attending church, sleeping, eating, and visiting friends, neighbors, and relatives to taste their Christmas baking and to look at their trees

## Legends

The most common Christmas figure in Denmark is the Christmas *Nisse* or *Julenisse.* A *nisse* is a gnome or sprite who is very small but strong, old but agile, gruff and grumpy but not without humor, helpful where respected, but perhaps a bit dangerous when ignored. His homespun breeches and smock made of unbleached wool are gray, and his cap and long stockings are red. He wears white clogs on his feet.

The stories of *nisser* are over 4,000 years old, but the idea of a Christmas *Nisse* or *Julenisse* is only slightly over 100 years old. They are known to like farms and farm folk as long as these people don't tease them. On Christmas Eve, they gather in the tower of the village church where they help the sexton toll the advent of Christmas.

The poor *Julenisse* seems to be extremely busy at Christmas carrying billboards, selling neckties in department stores, and posing for Christmas card illustrations. His likeness appears in magazines, in cartoon strips, on Christmas trees, in vendors' stands on street corners, and in many other places. A particularly creepy, almost sinister kind of *nisse* is found at Christmas time leering out from behind curtains, wall plants, chandeliers, and knickknacks. After Christmas, many of them are cruelly crumpled up and thrown into the fire.

*Julemand,* a relative of Santa Claus, was once thought to ride in a sleigh drawn by eight legs. He sped through the air across the icy waste and over *Jotunheim,* the realm of the dead, on his rounds.

Years ago on Christmas night, when the dead were up and about, all living things had to keep indoors. Anybody who stayed out might be carried off by the *Asgardsrejsen,* a surging train of dead souls that swept through the land headed by the god of death himself, Odin. These poor, lost souls were the *nisser's* kinsmen. No one would venture outside until sometime after midnight when people bearing blazing torches went out to meet the new sun. In later times, they went out to gather inside the churches for Christmas mass.

# Egypt

*Mboni Chrismen!*

Christians in the northeastern African country of Egypt make up about 7 percent of the population. The Egyptian Coptic Church adheres to the eastern calendar and celebrates Christmas on January 7. Because the majority of the country is Muslim, Christmas is not the public celebration that it is elsewhere.

Egypt's Christians are a very religious people, and Christmas is a very serious holiday. People fast the forty days of Advent as a means of purifying themselves in preparation for the holy day of Christmas. They fast by not eating during daylight hours and by abstaining from meat, eggs, and dairy products during the fasting period.

Christmas carols are sung by choirs, and international carols are mixed in with Coptic carols for a nice blend of Christmas music.

On Christmas Eve, Christians attend midnight masses wearing new clothes. The most famous of these masses is at St. Mark's Cathedral in Cairo and is presided over by the head of the Egyptian Coptic Church.

Families return home to eat their Christmas meal called *fata* that consists of rice, beans, garlic, and boiled meat. A special cookie *kahk* is made in the shape of a cross.

Parents distribute gifts and new clothes to the children.

# England

Merry Christmas!

The European island nation of England has contributed many customs to the worldwide celebration of Christmas: Christmas cards, the hanging of mistletoe, the hanging of Christmas stockings, the monarch's Christmas message to the world, caroling, the traditional Christmas dinner of roast turkey, mince pie, plum pudding, and the wassail bowl.

## Christmas Card

Henry Cole, the first director of the Victoria and Albert Museum in London, probably created the first Christmas card. In November of 1843, he wrote in his diary, "Mr. Horsley [John Calcott Horsley] came and brought design for Christmas card." A thousand lithographic copies of Horsley's design were made in 1846; it showed a family full of good cheer surrounded by a trellis type of design. Two smaller frames on either side showed Christmas charitable acts: "Clothing the Naked" and "Feeding the Hungry." The card was hand-colored and put on sale at Felix Summerly's Treasure House, a shop that Cole had helped to set up in Bond Street, London.

Some people credit W.C.T. Dobson with the first Christmas card. In 1844, he sent a friend a sketch he had made which symbolized the Christmas spirit. The next year he had copies of his lithograph sent to friends. This card is earlier than Cole's, but not many knew of it since it wasn't put up for sale. It was another ten years, around 1856, before the idea of the Christmas card caught on.

## Holiday Decorations

Homes in England display holly, ivy, mistletoe, and other greenery as well as brightly colored paper chains and streamers. Romans brought holy and ivy into their homes for good luck. Christians adopted the holly with its needle-sharp leaves and blood-red berries as a symbol of Christ's crown of thorns. Ivy was considered to be a woman's plant and holly a man's. In the Midlands of England, if the first holly brought into the home was prickly, the master would rule for the coming year, and if it were smooth-leaved, the mistress ruled. Holly was also thought to be hateful to witches and goblins and therefore good luck to the householder.

Mistletoe, known to be an important part of the Druids' rituals, was never accepted by the church except at York Minster, the only church allowed to use mistletoe for decoration, and where, each year, a bough of mistletoe was brought in and laid on the altar. Then a proclamation was made offering "a public liberty, pardon, and freedom to all sorts of inferior and even wicked people at the gates of the city to the four corners of the earth." The origin of the custom of kissing under the mistletoe, another British idea, is unknown.

The traditional Christmas tree was popularized in England by Prince Albert, Queen Victoria's German husband, in 1841. There had been Christmas trees before then, but Prince Albert made it an important part of the family-centered Christmas. After World War II, a huge, brightly decorated Christmas tree was placed in London's Trafalgar Square, a gift from the city of Oslo, Norway to commemorate Anglo-Norwegian cooperation during the war. Trees are decorated in England much as they are in most European countries and in America, with colored lights, tinsel, and fanciful, store bought or handmade decorations.

## Earlier Practices

The Feast of St. Nicholas falls on December 6 and was celebrated more in England in earlier times than today. Since he is the patron saint of children, often children are given small presents of fancy gingerbreads or toys. Parents ask the children to write letters to St. Nicholas or Father Christmas, asking for toys they would like to receive at Christmas. Traditionally, these notes should be left on a windowsill or just inside the chimney so that Father Christmas can reach them easily.

An interesting medieval custom on St. Nicholas Day was the election of Boy Bishops. In many Roman Catholic schools throughout the country, pupils would elect one of their friends to be the Boy Bishop from December 6 to Holy Innocents Day on December 28. This boy bore the name of a bishop, wore the ornate robes and the bishop's mitre hat, and carried the pastoral staff. He read the holy offices in church, and people held feasts in his honor. The Boy Bishop was allowed to appoint his friends as canons and priests. If he happened to die during this time he was a bishop, he was buried with the honors of a real bishop. There is the tomb of one such Boy Bishop in Salisbury Cathedral. The selection of a Boy Bishop was thought to encourage young boys to choose a career in the church. The whole idea was offensive to Protestants, and it was eventually abolished.

Another interesting medieval custom occurred on All-Hallows Eve, October 31, when it was traditional to choose the Lord of Misrule who would reign until February 2, Candlemas. His task was to ensure that there was continuous merriment from New Year's Eve through Twelfth Night on January 6. He was also called "The Master of Merry Disport," "The Abbot of Unreason," or the "Christmas King." Representing disorder, fun, and merrymaking, he made Christmas a welcome break during the long, hard, winter months of that time. Often noblemen had a Lord of Misrule elected from the lower classes in their homes at Christmas. The Sheriff, the Lord Mayor, the colleges at Oxford, and the Inns of Court practiced this same tradition that died out in the sixteenth century.

St. Thomas Day on December 21, honoring the patron saint of old people, was a time for giving the elderly small presents of money to help them buy their Christmas food. Just to prevent anyone from being forgotten, the old people asked for their money; this was called "Thomasing," "going a-gooding," or "mumpling." Poor children of the parish used to go around on this day asking for corn for their frumenty, cakes, or sweets. Frumenty was a kind of porridge made from grains of wheat boiled in milk and seasoned with sugar and cinnamon. In the county of Warwickshire, it was called "going a-corning." As they went around the villages, the children would sing:

"Christmas is coming and the geese are getting fat,
Please spare a penny for the old man's hat,
If you haven't got a penny, a ha'penny will do,
If you haven't got a ha'penny, God bless you."

The Boar's Head ceremony has taken place annually from medieval times at Queen's College, Oxford University, on the Saturday before Christmas. The ceremony honors a student from one of the Oxford colleges who once escaped from a boar in a very original manner. The student was walking in a nearby forest studying from a book of Aristotle, when suddenly a fearsome looking wild boar came rushing from the underbrush. The student rammed the book down the boar's throat explaining, *"Graecum est."* or "It's in Greek." During the college ceremony, the chef carries in on a silver platter a boar's head with an orange in its mouth and surrounded by rosemary, bay, and holly. The choir follows behind, singing:

"*Caput apri defero* (I carry the boar's head)
*Reddens, laudes, Domino* (Giving praises to God)
The boars's head in hand bear I,
With garlands gay and rosemary,
I pray you all sing merrily
*Qui estis in convivio*" (You who are at the banquet)

The orange is given to the chief singer and the sprigs of rosemary and bay to the guests. Boars' heads were displayed in a great many places at Christmas since boar hunts were very popular in the Middle Ages.

During medieval times, the most important celebration of Christmas Eve was the hauling of the Yule log; a log just the right size and shape was selected, trimmed, dragged home, and rolled onto the fire to burn through the Christmas season until January 6, Twelfth Night. The origins of the custom are pagan, but the church attempted to give the Yule log some Christian tradition by saying that the log should be ash because Jesus was first washed and dressed alongside an ash fire which the shepherds had made. They chose ash because it will burn while it is still green, so it may be used at a moment's notice, and it does not spatter when it burns. It was considered unlucky to let the Yule log fire go out, and it was also embarrassing to have to go to a neighbor to get a light; therefore, many towns and villages kept a communal bonfire going through the Christmas period. Many superstitions were connected with the Yule log. A maiden must wash her hands before touching the log, or the log would burn poorly. A squinting or barefoot person entering the house while the Yule log was burning was bad luck. If anyone threw ashes out of the house on Christmas Day, it was believed that he or she was throwing the ashes in Jesus' face. The ashes were also believed to have magical properties. They could cure a toothache, rid cattle of vermin, make the land more fertile, and protect the home from fire and bad luck.

Another interesting, ancient tradition is the making of Dumb Cakes, a dish made by single girls who wanted to know who their husbands were going to be. The girl must make the cake using "an eggshellful of salt, another of wheatmeal and a third of barley" while remaining absolutely quiet and alone. After putting it in the oven, she opened the door of the house and then went to bed, and her future husband would walk in at midnight and turn the cake. In the Cotswolds region, the cook wrote her initials on the top of the cake, and at midnight her intended would walk in and add his initials next to hers.

It used to be the tradition to toll church bells from 11:00 P.M. until midnight on Christmas Eve. This was called "The Old Lad's Passing" which tolled for the death of the Devil and the approaching birth of Christ. The custom of calling it that was forbidden after the Reformation, the name considered too affectionate for the Devil.

One superstition centered around animals on Christmas Eve; it was believed that even the lowly animals celebrated Christ's birth. The cows in the cowshed and the deer in the forest went down on their knees at midnight. Bees were supposed to awaken from their winter sleep and hum a song of praise to Christ. Animals were also supposed to be able to speak like humans. Only those who led a blameless life could hear them. Even the trees and plants along the River Jordan bowed in reverence at midnight. Ghosts, witches, and other evil creatures were supposed to have their powers suspended.

Games have been an important part of the English celebration of Christmas since medieval times. After Christmas lunch, medieval families entertained themselves; it was the only time that the working population was allowed to play games. Henry VIII issued a proclamation forbidding them at any other time. One game was called Snap Dragon; raisins, currants, and other dried fruit were heaped onto a shallow dish, and brandy was poured on top of them. The lights were extinguished, and the brandy was set on fire. The idea was to snatch the fruit out of the flames and eat it. Another game was Cross and Pyle, similar to calling head or tails, but it involved betting. Many games similar to ninepins were played. Archery and tilting were played outdoors. Hunt the Slipper, Forfeits, Blind Man's Buff, and Hoop and Hide (Hide and Seek) were other games played during Christmas. The last game of the day was Yawning for a Cheshire Cheese; towards midnight, everyone in the house sat in a circle, and whoever yawned the widest, the longest, the loudest, and the most times was presented with a Cheshire cheese.

## Christmas Crackers

Christmas crackers, another English contribution to Christmas, date back to Queen Victoria's time. The inventor was a pastry cook and confectioner by the name of Tom Smith. While on vacation in Paris, he noticed in some shop windows sugared almonds the French called *bonbons* or *dragees* that were sold in twists of colored paper.

He returned to London and created the cracker, a cylinder-shaped, decorated tube; eventually the bang, a tiny explosion caused by the friction of two chemically treated strips of cardboard being rubbed together, was added. Crackers today range from the simple, colored paper container with its weak bang and containing a rumpled paper hat and a very small, plastic toy to the very beautifully decorated masterpieces containing expensive jewelry or other costly items. They are usually placed beside the plates at Christmas dinner and opened after the main meal.

## Stir Up Sunday

Stir Up Sunday is the Sunday before the beginning of Advent, that is the fifth Sunday before Christmas. By tradition, this is the last day when Christmas cakes and puddings can be made if they are to be ready for Christmas. Many believe the day gets its name from the idea that everyone in the home takes turns stirring the pudding or cake while making a wish, but the name actually comes from the collection taken during the church service that day. "Stir up we beseech thee, O Lord, the wills of thy faithful people, that they plenteously bringing forth the fruit of good works, may of thee be plenteously rewarded." A coin placed in the Christmas pudding before it's cooked, as well as sometimes a ring and a thimble, brings the finder of the coin worldly fortune, the ring a marriage, and the thimble a life of blessedness. The Christmas cake is a much later tradition than the Christmas pudding, appearing in the mid-nineteenth century. The cake was really only plum pudding without the alcohol so as to make it suitable for family tea.

Wassailing, a centuries-old English tradition, was a harmless, pagan tradition that the church didn't try to stop. The word *wassail* comes from Anglo Saxon and means literally "the whole." If someone said to you, "Wassail," you would reply "Drinkhail" which means "your health." Families kept a wassail bowl steaming away throughout the Christmas season. One made the drink by mixing hot ale with the pulp of roasted apples and adding sugar and spices. In some parts of England, singers went from house to house with a wassail bowl decorated with ribbons, garlands, and sometimes a gilded apple. The singers invited the householders to drink wassail to the season and then to top up the bowl. Today wassail is served at holiday parties and get-togethers.

## Christmas Eve

On Christmas Eve in England, children hang stockings above the fireplace or at the foot of their beds so that Father Christmas can fill them. Parents often decorate the tree after the children have gone to bed. Midnight church services often feature carol singing before the beginning of the main service.

## Christmas Day

Special Christmas Day church services are held, and the beautiful carol service from King's College Chapel, Cambridge University, is generally televised on Christmas Day.

Dinner usually takes place in the early afternoon. The meal includes roast turkey or goose, roast potatoes, an array of veggies, mince pie, and plum pudding decorated with holly and flaming with brandy. In the early evening, tea is served, accompanied by a rich fruitcake with a thick marzipan (almond paste) icing.

The first reference to turkey at Christmas came during Henry VIII's time. Before that a good Christmas meal was fish, goose, cockerel, or bustard while the wealthy feasted on peacock or swan.

After dinner, the monarch's televised message to the people is broadcast to all parts of the British Commonwealth. King George V, Queen Elizabeth's grandfather, began this tradition, using the radio.

## Boxing Day

Boxing Day on December 26 was probably named after the old Christmas tradition of putting alms boxes around the church at Christmas. These alms boxes were opened on Christmas Day, and the contents were distributed the day after. This practice was called "the Box money" or "the dole of the Christmas Box." The term might also come from the old custom of apprentices and servants asking their masters and masters' customers for small amounts of money at Christmas. They collected the money in small earthenware boxes that were broken when opened. The opening was usually done the day after Christmas. Today Boxing Day is the day when people give gifts of money to those people who have provided services throughout the year, postmen, paper carriers, and dustmen.

## English Holiday Theatre

One of the most endearing Christmas traditions in England is the production of the pantomime. Boxing Day used to be the beginning of the pantomime season, but today pantomimes begin long before Christmas. An English pantomime, an idea begun in the eighteenth century, is a stage production based on a popular children's tale such as *Babes in the Woods, Cinderella, Aladdin,* or *Little Red Riding Hood.* A pantomime features men playing women's parts, women playing men's parts, lots of music and dancing, many jokes, and the inviting of audience participation by hissing the villains and cheering the heroes or heroines. The comic lead often referred to as the "Dame" is played by a man. The romantic lead or Leading Boy plays the hero, a character such as Prince Charming. Pantomimes are very popular and often feature famous actors and actresses in the lead roles in very lavish productions in the larger cities. Many villages and schools put on their own more modest but equally entertaining pantomimes.

One of the first pantomimes was *Harlequin Sorcerer* produced by John Rich at the Lincoln's Inn Fields Theatre in London in 1717.

Other theater productions popular during the holiday season are the annual production of *Peter Pan* in London and the National Theatre's version of *Pied Piper.* During the Middle Ages, the paradise plays were often presented on Adam and Eve's Day, December 24.

The tradition of the Mummers' Play is centuries old in England, and at one time mummers were found in nearly every village. In the Mummers' Play, lines are passed orally from generation to generation. The cast usually has six to eight men and no women. Women were expected to make the disguises that were very elaborate and meant to hide the identity of the wearer. Thus, they were called disguises and not costumes. Often they wore blackened faces or masks and fringes of cloth sewn to their inside out clothes. Father Christmas, wielding a club, leads in the characters. The hero is usually St. or King George, and his opponent is the Turkish Knight. Other characters are Bold Slasher, Quack Doctor, Valiant Soldier, Lawyer, Twing Twang, Little Johnnie Jack, Rumour, Hector, Alexander, and later, Nelson. The villain was given the name of a real person like Oliver Cromwell or Napoleon. The Turkish Knight confronts St. George, the patron saint of England, challenging him to a fight, and St. George kills the knight and is sorry. The doctor arrives and revives the Turk.

Today the Mummers Plays are done in good fun, all of the talking done in verse form with a lot of shouting and clashing of wooden swords, many references to the Bold Slasher and the Turkish Knight, and people feigning death only to be revived by some magic potion.

As in other countries, the cinema or movies have become an important part of the Christmas season. In the 1930s, each child had a cinema card, and if he had fifty-two marks on his card showing that he had been to the cinema fifty-two times during the year, he got to see a free Christmas show. Cinemas often put on special shows for young children and the unemployed at Christmas. Even in British gaols (jails), films are shown on Christmas Day. People look forward to the special movies created for the holiday season.



3282-TUCK

## Holy Innocents Day

Holy Innocents Day, December 28, is remembered because of King Herod's slaughter of the babies in Bethlehem when he learned of the birth of Jesus. Many superstitions are connected with this day. Traditionally an unlucky day, no fingernails or toenails should be cut, and no new clothes should be put on. If anything of importance were to begin on this day, it would never be finished, or it would come to an unhappy end. The coronation of King Edward IV had been planned for this day, but it was changed.

## New Year's Day

Gifts were given on New Year's Day until the reign of King James I when it was changed to Christmas. Today New Year's Day is a bank holiday and is celebrated much as it is throughout the western world. There are numerous superstitions connected with New Year's Eve and Day. During the eighteenth century in the south of England, glasses were raised just before midnight on New Year's Eve, and all would say, "To the Old Friend! Farewell! Farewell! Farewell!" When bells rang at midnight, a toast was drunk, "To the new infant! Hip-hip-hoorah! Hip-hip-hoorah!" When all the toasts had been drunk, everyone marched off to the farmyard and barns to wish all living creatures good luck in the coming year. They would eat special triangular shaped mince pies called God Cakes, the shape being symbolic of the Trinity. Before going to sleep, bachelors and spinsters put nine holly leaves into a handkerchief, tied it with nine knots, and put it under their pillows to guarantee that they would dream of their future wife or husband.

One old tradition of this day was that spinsters hurried to the village pump or well in the hope of being the first to draw water. This bucket of water was called the cream or the flower, and whichever spinster drew the flower would be married to the handsomest bachelor in the district before the year was out. If the first person to the well were already married, she would wash her milking pail in the flower and carry a pail of it to her cows so they would produce milk abundantly throughout the year. Another custom allowed children to dash about with newly drawn water that they would sprinkle on anyone they met.

## Twelfth Night

Twelfth Night, January 6, usually ends the holiday season for people in England. It's the traditional time for taking down the tree and decorations. Failure to do so would bring bad luck. A ceremony takes place in the Chapel Royal at St. James Palace in London to commemorate the three gifts of the Three Kings. The reigning monarch rides in a procession to the chapel and presents gold, frankincense, and myrrh to the officiating clergy who holds out an alms dish. Two men from the Lord Chamberlain's Office have represented the monarch since the reign of George III.

On Twelfth Night in the counties of Herefordshire and Gloucestershire, farmers used to light twelve small bonfires and a large one in their main wheat fields. Then they would gather together with their farmhands and stand in a large circle toasting the harvest to come. This was thought to protect the wheat from disease.

Twelfth Night cakes were often baked in honor of the Three Kings. Sometimes a coin was put into the cake with the person getting the coin named as the Twelfth Night King. Sometimes a bean and a pea were put into the cake mix, and the man who got the bean was king, and the woman who got the pea was queen. If a man found the pea, he could pick his queen. In the nineteenth century, special cards were sold with the cakes. These were used to elect an entire court to go with the king and queen. The cards were put into a hat and drawn. In 1795, a pastry cook turned actor, Robert Baddeley, left a sum of money in his will which was "to provide cake and wine for the performers in the green room of Drury Lane Theatre on Twelfth Night." The Baddeley's Cake continues to this day.

In Brian Shull's book for the National Trust called *The National*

*Trust Guide to Traditional Customs of Britain,* he lists some very interesting events that take place during the Christmas season:

On Christmas morning at Sherborne Castle, Dorset, they distribute pennies at the castle gate.

On Christmas Day, which is usually freezing, at the Serpentine in Hyde Park in London, there is a swimming race for the Peter Pan Cup.

On Christmas Eve in Uttorer, Staffordshire, a mumming play called *The Guizers* is performed twelve times between 8:00 P.M. and 12:00 P.M.

On Christmas Eve in Dewsbury, West Yorkshire, the bell ringers "Toll the Devil's Knell" in which they ring the tenor bell once for each year since the Nativity. They must regulate the ringing to reach the final toll at exactly midnight.

# Ethiopia

*Melkam Yelidet Beaal !* or *Poket Kristmet!*

In the Ethiopian Coptic Church, Christmas or *Leddat* is celebrated on January 7. In spite of the Egyptians' ancient Christian heritage and the fact that 40 percent of the population is Christian, Christmas is not a very important holiday.

In the thirteen century, King Lalibela ordered the construction of magnificent churches carved out of solid rock in a town that now bears his name. Today Ethiopian Christmas observances include pilgrimages to these churches. Thousands make the journey to Lalibela each year though it means walking for days, weeks, or months. Those gathered there on Christmas morning share a meal. Then church services are held at *Beta Mariam,* one of the underground churches whose name means "House of Mary." During the lengthy service, a cross is passed among the worshippers so that each may kiss it.

In the modern, circular churches, the men and boys sit separately from the women and girls. In the outside circle sits the choir; the second circle seats the congregation, and Holy Communion is served in the inner circle.

People fast for a day before Christmas, and they attend early morning mass all dressed in white. As they enter the church, people are handed candles, and everyone walks around the church three times. People stand during mass that sometimes lasts up to three hours.

Processions take place in which revered icons or religious images are removed from the churches and carried through the streets. Many take part in an all-night vigil on Christmas Eve. A meal of beans and bread is served to worshipers through the night of singing, dancing, and praying.

Christmas Day church services include religious dances. Percussionists playing drums, prayer sticks, and *tsenatsel* create a rhythm for the dancers.

The name of a game played only on Christmas Day by Ethiopian boys is called *Ganna* or Genna. Some people call the day *Ganna* or *Genne* after the popular game. The game, similar to hockey, is played with a stick and a wooden puck. A very rough game, minor injuries are common. The game ends as night settles in, and the teams shout naughty limericks at each other.

Christmas fare usually includes *injera,* a sourdough crepe or pancake bread often cooked over an open fire. People use the *injera* to put the other food on and to scoop up other food to eat. *Doro wat,* a spicy chicken stew, often serves as the main course. A piece of the *injera* is used to scoop up some of the *wat* that is served from intricately designed, basket-like stands.

Gift giving is not as important in Ethiopia as it is in other places. Children usually receive practical gifts such as clothing.

## Timkat

*Timkat* is a three-day celebration unique to Ethiopia. It commemorates the baptism of Jesus Christ, and it begins on January 19. Adults wear a rectangular shawl called a *shamma* to church services. Children walk in a procession wearing crowns and robes that represent their particular church youth groups. Priests, dressed in red and white robes, wear turbans and carry fancy, embroidered umbrellas.

Music for the celebration is provided by the *sistrum* that is a percussion-type instrument shaped like a pear. It has small, metal disks that make a tinkling sound when shaken. A *makamiya* or prayer stick, a long pole that is T-shaped and used as a support stick for the clergy during the long church services, taps out the rhythm. During the celebration of *Timkat,* people play a sport called *yeferas guks.* On a large field, players chase each other on horseback, throwing ceremonial lances. The young men on the teams wear white and lion mane capes and headdresses. Hippopotamus hides are used as shields. Thus ends the colorful Ethiopian holiday celebration.

# Finland

*Hauskaa Joulua!*

Christmas in the Scandinavian country of Finland is the biggest festival of the year, a turning point, a time when light finally overcomes the dark season. Christmas is anticipated long before the actual day; even as far back as October, many associations and organizations begin preparations. Women's groups plan bazaars and, in keeping with tradition, make many of the Christmas decorations. These evenings have been popular since the 1920s and could be regarded as the first Christmas parties of the season. They are called *Pikkujoulu* meaning "Little Christmas" since they always include some type of Christmas program such as talks or music and special seasonal delicacies. There may be a play or sketch performed for everyone's amusement. Every employer of any size arranges a *Pikkujoulu,* as does just about every organization; even town councils host these parties.

On December 13, the Swedish-speaking schools and homes celebrate St. Lucia's Day, a practice that spread from Sweden in the 1920s. The oldest daughter of the family, dressed all in white with a red belt and a crown of candles, wakes her parents with morning coffee. Lucia, accompanied by her brothers and sisters in the roles of servants and pages, sing together. This custom is becoming popular among Finnish-speaking people too.

## Advent Season

The first Sunday in Advent, the pre-Christmas period beginning with the fourth Sunday before Christmas, officially marks the beginning of the Christmas season. All over Finland, there are concerts with Vogler's "Hosanna" resounding throughout the country.

Advent wreaths made of fir, often decorated with ribbons and berries and holding four candles, are seen in most homes. The first Sunday, one candle is lit, the second Sunday two are lit, and so on. The idea of Advent candles originated from Sweden and Germany and did not become popular in Finland until the 1930s. Advent calendars are also popular. This is a calendar with the first twenty-four days of December marked on little doors or windows. Each day a child opens one of the flaps, revealing a picture, a saying, or sometimes even a treat.

It is at the beginning of Advent that Christmas lights come on in shops and offices. The town centers are ablaze with lights. In Pietarsaari, a town on the west coast of Finland, there has been a Christmas Street, *Storgatan,* since the 1840s. Suspended over the street are three giant decorations: a cross symbolizing faith, an anchor representing hope, and a heart symbolizing love

People mail Christmas cards. On the last Sunday before Christmas, it is time to find a tree. They are usually decorated with rows of national flags representing the friendship among nations. Another popular decoration is the *himmeli,* a geometric mobile made of straw. The straw must be nice and straight and is softened in the sauna. It is then cut into sections of equal length and threaded together to make triangles, squares, and eight-sided figures which are combined to make even larger, more intricate shapes. Wood shavings are often glued together to make clever decorations also. Since the fifteenth century, families have made gingerbread or *pepparkakor* in the shapes of stars, hearts, moons, pigs, and other shapes plus gingerbread houses. Other decorations are candies, nuts, cotton, and tinsel. The tree's candles are lit for the first time on December 23 when the tree is brought into the home.

An old custom still practiced in parts of Finland is the plaiting of a canopy of straw that is suspended from the ceiling. Paper stars hung from this ceiling reflect the light of the lamps and fire below, suggesting a starlit sky. In earlier days, straw was spread on the floors of farmhouses to imitate the manger.

Everyone puts out a bundle or two of oats for the birds. In the country barnyard, animals are given extra portions of food. Presents of tulips, hyacinths, or poinsettias are often taken to friends.

## Christmas Eve

On Christmas Eve, the highlight of the year, grownup children who have moved away join their families. Shops close at midday, and exactly at noon, the "Peace of Christmas" is declared in Turku, the former capital of Finland. This declaration, accompanied by advice and greetings, dates from the Middle Ages. Most Finns listen to this ceremony on the radio, and it marks the beginning of the Christmas Eve celebrations. Many people eat the first part of the Christmas meal at this point.

The sauna plays an important part in the Christmas season. As far back as the beginning of the twentieth century, people were expected to "attend" the sauna on Christmas Eve. At sunset, families make their way to the churchyards where they hold a service at about 5:00 P.M. They place candles and sometimes wreaths on the graves of loved ones. Thousands of candles shine out over the snow. In some towns, former soldiers go in procession to visit the graves of their fallen comrades, and a guard of honor stands with drawn swords by the large cross, dedicated to the memory of these soldiers. In the city of Helsinki, representatives of social organizations and army officers stand guard by the tomb of Marshall Manneheim. They usually sing a hymn or two including Martin Luther's *"Ein' Feste Burg."*

Excitement grows as children await the arrival of Father Christmas who comes in person to each home and usually resembles, although dressed in the traditional way, the father, a neighbor, or a relative. He is accompanied by his elves, children dressed in red tights, large, red caps, and gray, cotton suits decorated with red. When he arrives, he always asks the same question, "Are there any good children here?" The reply is always a resounding "Yes!" Father Christmas usually brings in a large basket with all the presents. The children sing to him, and he tells the children how far he has come, all the way from Lapland, a very, very long journey. He lives at Korvatunturi, a high hill in eastern Lapland, at least according to The Finnish Broadcasting Company who declared it so in 1927. As soon as the children and adults have sung him one last song, Father Christmas must be off. He leaves his little helpers to pass out the presents.

Christmas dinner is served at last! Hors d'oeuvres, many casseroles made days in advance, *lipeakala* or the Christmas fish, salted salmon, *joulukinkku* or the Christmas ham, rye and white breads, *tortuja* or a kind of plum cake, and a rice pudding with a hidden almond are included. The finder of the almond has the assurance that he or she will be married by the following Christmas.

## Christmas Day

Traditionally, Christmas is a day of quiet, about the only activity is attending church. The services are packed, even at the 6:00 A.M. services. Some prefer to read the Christmas story and sing carols and hymns at home.

## St. Stephen's Day

The day after Christmas, St. Stephen's Day, is a national holiday. Once a time for sleigh rides and races through the countryside, this has changed as the Finnish population of horses has diminished. There were and are many parties and dances on this day.

## New Year's Eve

Again, feasting is an important part of the celebrating. This is also a time for magic. Fortunes in the coming year are told by interpreting the meaning of tin melted over the fire and then dropped into a bucket of cold water. The resulting shapes are held up to the wall, and the shadows' images are omens of the future.

Christmas in Finland ends on Twelfth Night, January 6.

# France

*Joyeux Noël!*

In many parts of the European country of France, St. Barbara's Day on December 4 marks the beginning of the Christmas season. On St. Barbara's Eve in southern France, especially in Provence, wheat germs are soaked in water, placed in dishes, and set to germinate in a warm chimney corner or sunny window. According to old folk belief, if the grain grows fast, crops will do well in the coming year. If the grain withers and dies, the crops will be ruined. The "Barbara grain" is carefully tended by the children, who, on Christmas Eve, place it near the crèche or manger scene as a living symbol of the coming harvest.

On St. Nicholas Day, December 6, according to French legend, the Virgin Mary gave the area of France called Lorraine to St. Nicholas as a reward. He became patron saint of the area and visits each year. On St. Nicholas Eve, children in Lorraine and some other parts hang their stockings near the fire and go to bed with a prayer to the saint, *"Saint Nicolas, mon bon patron, Envoyez-moi quelque chose de bon."* (Saint Nicholas, my good patron, bring me something good.) Well-behaved children get toys and bonbons, and the bad get stout rods. St. Nicholas, a strict disciplinarian, remembers how children behave. As a reminder that he is watching, he leaves small ribbon-tied branches of birch twigs with the gifts.

## Christmas Eve

Christmas or *le Noël* is limited to a distribution of gifts mainly among the children, to church attendance, and to family dinners. Before going to bed on Christmas Eve, children carefully arrange their shoes by the fireside; some prefer to leave boots to make room for more presents. Others wait for their presents that are placed under the tree. *Le petit Jésus,* sometimes called *le petit Noël,* used to be the figure who delivered presents. Today he is replaced by *le Père Noël,* accompanied by *le Père Fouettard* who gives the naughty children a whipping instead of toys. In France *le Père Noël* does not travel by sleigh pulled by reindeer, but he goes on foot, accompanied by a little donkey who carries the load of presents. While the children are asleep, little toys, candies, and fruits are hung on the Christmas tree along with the other decorations to add to the gifts from *le Père Noël.* Frequently in places such as city halls, schools, and factories around Christmas Day, there is a celebration during which *le Père Noël* appears in person and brings toys, says a few words to the children, and listens to songs and poems they have prepared for him.

In the larger cities, people attend very lively parties on Christmas Eve. In Paris, wining, dining, and dancing are more common than in the smaller towns and cities where a more religious mood prevails. Reservations must be made weeks in advance for the exclusive Parisian restaurants where special dishes are prepared for the occasion.

At midnight on Christmas Eve, masses are celebrated, the majority of Frenchmen being Roman Catholic. Churches and cathedrals are beautifully lighted, and joyous sounds of carols, bells, and carillons are heard. Ordinarily, children do not attend midnight mass.

When the family returns from church, they have a special dinner or *le réveillon.* This usually consists of baked ham, roast fowl, salads, cake, fruit, bonbons, and wine. It often varies from region to region: traditional goose in Alsace; buckwheat cakes with sour cream in Breton; in Paris oyster, white sausage, a meat pie called *tourtière,* roast partridge, or perhaps turkey with pureed chestnuts may be served. The entire country enjoys the traditional cake in the shape of the Yule log,

*La Bûche de Noël.* In earlier times, while the family was away at midnight mass, a real Yule log was left burning. In many parts of the country, a meal was cooked over the fire from the log. That tradition had pagan origins from the "feast of fire" which commemorated the winter solstice. Today the Yule log tradition is kept alive by the symbol of the *La Bûche de Noël.*

## La Crèche

France's most important contribution to the worldwide celebration of Christmas and the most popular Christmas symbol in French homes and churches is the crèche or the manger scene. The idea of the manger scene originated in twelfth century France. At first, the scene was put on as a drama in the cathedrals and churches; the manger itself, resembling an altar, was placed inside the church or beside the door. The manger as we know it today was started by beloved St. Francis of Assisi between 1316 and 1334 in Italy. The idea of the crèche did not become popular until the sixteenth century.

Today the family arranges a small stage in a prominent part of the house. Children then bring rocks, branches, and moss to make the setting. Little terra cotta figures known as *santons* or 'little saints" are put around the manger to represent the holy family, the other characters of the Nativity story, and the people of the villages like the mayor, the priest, the policeman, the butcher, and the farmer. In many French homes, the crèche is put up several weeks before Christmas, but the Baby Jesus is not placed in His little bed of straw until Christmas morning. The Magi or Three Wise Men are not added to the scene until the sixth of January, the feast day of Epiphany, celebrating the visit of the Magi to the Baby Jesus. Since 1803 a special fair for the sale of les *santons* has been held in Marseilles during the month of December. The undisputed capital of les *santons* is the town of Aubagne near Marseilles where the making of these little figures has become quite an art.

## Christmas Tree

The popularity of Christmas trees was rather late in coming to France. The evergreen tree was first presented as the holy tree of Christmas in the city of Strasbourg in 1605 and was decorated with artificial colored roses, apples, wafers, gold foil, and sweets symbolizing the tree in the Garden of Eden. This custom did not become popular until, on Christmas Day, 1867, in order to amuse his son, Napoleon the Third planted the first Parisian Christmas tree in the Tuileries Garden.

Decorations today vary: shiny, colored glass balls, tinsel called *les cheveux d'anges* or angel hair, and artificial snow. Opinions differ as to what should be placed at the top of the tree: *le Père Noël,* an angel, a star, or the Infant Jesus. Trees are found in many public places. Department store windows, especially in Paris, have very elaborate Christmas displays, many of which are animated and very elegant. Champs Elyssés, an avenue in Paris, has a beautiful lighting display.

Each part of France has its unique Christmas customs. Children in Burgundy put out alms for the poor in little paper bags. In the Maritime Alps, there is a torchlight procession on skis to midnight mass. Auvergne has the unique tradition of the Christmas candle in which the candle is lit by the eldest member of the family present at the celebration; it is used to make the sign of the cross, extinguished, and passed on to the eldest son who does the same and passes it on to his wife. The candle is finally handed to the last born child, lit, and placed in the middle of the table. The family can then sit down to dinner. In the small village of Solliesville in Provence, the whole population gathers in order to give bread to twelve children who are selected as symbols of the twelve apostles, each one receiving an obol of bread, meat, and candies. Then a supper is offered to the important townsmen and people and their guests.

## New Year's Day

The largest, most common exchange of presents is made on New Year's Day, *Le Jour de L'An* or *Le Jour Des Etrennes.* The first of the year is to Frenchmen what Christmas is to Americans, a great family day and the most cherished holiday of the year. The children get another round of presents from St. Nicholas. Gifts are presented to family, relatives, servants, and tradesmen who have served the family for the past year.

Early in the morning on New Year's Day, children give their parents little, handmade gifts and wish them *"Bonne Anné!"* Tradesmen and their errand boys or girls go to patrons with season's compliments and gifts representing their businesses. It's customary to give wine or money to those who bring the gifts. Servants and clerks usually get a double month's pay as a New Year's gift. Little sweetmeat boxes called *les bonbonnières* are filled with chocolates or other sweets, flowers, and all kinds of fresh and glacéed fruits are customary gifts exchanged among family and friends.

After the New Year's dinner has been enjoyed with the family, the streets are filled with laughing crowds exchanging greetings and hurrying to their next get-together. The younger family members assemble at the home of the oldest for an evening feast, a homecoming for dining and saluting the New Year.

The greeting card is very popular in France at the New Year. One considers it almost a duty to send a card to every acquaintance one can think of; in fact, the average person will feel neglected if he or she does not receive at least a hundred cards.

## Epiphany

In Provence and some other parts of southern France, the children go out on Epiphany Eve, January 5, to meet the Three Kings. Sometimes they carry offerings of cakes and figs for the Magi and hay for their weary camels. Even though the children fail to meet them, they



3282-TUCK

will see the stately figures near the altar at Epiphany Mass celebrated at midnight. In small towns and villages in Normandy on Epiphany Eve, it's customary for bands of boys and girls, carrying illuminated Chinese lanterns and empty baskets, to go from house to house singing traditional songs and begging from the rich to share their bounty with the destitute. Householders give the singers gifts of food and drink, money, or clothes.

*Le Jour Des Rois, Fête Des Rois,* Day of the Kings, or Feast of Epiphany is January 6.This day is celebrated in Normandy with parties. The Cake of the Kings is the crowning glory of an elaborate feast. The thin, round cake is cut in the pantry, covered with a white napkin, and carried into the dining room on a small table. The cake is always cut into one or more pieces than there are people in attendance, this extra called *le part à Dieu,* God's share, intended for the first poor person who comes to the door. The youngest member of the group, who often hides under the table, is asked to select which piece of cake shall go to each person. Great excitement goes on during the distribution because a small piece of china or a dried bean has been baked into the cake. The one finding it becomes king or queen of the party, and he or she chooses a partner. Together they rule the feast. Every move the royal couple makes is commented upon and imitated with mock ceremony by the entire group who shout loudly such things as "The queen drinks," "The king laughs," or "The queen drops her handkerchief."

## Legends

Alphonse Daudet, famous for his stories of Provence, wrote the story of the greedy priest who had to celebrate the three Christmas Masses. His mind was on the coming *le réveillon* or meal waiting for him after the masses. The Devil, who had taken the place of the altar boy, encouraged the priest to skip over parts of the mass. Later, at the *le* réveillon, the priest ate so much that he died, and his soul was taken by the Devil. He was condemned to return every Christmas night to celebrate the three masses.

Another such legend tells of the dancers who were condemned to dance throughout the year because their movements had turned the priest's thoughts during the midnight mass.

# Germany

*Fröliche Weihnachten!*

It has been said that if anyone wants to understand the German people, that person should spend Christmas in Germany, the European country well known for its "Christmas keeping." No other German celebration has such a deep influence on the country's life.

## St. Martin's Day

The winter holiday season begins with St. Martin's Day on November 11. Children march in procession in the streets, carrying Chinese lanterns, homemade lights, torches, and hollowed-out turnips with candles inside. They are accompanied by groups of musicians and singing children. Then there is an enactment of St. Martin's famous act of charity when he met a poor beggar and cut his own cloak in half and gave half to the beggar. On the eve before St. Martin's Day, bonfires light the hills, and in some areas, younger children are given buns shaped like people, animals, plants, rings, or horseshoes. After leaving the bonfires, the children split into small groups and go about singing and asking for gifts; they usually receive cookies, sweets, apples, nuts, or money.

## St. Barbara's Day

St. Barbara's Day on December 4 marks the next day of celebration. St. Barbara, known for her very painful martyrdom, wanted to become a Christian, and her heathen father forbad it and took her to court. The court couldn't bring itself to execute her, so her father cut off her head himself. When he did this, there was a mighty clap of thunder, and a huge flash of lightning struck the father dead. Barbara is the patron saint of all jobs concerned with fire and explosions such as firemen, miners, and the artillery. People honor her by placing branches of cherry, elder, or pear trees into a jug of water and keeping it in a warm place. The branches must have good buds so they will bloom on Christmas Eve. These blooming branches are thought to keep misfortune away for the coming year.

## St. Nicholas Day

St. Nicholas Day on December 6 honors the saint known for the many miracles he has performed. Many of these were at sea or in harbors, so he is the patron saint of sailors and also the patron saint of students, and indeed, of all children. One legend tells how he brought back to life three children who had been murdered and stored as pickled meat in vats in the house of an evil butcher. He is also known for having provided the necessary dowry for three sisters whose father couldn't afford to provide the much-needed dowry that had to be paid to the future husbands of the poor but proud sisters. This is how he came to be known for gift-giving.

On the evening of December 5, an adult, usually the father, a relative, or a friend, dresses up as St. Nicholas in his bishop's robe, his tall mitre, and his staff and hands out gifts from a large sack. The children sit and pray and sing until a bell announces the arrival of St. Nicholas who asks questions such as "Have you been good? Have you prayed faithfully? Have you been well-behaved towards your parents and teachers?"



3282-TUCK

St. Nicholas is accompanied by a dark figure wrapped up in old clothes, sacks, or furs. He goes by different names all over Germany, the *Krampus, Pelzebock* or *Pelznickel, Hans Muff, Stappklos*, the Wild Boar, or most commonly *Knecht Ruprecht.* With the sack of gifts on his back, he carries a rod in his hand with which to punish disobedient children, and he growls, rattles some chains, and shows his teeth fiercely. German mothers often say, "Just wait until Ruprecht comes!"

Children put their shoes under the bed or near a radiator on December 5, and St. Nicholas comes secretly to fill them with gifts. Sometimes children find a little rod as a warning. In one area, St. Nicholas comes down from heaven on a golden cord to visit the sleeping children. On the North Sea, he comes by ship, but in most places he comes riding through the sky on either a donkey or a white horse. Since the animal must travel a long way, children leave a small bundle of hay alongside their shoes.

In larger cities the people have been influenced more from other countries, from television, and from the large department stores, so Father Christmas or Santa Claus has replaced St. Nicholas. In some areas he still delivers presents on December 5, but more and more he delivers them at Christmas. In a few areas, it is the Christ Child who delivers the gifts.

## Advent Season

Christmas markets are an important part of a German Christmas, the most famous one being at Nuremberg. From the beginning of Advent, the four Sundays before Christmas Eve, booths and stalls are set up at the marketplace to sell decorations, candles, Nativity scenes, gingerbread trees, and presents. The smells of fir trees, roasted almonds, fried sausages, and roasted chestnuts mix with the music to fill the holiday air. The Munich Christmas market called the Christ Child Market dates back over 600 years.

Children write Christmas wish lists about a month before Christmas. Lists include items such as clothing, toys, books, sports equipment, bicycles, cameras, cassette and CD players, musical instruments, and construction kits. The lists are often sprinkled with sugar to make them shine so that they will not go unnoticed on the windowsills where they are placed. Some children in northern Germany send them to places like *Himmebreich* or heaven.

Sending lots of Christmas cards to all your friends and relatives is very important, for such greetings are thought to bring good luck to the people to whom they are written.

Popular Advent calendars hang alongside children's beds. These calendars show the first twenty-four days of December, and each date has a little door or flap that is opened daily to reveal a scene, symbol, saying, or sometimes even a treat. Advent calendars made of a chain of candles have become popular. Small balls of wax are numbered one through twenty-four, and each evening one is lit and burns down. Some now use the Advent star on which twenty-four little stars are attached to a large, six-pointed star. Each day a little star is removed until on Christmas Eve, the large star hangs on the wall as a symbol of the light of the days to come.

Advent wreaths made of bound fir twigs and adorned with bows or other decorations are popular. Four candles are attached, and each Sunday of Advent another candle is lit until the fourth Sunday, all four are aglow. In large houses, shops, and churches, these wreaths hang from the ceilings.

Lots of greenery is used to decorate during the holidays. The poinsettia is used, and ever popular is the queen of all plants that bloom for Christmas, the Christmas rose; it will show its pinkish blossom even amid the snow and ice.

## Christmas Trees

The focal point of the entire season is Germany's much-loved, special contribution to the worldwide celebration of Christmas, the beautifully decorated Christmas tree. There are several legends as to how and when Christmas trees were first used. One rather doubtful legend tells of the great religious figure Martin Luther walking on a Christmas Eve under the cold, December sky which was brightly illuminated by the stars. Luther returned home and set up a tree for the delight of his wife and children, using the glowing symbol to tell his children the true meaning of the Christ Child, the light of the world, whose birth had so gloriously brightened the sky on the first Christmas Eve.

Henry Van Dyke wrote in *The First Christmas Tree,* of St. Boniface who brought Christianity to Germany in the eighth century. Boniface learned that the oldest son of a chieftain was to be sacrificed to the gods on Christmas Eve. A giant oak that was sacred to the god Thor was to be the scene of the execution. Boniface wanted to destroy the oak, the symbol of such pagan rites; therefore, after striking the mighty oak with one blow after which he caused it to tumble, Boniface pointed to an evergreen and said, "This is the word, and this is the counsel. Not a drop of blood shall fall tonight, for this is the birth-night of the Saint Christ, Son of the All-Father and Saviour of the World. This little tree, a young child of the forest, shall be a home tree tonight. It is the wood of peace, for your homes are built of fir. It is the sign of endless life, for its branches are ever green. See how it points toward heaven. Let this be called the tree of the Christ Child; gather about it, not in the wild woods, but in your homes; there it will shelter no deeds of blood, but loving gifts and lights of kindness." The wood of the fallen oak was used to build a little monastery and a church dedicated to St. Peter. The fir tree was cut and taken to Chieftan Gundhar's great hall where it was set up for the Christmas observance.

Another explanation for the beginning of the Christmas tree states that the idea of a Yule tree came from a pagan custom which required an evergreen to be set up indoors or near the house's entrance to dispel the gloom of winter and to remind the people that the evergreen branches represent the continuing cycle of the Earth's seasons.

The first written report of a Christmas tree as we know it today was in 1605. It read, "At Christmas, fir trees are set up in the rooms at Strasbourg, and hung with roses cut from paper of many colors, apples, wafers, spangle-gold, sugar, etc. It is customary to surround it with a square frame."

From the mid-seventeenth century on, the Christmas tree grew in popularity, but it wasn't until the beginning of the nineteenth century that the use of the Christmas tree grew into the custom that it is in Germany today.

Trees are found in every home, in churches, in public squares, in shops, in offices, at airports and railway stations, and at schools. Decorations for the trees vary: silver or gold painted nuts, tinsel, paper roses, cookies, candies, beautiful, blown-glass ornaments, candles, and electric lights.

About ten days before Christmas, children sometimes go to the woods to look for moss. They spread it out to dry in the cellar or someplace warm. It disappears and is taken by the Christ Child who needs it for a crib.

## Christmas Music

Music plays a very important part in the German Christmas. Beginning with Advent, religious carols and the more secular Christmas songs are heard everywhere. Well-known German composers such as Wolfgang Amadeus Mozart, George Frederic Handel, and Johann Sebastian Bach created masterpieces of Christmas oratorios, masses, and concert arias which are unexcelled and heard all over the world at the Christmas season.

During the Middle Ages in Germany, students traveled from house to house singing in the hope of receiving small gifts. Wandering singers known as *Kurrende-Sanger* still go caroling in parts of Germany such as Saxony and Thuringia.

Martin Luther wrote many hymns and a Christmas song "From Heaven Above to Earth I Come" to his daughter while rocking her to sleep. This song is heard today from the dome of the *Kruz-kirche* in Dresden on Christmas morning.

Christmas cribs or manger scenes are popular. They may be

wooden, clay, or plaster of Paris. They can be tiny or huge displays filling an entire room. Festively decorated churches with altars flanked by decorated and undecorated firs have lots of lights, and there are graphic depictions of the Nativity scene. Midnight church services often end with the singing of "Silent Night, Holy Night."

## Christmas Eve

All shops close at 1:00 P.M. on December 24, and only necessary public services remain open. Everyone hurries home to put on his or her best clothes, and as soon as evening comes and the first church bells sound, the celebrating gets underway. In many larger homes, a room has remained locked during the weeks before Christmas, and adults whisper together, everything being very mysterious. In homes where there is no locked door, the family is kept out of one room on Christmas Eve. To begin the festivities, one of the parents sneaks into the locked room and rings a bell to indicate the Christ Child, Father Christmas, or *Weihnachtsmann* has brought gifts. The youngest child opens the door, and everyone admires the beautiful, lighted tree. They sing some Christmas songs, and the presents are opened.

A unique custom exists in some areas in which the door of the room where the family is gathered suddenly opens just wide enough for nuts, parcels, and presents to be thrown in as if by magic. When the parcels are opened, they are found to be for someone else other than the person to whom they are addressed. This second person may not be the intended recipient either, and the parcel gets smaller and smaller as it goes from person to person and the person for whom it was actually intended finally gets it. The gift giver's identity must remain a secret in order for the gift to bring good luck.

After presents are opened, the children are asked to recite poems, and the family sings more songs, plays Christmas music, listens to a Christmas concert on the radio, or watches a Christmas program on television.

It differs as to when Christmas dinner is served, before or after the opening of the presents. In southern Germany, traditionally the meal is eaten after midnight mass. The Christmas season is a time for considerable eating and drinking, and in northern Germany, Christmas Eve is called "Full Belly Eve" or "Fat Belly Eve." Food differs slightly from region to region. There are many different baked goods such as cookies of every imaginable kind shaped like saints, ordinary people, animals, stars, rockets, cartoon characters, or sports figures. The favorites are animals. Other goodies include spiced cake, gingerbread, waffles, or deep-fried doughnuts. Roast goose and pork are popular for Christmas dinner as is carp.

Germans usually spend Christmas Day quietly at home with relatives and friends.

## Boxing Day or St. Stephen's Day

Boxing Day on December 26 is the day for paying visits. Often relatives gather at the home of the eldest relative. Parents may take their children to the churches to gaze quietly at the Nativity scenes. The evening is often spent going to the theater or to the Christmas meetings of sports clubs or similar organizations.

The Catholic Church celebrates St. Stephen's Day on December 26; St. Stephen was the first Christian martyr. Parades take place in areas where there is a lot of horse breeding or many riding clubs. In some areas, horses are blessed on this day, the horses representing all of the animals.

## Holy Innocents Day

Holy Innocents Day on December 28 is the anniversary of King Herod's slaughter of the babies of Bethlehem when he learned of the birth of Christ. Boys and girls of Thuringia and other areas go about the streets with switches and boughs of green with which they spank passers-by and demand little gifts of coins. This custom is called "whipping with fresh greens."

## New Year's Eve or St. Sylvester's Eve

On St. Sylvester's Eve or New Year's Eve, food again plays an important part in the celebration. Even in the fashionable, big city restaurants, people think that it is lucky to eat the traditional St. Sylvester's carp and to keep a few of the fish's shining scales as a New Year's charm. In many places, traditional Sylvester punch, a hot toddy of red wine flavored with cinnamon and sugar, is served with *pfannkuchen* or doughnuts. In Baden they eat a dried pea soup said to bring good luck. Other special New Year's foods are *noujoer,* little cakes baked in the form of spiral wreaths, pretzels, or circles, and *ballbauschen,* a cake with currants and raisins. Tradition demands that a little of each kind of food be left on the plates until after midnight to insure a well-stocked larder for the coming year.

At midnight everyone shouts, "*Prosit* Neujahr*!*" According to an old German custom, the first day of the year must be lived as one would like to live the next twelve months. The housewife puts the house in order; everybody wears at least one new garment; no money is spent, but the coins in one's pocket are rattled for good luck; no unpleasant work is begun; the doctor and pharmacist are avoided, and everyone keeps on good terms with his neighbors.

Greeting cards are exchanged also at New Year's. Money gifts are often given to the postman, janitor, or others who have served the family during the year. Shooting parties are popular pastimes in the Bavarian Alps. Card games are popular as are lead pouring parties where molten lead is poured into a container of water, and fortunes are told by studying the lead's formations.

## Epiphany

On Epiphany, January 6, the day when the Three Wise Men came to visit the Baby Jesus, the custom of Star Singing was quite common in earlier times, but it became even more popular after World War II. On the Sunday nearest to Epiphany, groups of younger singers gather in front of the churches to sing Epiphany carols to the accompaniment of guitars and other instruments. Three boys or girls play the Three Kings, dressed in exotic costumes and crowns of gold and cardboard. They go from place to place collecting money for missionary work in the Third World countries.

In some areas, the pastor makes the rounds of homes in his parish, blessing them. Two assistants accompany him carrying incense and holy water. He blesses the family, prays for peace and security, and writes C+M+B and the year on the door beam or post. This stands for the names of the Magi: Caspar, Melchior, and Balthasar.

# Ghana

Merry Christmas!
*Afishapa!* (Akan)

In the African country of Ghana, approximately one-third of the people are Christian. Many take Christmas quite seriously as a religious holiday, and everyone seems to celebrate Christmas, regardless of his or her religion.

Christmas is one of the most important and joyous religious festivals. It is a time for beautiful Christmas music on the streets, on radio, television, and everywhere.

Christmas, lasting eight days, is a time of festivity with rounds of parties. Santa Claus has become very popular, and many of the large stores use his image to promote the holiday.

Christmas coincides with the main cocoa season, a time of prosperity and plenty. About a day or two before Christmas, workers cease work and return to their homes they have not seen for perhaps a year. They travel by brightly decorated cars, trucks, buses, or boats or by horse or on foot. Traffic is heavy at this time as the people travel almost as pilgrims trying to get to their ancestral homes to visit with family and friends..

## Christmas Eve

On Christmas Eve, children march up and down the streets saying, "*Egbona hee, egbona hee! Egogo vo!*" which means "Christ is coming, Christ is coming! He is near!" Fireworks are set off. At about

7:00 P.M., church bells summon people to church where the Christmas tree, usually a large evergreen or a palm, is decorated with candles. Children present their programs. The churches are filled, and everyone eagerly wishes each other the best after the service. There is often a procession through the streets led by local bands and Christmas revelers. The dancing in the streets may continue until the wee hours of the morning.

The traditional Christmas Eve dinner consists either of a specially cooked rice and goat or chicken stew or soup and is eaten before the church service. All friends, relatives, and even strangers are invited to dine.

## Christmas Day

Christmas Day proves very festive. About 4:00 A.M., a group of children and adults representing the angels who heralded the coming of Christ to the shepherds go from house to house singing carols. Sometimes this is done on Christmas Eve. Families give small gifts to the singers. The early morning meal may consist of mashed yams cooked with eggs and palm oil. Christmas morning church services are at 10:00 A.M., and again the churches are filled, and the Christmas story is told again in all of the ethnic languages along with singing traditional carols in the many languages. After the services, children receive special gifts such as imported chocolate, cookies, and crackers. They are told that this has all come from Father Christmas. The young may also receive new clothes and perhaps new shoes, a diary, or a book. Feasting and dancing occupy the rest of the day.

Christmas trees are an important part of the holiday, but they are often not whole trees, but parts of trees. Some families have only a branch, but they decorate it with imported lights. Often a tree in the courtyard is decorated; it may be a mango tree, a guava tree, or a cashew tree. Children and young people usually decorate these. Houses are often brightly decorated with beautiful paper ornaments specially made by the families. Schools and neighborhoods are brightly decorated with colorful crepe paper. Churches are decorated, and homes are often decorated with flowers and palm branches from Advent that begins four Sundays before Christmas Eve. The national radio plays carols all day, often in English

Christmas fare is often a dish like mashed potatoes with peanut soup followed by ice cream and a beer because the weather is so hot. Another favorite is rice and *fufu,* a dish of yam pounded into a paste, with stew or soup and porridge with beans or okra soup. Meat for the day may be sheep, goat, beef, pork, or chicken. Fish may also be eaten. There may be mangoes, oranges, paw-paws, and cashew fruits. Often families eat with their neighbors. Gifts are distributed, and everybody enjoys himself.

Christmas serves as a time to reflect on the past and think of the future. Those who have died are often remembered with the libation ceremony, which is a former pagan festival of ancestor worship that has become blended with Christmas. Each family has a drink in the hall of their home and spills a little on the ground so that the dead ancestors will drink too and not miss out.

In every town, groups of children from various ages go from house to house singing or chanting. They sing original songs, some about Christmas. If an adult at a house gives them gifts after they sing, they reply with a song of thanks. The groups continue house-to-house visits for eight days. Occasionally, instead of singing, the children play homemade trumpets.

# Greece

*Kala Christougenna!*

In the beautiful Mediterranean country of Greece, food plays a major role in the celebration of Christmas, with many superstitions and customs connected with food at this time of year. Because the Advent season beginning the fourth Sunday before Christmas Eve serves as a four-week period of fasting, elaborate preparations are made for the Christmas table. Most Greeks eat pork as the main dish for Christmas, but some people in villages choose chicken instead. Chicken pie is usually eaten the day after Christmas.

Every housewife bakes a *Christopsomo,* a Christ Bread, decorated with elaborate, frosted ornaments usually representing some aspect of the family occupation. In Drymos in the area of Macedonia, the farmer's Christmas loaf usually has a plow and oxen on it, a wine barrel, and a house. The shepherd's wife uses lambs, kids, and a sheepfold to decorate her loaf. In the Kozani area, a bun dedicated to the land and sheep and made in the shape of a harness is kept in the house all year, nailed to the wall. Buns dedicated to the cattle are usually reduced to crumbs, salted, and given to the beasts to eat as a protection against illness.

## Christmas Trees

Years ago the Greeks decorated small boats with lights for the season instead of trees. Today people put up trees. Large cities erect trees in the middle of the city, such as in Athens where the mayor puts up the tallest tree in Europe. On New Year's Eve, Athenians go to



3282-TUCK

where the tree is and count backwards to welcome the New Year. City streets are decorated with lights and garlands.

## Christmas Eve and Day

On Christmas Eve the housewife first places on the table the Christmas loaf and a pot of honey. Around it she arranges various dried fruits, walnuts, hazelnuts, almonds, and sweets. Then the master of the house makes the sign of the cross over the loaf with his knife, wishes everyone *"Chronia polla,"* cuts the loaf, and gives everyone a slice. Honey is eaten, and then the family lifts the table three times with their hands.

In Sisope in Pontus on Christmas Eve, it is the custom to insert a sprig of olive into the center of the Christmas loaf. On the sprig are hung dried figs, apples, and oranges. When the family sits down, they lift the table three times saying, "Christ is born, joy has come to the world, our Lady's table, Mary's table." The meal finished, loaf, sprig and all, is placed on a shelf or hung in front of the household icons until Epiphany on January 6 when it is taken down and eaten.

In the village of Simitle near Raidestos in Thrace, the housewife prepares nine dishes on Christmas Eve. They are set on a low table, and burning incense is swung over them. Then they are placed in front of the household icons so that Mary may eat and be content.

In Koroni in Missenia, the people reserve the first slice from the Christmas loaf for the first beggar who happens by. Since the bits and crumbs left from the Christmas dinner are considered sacred, they are scattered near the roots of fruit trees to help the trees to bear a lot of fruit.

In rural areas of Greece, many practices intended to assure good crops are connected with the hearth. The plow and the Christmas table are placed near the hearth. The Christmas cake is put in the middle of the table and covered with a plate filled with wheat grain, garlic, silver coins, pomegranates, dried fruit, grapes, watermelon, and a glass of wine into which the housewife dips the *Kallikantzaros* buns. This rite is performed three times: at Christmas; at New Year's; at Epiphany or Twelfth Night.

At Klos near Mrmora on Christmas Eve, it was the custom of village girls to gather at a friend's house, to open the shutters, and to place a basin of water with a sprig of dried basil in it on the windowsill along with an icon of the Virgin Mary. They put incense in a censer and censed the basin and the whole room and read and sang Christmas carols while glancing at intervals through the window in the direction of the east. It was believed if they were true Christians, at the moment of Christ's birth, they would see a great flash like lightning on the horizon. Some girls are said to have had visions of the Virgin Mary herself holding Jesus.

In some villages, women stay up all night Christmas Eve to see the heavens bursting in glory. They believe any wish made at this time will come true.

On Christmas Eve before going to mass, groups of boys go around to homes singing carols, accompanied by the beating of small drums and the sound of steel triangles. They are often rewarded with walnuts, almonds, dried figs, cookies, and sometimes in the larger towns with money. They repeat this ritual on St. Basil's Eve, December 31. Only children and the poor receive Christmas presents in Greece; most gifts are exchanged on St. Basil's Day on January 1.

Mass on Christmas begins at 4:00 A.M. and ends shortly before daybreak. When the family returns home, they dine on nuts, oranges, tangerines and pomegranates. *Christopsomo* or the Bread of Christ and *kourabiedes* are served also. The former is a simple cake decorated with nuts while the latter are small cakes covered with powdered sugar and sometimes soaked in diluted honey. When soaked in honey, they are called *melomacaroma.*

## New Year's Day

January 1 is St. Basil's Day. As protector of the poor, the orphaned, and the widowed, St. Basil is said to provide dowries for poverty-stricken young girls by inserting coins in little cakes and tossing them through the windows at night. St. Basil called *Agios Vailios* is like Santa Claus to Greek children. As was mentioned, before, most gift exchanging occurs on St. Basil's Day. Either on the eve of St. Basil's Day or on the day itself, the New Year's cake, the *Vasilopitia,* is cut. A coin is hidden in the round, thin cake which brings the finder good luck. The cutting of the cake proves to be a tradition in itself. The first slice belongs to the saint or to the church; the second piece to the poor; the third to the eldest member of the household; the other pieces to the master of the house, the mistress, and to the guests, with age or family relationship ranking them. Last come the children and the servants.

## Epiphany

Because it is a maritime nation, in Greece the blessing of the waters is an important ritual during the holidays. On Epiphany Eve, January 5, special church services are held in which the priest blesses the water, and worshippers kiss the cross and drink from the blessed, holy water. Bottles of the water are carried home and placed near the family's icons. The priest also blesses people's homes with the holy water.

At 12:00 P.M. on Epiphany, in each coastal town or village, the archbishop, bishop, or priest leads a procession from the church to the waterfront. Clothed in magnificent vestments, he holds a crucifix of gold or ebony with a silver image of Jesus. Acolytes and the lesser clergy, clad in beautiful vestments, accompany him, chanting as they march. A procession follows, and at the water's edge, the priest says a prayer of dedication, and after tying a scarf around the cross, he hurls it into the water. From the shore and from boats, boys and men dive after the cross. The one who recovers the cross receives a special blessing from the priest and sometimes money from bystanders.

On Epiphany, many housewives make *teganites,* fancy, unsweetened bread fashioned into all kinds of geometrical shapes such as triangles, figures-of-eight, or circles. These are fried in hot oil and eaten with cheese. This day marks the end of the Christmas holiday season.

## Christmas Legends

During the twelve-day period from Christmas to Epiphany, the *Kallikantzaroi* make their appearance. They are goblins or a kind of spirit who appears only at Christmas, emerging from the bowels of the earth. George A. Megas in *Greek Calendar Customs* writes, "All year round equipped with axes, they strive to cut away the [world] tree which supports the earth; but by the time they have nearly done, Christ is born, the tree grows anew, and the spirits leap to the surface of the earth in a rage. The appearance of these spirits differs by source. Some say they are like humans only dark, ugly, and very tall and wear iron clogs. Others say they are lame, squint-eyed, very stupid creatures. They feed on worms, frogs, snakes etc. They slip into houses through chimneys; they pee on the fire, ride astride peoples' backs, force people to dance, and pester them in every imaginable way."

During these twelve days also, people believe that all waters are unholy and not blessed. Villagers never go out into the street without carrying a candle or a torch. They believe the only way to get rid of the *Kallikantzaroi* is by blessing the waters at Epiphany. Then all the evil spirits scatter in a hurry, pursued by the priest's sprinkler (a cluster of sweet basil dipped in holy water).

Many superstitions are associated with children born at Christmas. It is believed that they turn into strange creatures. If a child is born at Christmas, his mother must bind him in garlic tresses or straw to prevent him from joining the *Kallikantzaroi.* Another way to prevent this is to singe the child's toenails, for a person can't become one of these goblins without toenails. Some people believe that these spirits or goblins are linked with the departed souls who return to earth once a year. The people of Pharasa long believed the dead visited homes during the twelve days of Christmas by entering through the chimney.



3282-TUCK

People hung incense in the fireplace to keep them away. Today the lower jaw of a pig is sometimes hung behind the front door or inside the chimney, and people throw salt or an old shoe into the fireplace, for the stench of the burning salt or leather keeps them away. The best way to keep them away from the house is to use fire that evil spirits can't abide. So the hearth fire is kept going throughout the twelve days with a stout log cut from a thorny tree. It is called the Christmas log, the twelve-day log, or *Skarkantzalos.* Before being placed on the hearth, the log is sprinkled with various kinds of dried fruits. The charred wood and ashes left in the grate have powers of protection and are used to preserve the house and the land from evil demons, bugs, and hail. In a rite called "coupling of fire," two or more logs are placed on the grate in pairs and lighted together. Wild asparagus, pine thistle, and other plants are known to make bursting noises and thick smoke when burning, so they are thrown into the fire to drive evil spirits or demons away. In northeastern Greece, bonfires are lighted in village squares on Christmas for the same reason.

# Grenada

Merry Christmas!

About a month before Christmas, a definite mood change occurs in the beautiful country of Grenada, a Caribbean island in the British West Indies. A feeling of expectation fills the air; people begin to prepare as if in anticipation for an honored guest. Walls are painted; new curtains are hung; yards are cleaned and swept; doors are opened to welcome visitors, and music fills the air.

Decorations adorn city streets, shops, and stores. Shelves are restocked, and a sense of urgency permeates. Preferred decorations are ferns, flowers, colored tissue paper, silver paper, glitter, and colored lights. Many homes have Christmas trees made from branches or very young trees decorated with mainly homemade ornaments.

People exchange Christmas cards, quite often made by the sender. Gifts, tending to be of a practical nature, are exchanged. Garden produce, meat from livestock slaughtered for the holidays, and handcrafted woodwork are all typical gifts.

Churches take their roles as the focal point of the holiday celebration. The two main churches, the Anglican and the Roman Catholic, hold midnight masses. A pageant of peace is presented in most churches during mass. The play *A Christmas Carol,* based on a story by Charles Dickens, is presented in many parishes.

The Christmas season is one huge feast lasting for days. Four main items dominate the Christmas dinner table; rice, peas, ham, and bread. Local drinks like mayby, sorrel, and rum punch are served as well as homemade cakes.

Christmas Day, people spend welcoming family and friends, eating, remembering the good old days, and just having fun. New Year's Day offers more of the same

# Guatemala

*Feliz Navidad!*

Christmas in the Central American country of Guatemala is a fiesta of bright, blooming flowers, unique musical sounds, and lots of merrymaking.

## Days of Guadalupe

Before the Christmas season begins, the people of Guatemala celebrate The Day of Guadalupe or *El Dia de Guadalupe* on December 8. This day honors the bronze-skinned Virgin of Guadalupe who first appeared to a little Indian boy named Santiago a long time ago. She later became the patron of Mexico, of all Indians, and indeed, of all North America. In Guatemala City, children dress in very detailed, traditional Indian costumes. Days before the feast, local markets sell miniature *cascastes* or baskets which Guatemalan Indians use for carrying produce. The boys' *cascastes* are filled with miniature chickens, vegetables, sausages, eggs, and other foods, while the girls carry small water jugs on their heads or balance baskets of tortillas covered with brightly colored cloth in the same manner.

Among the streets near the Church of Guadalupe, stalls are set up where crisp, tasty *bunelos* or fritters made with honey are sold, and spicy *batidos,* a drink flavored with ginger and achote, is served in gaily painted gourds. A big parade is held, and along the route elaborate settings for photographs are staged. The costumed children may have their pictures taken against backgrounds such as a bamboo Indian hut,



3282-TUCK

or they may watch the making of tortillas, listen to the playing of the marimbas, or observe or take part in some other Indian activity. During the day, there are firecrackers, and at night adults dress up in Indian costumes to attend parties or dances at private homes or clubs.

## Posados

Nine days before Christmas, the *posados* begin. They are similar to the Mexican *posados.* Each of the nine days before Christmas, it is customary in Guatemala for many families to place statues of Mary and Joseph on a large platform and to invite their friends to join them for the evening *posado.* The platform is carried through the dark streets on the shoulders of two men, accompanied by family members and maybe twenty or thirty friends. As they march along, one of them plays the turtle drum, and the "ticka, ticka, too, ticka, ticka, too" beat used only for Christmas *posado* can be heard for blocks. All carry lighted *farolitos* or gaily painted tin lanterns lighted with candles, and often some members of the groups have firecrackers.

They arrive at a pre-arranged home and sing a carol asking for shelter. The family inside refuses to let them in and asks questions as to whom they are and why such strangers should be let in. The question and answer carol continues until the outsiders explain that they are Mary and Joseph. At this, the family inside sings, "Open the door and let them in."

The members of the *posado* enter, carrying the figures of Mary and Joseph to a *nacimiento* or manger scene. Then all join in reciting the rosary and the novena for the day. After this ceremony, hot punch and tamales are served. Guests dance to the music of the marimbas.

The next evening the family who has sheltered the statues of Mary and Joseph remove them from the *nacimiento,* gather their friends, and start their own *posado.* Thus, the figures of Mary and Joseph visit nine homes. On Christmas Eve, the *posado* ends at a home large enough to invite all the people who have taken part in the nightly processions.

## Christmas Eve and Day

On Christmas, the figure of the Christ Child is added to the *nacimiento.* Family and friends assemble in a dark room carrying lighted candles and some type of noisemaker or rattle. One member holds a large, silver tray mounded with yards of fluffy, pastel tulle representing clouds with the Christ Child resting in the middle. After a procession around the patio, the group surrounds the *nacimiento* and places the Child in the crib. Many children in Guatemala love the *nacimientos* so much that they have their own little manger scenes.

Because of the large population of German descent in Guatemala, Christmas trees are very traditional and are usually long-needled pines imported from the United States. The presents brought by the Christ Child are usually placed under the tree, and often the *nacimiento* is placed there also. The tree ornaments are often imported from Germany.

On Christmas Eve people attend midnight mass, and they return home to the *ceno* or elaborate supper.

Christmas Day, children get up early to see the presents. Christmas dinner is an informal affair, the family usually eating leftovers from the *ceno* the night before.

New Year's Day is the occasion for many parties and lots and lots of firecrackers. On this day, adults receive presents. Employers give their employees money or gifts on this day too.

# Haiti

*Joyeux Noël!*

The beautiful Caribbean country of Haiti was once a French colony but won its independence. The country has been ruled by a series of dictators and has suffered severely economically, now being considered the poorest country in the western hemisphere.

The celebration of Christmas begins on Christmas Eve in Haiti. Often members of a family take turns hosting the Christmas dinner, and the whole family shares the expense.

Some homes have Christmas trees. They were introduced into Haiti from America about sixty years ago. Presents for the family are placed under the trees.

Haitians decorate their *tonelles* for the holidays. A *tonelle* is a shelter made from bamboo, the stems of coconut palms, or just plain twigs and shaped like an arch. People use it as shelter against the rain or sometimes as a place for dancing. At Christmas, children and grownups decorate the *tonelles* by hanging gourds and strips of colored paper on them.

Months before Christmas, children begin working on a special design called a *fanal* or a cardboard design of a church or a house. Holes are punched in the structure, and candles or a small kerosene lamp are placed inside each *fanal.*

On Christmas Eve, boys and girls carry their *fanals* down the mountains and into the streets of the cities and villages. It is said that this custom began as a way to show the Three Wise Men the path to the manger and the Infant Jesus. When the children return home, many place their *fanals* in their windows.

Boys and girls begin making their crèches or manger scenes for their schools and churches in October, pasting up cardboard figures of Mary, Joseph, and the Infant Jesus. Small shops also sell the figures. The crèche is placed in a special place in the home. Sometimes you see not only the traditional figures, but also people like the town's mayor or the tax collector.

The Santa Claus figure is called *Ton-Ton Noël* in Creole, and some call him *Bonhomme Noël.* He visits only good children. Bad children also get a visitor; his name is *Père Fouettard,* and he brings a whip to give to the parents of bad boys and girls.



3282-TUCK

# Hungary

*Kallemes Karacsonyi Unnepeket!*

The people of the country of Hungary, often called the breadbasket of Europe, begin their holiday celebrations with St. Nicholas Day on December 6, as many European countries do. The saint in his bishop's robes goes about distributing rewards to good children and warning the naughty. The Hungarian Santa Claus is sometimes called *Mikulás.* Children place their shoes or boots on their windowsills so that St. Nicholas might leave gifts of candies, tangerines, walnuts, apples, dates, and chocolate *Mikulás* figures, or if necessary, some birch switches with a Devil figure attached to them. Since most children are not all good or bad, they usually get goodies and a switch.

*Mikulás'* day *is* celebrated in schools and in workplaces for the workers' children. Children sing songs, and the bravest children sit on his lap and tell him a poem or sing a song. Then *Mikulás* calls them one by one, praising them for the good things they did and mentioning bad things as well. These personal messages are based on previous parents' notes. *Mikulás* plays with the children, or they watch a movie together. *Miklulás* often comes with one or two small, evil boys called *krampusz.*

The official season starts with the Advent season beginning the fourth Sunday before Christmas Eve. Advent wreaths can be seen in stores, schools, offices, and in almost every home. Candles are decorated with red and gold ribbons symbolizing life and brightness. Most children get Advent calendars with a small gift or candy for every day before Christmas. Lights and decorations are mostly inside the houses, and the streets are not as brightly decorated as in other places.

Christmas trees in homes are not usually decorated until Christmas Eve, but trees appear in stores during Advent.

The religious and nonreligious celebrate Christmas in much the same way except for attendance at church services. Christmas lasts for two days, December 25 and 26. Families get together to enjoy each other's company, and it's very much a family-oriented time.

## Christmas Eve

On Christmas Eve, Adam and Eve Day, or *Karacsony Vigillaja,* when the first star appears, the celebrating begins with the evening's meal consisting of such treats as cabbage soup, fish, cakes shaped like horseshoes and filled with poppy seeds or walnuts, special, twisted, Christmas bread, and small dumplings sprinkled with seeds and sugar.

Right after the meal, the family assembles around the lighted Christmas tree. A short prayer is offered, carols are sung, and gifts are distributed.

One of the main decorations on the Christmas tree is the *szaloncukor* or homemade, fudge-like candy wrapped in colorful papers. Sparklers are placed on the tree and lit. Children play with their toys; people sing and eat, and then many attend midnight church services.

## Christmas Day

On *Karasony* or Christmas Day, dinner usually consists of wild game like hare, roast meat, and stuffed cabbage. Poppy seed dumplings, poppy seed and nut cakes, and choice pastries with poppy seed fillings are served. Christmas Day resembles Thanksgiving Day in the United States with people either going home or staying home to be with family and friends.

## St. Stephen's Day

*Vertanu Szent 1st van Napja* or St. Stephen the Martyr's Day on December 26 marks the second day of Christmas. This day features more feasting, merrymaking, and visiting.

During the holidays, singers go from house to house carrying a huge star lighted on the inside. After the carols, some of the groups reenact scenes from the Nativity, the visit of the Magi, or the court of King Herod, a custom called "Bethlehem."

## New Year's Day

On *Ujev Napya* or New Year's Day, chimney sweeps with their brooms go from house to house, singing New Year's songs and receiving gifts of money. According to ancient custom, one must break twigs from their brooms without being detected by the sweeps who shut their eyes and pretend not to notice what is going on. People tie the tiny branches together with ribbons and keep them for good luck.

The traditional New Year's Day feast features roast pig with an apple or a four-leaf clover in its mouth. Eating pig brings good luck.

## Three Kings Day

*Vizkereszt* or the Blessing of the Water Day, occurs on January 6 or Three Kings Day. In the churches, priests sanctify and mix salt with holy water they use to bless their parishioners. In smaller villages, the priest goes from house to house with his helpers, blessing each household. The house is sprinkled with holy water, and each door is marked with the initials GMB in memory of the Three Wise Men, Gaspar, Menyhert, and Boldizsar.

In some areas, young boys masquerade as the Three Kings and make the rounds of the village singing about the shepherds and the birth, receiving food and money as gifts. Sometimes groups of white-clad girls, led by a girl dressed as an old hag, make the rounds of the village singing songs.



3282-TUCK

# Iceland

*Gledileg Jol!*

Christmas on the dark, cold island nation of Iceland is heralded as a festival of light for two reasons: first, it is a religious holiday celebrating the triumph of the spirit over darkness and the birth of the "Light of the World," Jesus Christ; second, it's also the season which ushers in a time of gradually lengthening days. Iceland is located very far north, and it is dark most of the daylight hours in the winter.

Strictly a family affair, Christmas centers very much on the children. Christmas means dining on good food, wearing one's best clothes, decorating inside and outside the house, and above all, experiencing family closeness with family reunions and visiting old friends.

Around mid-November, people begin to prepare for Christmas. Sprucing up for Christmas by painting the home, buying new furniture and carpeting, and cleaning remains a strong Icelandic tradition. Years ago, women spent many hours sewing so that each household member would have at least one new garment for Christmas. It was said that any person not receiving something new was in danger of being eaten by a malicious beast called the Christmas Cat. The threat of the cat is no longer used, but it is still traditional to get something new to wear at Christmas.

Advent calendars are a fairly recent custom in Iceland. Advent is the season beginning the fourth Sunday before Christmas Eve. Advent calendars represent the first twenty-four days of December, and the dates are on little windows or flaps that are opened daily. Behind each flap is usually a chocolate treat.

Students get a two to three week Christmas vacation from school.

The youngest children are the first to get out for the holidays after a day at school known as "Little Christmas" in which candles are lit in the decorated classrooms, stories are read, and hymns or carols are sung.

A lot of time is spent buying presents and stocking up on enough food to last for three days of a lot of eating, Christmas Eve, Christmas Day, and the Second Day of Christmas or Boxing Day on December 26. Stores are closed at this time; thus, making sure that one has enough supplies to last the three days is important.

## Christmas Trees

Many families have a tree usually imported since there are few evergreens that grow normally in Iceland. In recent years, locally cultivated trees are used as well. A star or a crown usually sits atop the tree, and the trees are usually decorated on December 23 or 24. In years past, children helped their fathers create trees by tying branches and foliage from shrubs to center poles painted green to assist Mother Nature. Often small pouches containing treats were attached to the tree. Decorating the tree ranges from mutton tallow candles and homemade creations to more sophisticated electric lights and decorations bought from stores. Many strings of lights are put on the outsides of houses or on the sides of buildings.

## Porláksmessa

The major, native saint of Iceland is St. Thorlakur Thorhallsson, Bishop of Skáholt. December 23 or *Porláksmessa* is the day commemorating his death in 1193. The main custom associated with his day is the partaking of a simple meal of skate. This custom began in the West Fjords and has become traditional all over the country. The Yule tree is often decorated on this evening, and this is also a big shopping day for last minute gifts; the stores remain open until midnight.

## Christmas Eve

Christmas Eve or *Aðfangadagur* serves as the high point of the holiday season. Television broadcasts stop at 5:00 P.M. and do not resume until 10:00 P.M. Christmas lights are never turned on until 6:00 P.M. The ringing of the bells of the Lutheran Cathedral in the capital city of Reykjavik is broadcast nationally as the beginning of a special religious service. This is the signal for all to rise, hug each other, and wish each other *Gledilig Jol.* All regular, public services have come to a standstill; no buses are running; no restaurants or places of entertainment are open; fishing vessels are moored in port; even the hospitals are half-empty, for patients are allowed to go home for Christmas if it can be done safely.

With the lights lit, Christmas Eve dinner begins. After the table is cleared, and the dishes are washed, the time the children have been waiting for so long arrives, the opening of the presents! Gifts at this time of year didn't become popular until the late nineteenth century; before that, summer gifts were more common.

Books have for decades been among the most popular items for Christmas gifts in Iceland. Parents often give children something useful also, such as clothes or study aids or skis and related gear, radios, or cassettes and CDs. There are exchanges of gifts between children, between husbands and wives, and between visiting grandparents and the young.

People rarely leave the home on Christmas Eve unless going to church, a practice that is not very widespread. Most families end the evening by watching a late religious service on television. Sometimes refreshments such as homemade pastries, coffee, and soft drinks are served before bedtime.

## Christmas Day

People usually sleep in on Christmas morning and eat a festive Christmas Day luncheon or brunch. Recently a preference has grown for a large Christmas dinner as the day's main meal. In most homes, smoked lamb or mutton is the main course for dinner. For the other two days, the food varies, with pork, beef, lamb roast, ptarmigan or grouse, and chicken being popular. One would expect to see a lot of seafood on the table since Iceland is a nation of fishermen, but this is not so these days. *Laufabraud* or fancy, fried cakes and *ponnukokur* or thin pancakes are often a part of the Christmas feast as well as a Christmas cake filled with raisins and currants.

Christmas Day usually means visiting family, for no public services are running. The Second Day of Christmas on December 26 is a major holiday also and is celebrated with additional family visiting. It is much like an ordinary Sunday. Buses are running again on regular schedules, and restaurants and places of entertainment attract large crowds.

## New Year's Eve and Day

New Year's Eve is one of the most magical nights of the year. This night, the eighth night of the Yule season, sees cows gain human speech, seals take on human form, the dead rise from their graves, and the elves move house. The housewife chants this rhyme to the elves on this night:

"Let those who want to, arrive
Let those who want to, leave
Let those who want to, stay
Without harm to me or mine."

On this evening one can receive gold from elves by sitting at a crossroads and waiting for them to pass.

Bonfires are popular on New Year's Eve. Another custom is "blowing out the year" involving the setting off of fireworks, sometimes very elaborate displays.

Families usually spend the first part of the night together, but often dances start shortly before midnight.

## Jólasveinar

One of the most delightful of Christmas legends is the Icelandic tradition of the thirteen Christmas goblins or *Jólasveinar.* They take the place of Santa Claus for children. These goblins are jolly little fellows with names like Window Peeper, Doorway Sniffer, Bowl Licker, Pot Licker, Pot Scraper Licker, *Skyr* or Yogurt Licker, Sausage Snatcher, Meat Hooker, Candle Beggar, Gimpy, Gully Imp, and Itty Bitty. Some other interchangeable names used for this group are Bundle, Strap Loosener, Idiot Child, Skirt Blower, Fat Gobbler, Barn Roll, Donut Beggar, Lamp Shadow, Moor Charlie, and Smoke Gulper. As Christmas draws near, they come down from the mountains to the villages to enjoy the festivities. One comes each day, with the last one arriving on Christmas Eve. They bring little presents, leaving them on the windowsills. Naughty children are left a potato or some other reminder to improve behavior. When the festivities are over, back to their homes they go, one by one, just as they came. Children like to believe that the goblins bring the Christmas gifts, and grownups enjoy dressing up to represent the goblins.

The idea of these delightful goblins has changed considerably through the years. Long ago these thirteen "Christmas Lads of Iceland," sons of the ancient, bloodthirsty ogres Gryla and Leppalúði, arrived one at a time the thirteen days before Christmas. They stole candles and sausages, took away the good grain, and wrecked the tidy households. One by one, beginning on Christmas Day, they left, taking with them the naughty children stuffed in sacks.

## New Year's Day

The liveliest partying occurs on New Year's Eve. Bonfires are lit for the youngsters. Fancy dinners are served in homes, or many people go out on the town for the evening. Midnight arrives with exchanges of Happy New Year, kissing friends, blowing vessel foghorns, and setting off fireworks. New Year's Day serves as a day of rest, with perhaps a bit of visiting in the late afternoon or a dance that night.

Christmas decorations usually come down after the Thirteenth Day, January 7, when the holiday season ends in Iceland.

# India

*Shut Naya Baras!* (Hindi)
*Naya Saal Mubarak Ho!* (Urdu)

In the huge Asian country of India, Christians are a minority. The Christmas celebration reflects a mixture of eastern and western traditions.

In villages, Indian Christians send trays of fruit, nuts, sweets, and flowers to friends and relatives. In larger towns, the western custom of exchanging cards has become popular. The cards often depict the holy family as Indians in an Indian setting.

There are new clothes for the family, gifts, and many Indian festival dishes. Children receive most of the gifts. Servants receive *baksheesh* or coins, and in turn, servants present a lemon to the head of the household on Christmas morning. This shows respect and high esteem, bearing wishes for a long life and prosperity.

In most churches, there are cribs or manger scenes. In many areas, shops are decorated with lights, ribbons, and simulated snowflakes. Recorded Christmas carols are played. Candles and floral arrangements of scarlet poinsettias and other tropical plants are everywhere. Outside decorations are often put on banana trees. People sometimes decorate mango trees also and use mango leaves to decorate their homes.

Indian Christians like long church services. The main Christmas service is a midnight one lasting two to three hours, with hundreds of people sitting on the floor.

In northwest India, the tribal Christians of the Bhil people, an aboriginal tribe, go out nightly for a week to sing Christmas songs the whole night through. They go to surrounding villages where there are Christians or inquirers into the faith. A drum and cymbals may accompany the songs that are often set to a hot, tribal rhythm. If there are many houses to visit, they may not sing more than five or six songs in one house. Each hymn usually has thirty to forty verses, so it doesn't take many visits before the rooster crows at 4:00 A.M. or the sun rises at 6:00 A.M. The host, however poor, will try to bring out a tray filled with chunks of sweetmeat for the forty or fifty people crowded onto his veranda.

In southern India, Christians fill little clay lamps with oil and put a piece of twisted cotton into each for a wick. Towards the evening, they light these lamps and place them along the edges of low, flat-roofed houses and along the outside walls.

## The Santals

The Santals, one of the largest tribes in India, call Christmas *marai din,* the biggest day of the year. They connect Christmas with their harvest festival and use many of their harvest festival customs.

Before Christmas, they clean their villages and houses and decorate their homes with flowers, flags, and ribbons, and buy new clothes. Santals do not buy cards and exchange gifts since they are rather poor. They prepare ice beer, tea, and fried rice and invite their friends to celebrate. Most Santals eat pork for Christmas dinner, while some eat beef.

Santals celebrate Christmas for five days. During this time, they sing, dance, and rejoice. Young girls gather on the streets, join their hands, and dance vigorously from one end of the street to the other. The boys play musical instruments, and the girls sing songs. These singing and dancing groups are given tea and fried rice by appreciative watchers.

Boys in the villages go fishing and hunting during the Christmas season, enjoying their comradeship.



3282-TUCK

# Ireland

Merry Christmas!
*Noflaig Nait Cugat!* (Gaelic)

St. Patrick brought Christmas to the beautiful, green island of Ireland late in the fifth century, and it continues to be celebrated in a mainly religious manner. Since Ireland is predominately Roman Catholic, the celebration of Christmas begins with Advent. From the four Sundays before Christmas Eve, the celebration tends to be mostly religious, whereas the period from December 26 through January 6 becomes a time of merriment as Ireland closes down for a national vacation.

## Superstitions and Sayings

An Irish Christmas has many superstitions and wise sayings. "A green Christmas makes a fat churchyard" means that a Christmas without snow hints of hard times to come, an omen that the village churchyard will have a lot of new graves in the coming year. Another saying goes "When it snows on Christmas Eve, the angels in heaven are plucking geese for the feast on the morrow." Another belief allows that the gates of heaven open at the hour of midnight on Christmas Eve, so if anyone dies at this time, he will go straight up into heaven.

Years ago in Ireland, circular cakes flavored with caraway seeds were baked on Christmas Eve for every household member. If anyone's cake broke, it was an omen of bad luck. The Irish have a Gaelic name for Christmas Eve, *Didhche na ceapairi,* which means "Night of Cakes."

The main contribution of the Irish to the worldwide celebration of

Christmas is the idea of putting candles in windows on Christmas Eve to light the way for Mary and Joseph who wander forever on that night. In the days when Ireland was under English rule, the English tried to suppress Roman Catholicism, and the candles were a signal to passing priests that the home was a safe place in which to say mass. Today the Irish put candles in each window at the front of the house, and these candles are lit from the main candle that is put in the home's principal window. It may be white, red, blue, or green and is often as tall as two feet. Prayers are said when the candles are placed in the windows, and the privilege of lighting them is given to the father, to the youngest child, or to a daughter named Mary.

In many Irish villages, a long-standing tradition after the evening meal on Christmas Eve and before going to bed was to bank the fire, sweep the floor, and set the table with a loaf of bread filled with caraway seeds and raisins, a pitcher of milk, and a large, lighted candle. The door was left unlatched, and hospitality was extended to the holy family or to any travelers who happened along. In earlier days, a dish of water was placed on the windowsill for the holy family to bless; then this water was used all year to cure illnesses.

Years ago, church bells tolled from 11:00 P.M. to midnight on Christmas Eve for the funeral of the Devil, for it was believed that the Devil died when Jesus was born. Houses and churches in Ireland were decorated with holly, for on this night an angel sprang from every spike of the holly and danced for the Christ Child. Barnyard animals were blessed with the gift of speech and knelt in prayer from 11:00 P.M. to midnight. Roosters, filled with Christmas joy, crowed throughout the night, and to hear the cock crow at midnight was considered to be good luck.

## Today's Traditions

Christmas shopping begins a few weeks before Christmas, and people tend to purchase fewer and less lavish gifts than in places like the United States. Many people give gifts only to those residing in the same household, and it is one gift per person on one's list. Father Christmas appears in the stores and in the streets and comes to fill children's stocking which are usually hung on the children's beds. Cards are sent only to those who won't be home for Christmas or won't be seen. Unmarried, and often, married children are expected to come home for Christmas.

Decorations in homes usually include holly, ivy, and bits of greenery stitched to fabric to make seasonal mottoes such as "Happy Christmas" or "Season's Greetings." These are often bought ready-made in the larger cities. Schoolrooms, office buildings, plazas, and hotels are decorated for the season. Churches are usually decorated simply with holly leaves stitched together and wound around pillars and placed along the altar's edges. Christmas trees have become popular only recently and are decorated much as in England or the United States.

Nativity scenes are also fairly new in Ireland, with each church having a Nativity scene, crib, or Bethlehem scene. Families often approach the church's Nativity scene as a group before being seated for mass, and some people pray and meditate in front of the crib. Worshippers sometimes take a few wisps of the straw from the Nativity scene; these are sewn into a piece of ribbon or other cloth and carried around for a blessing or good luck charm. Nativity scenes are found in most homes today. They are set up in a prominent place, families saying the rosary every night in front of them. The Three Wise Men are added to the scene only on January 6, Three Kings Day, or Epiphany when the Kings arrived to see Christ.

Attending midnight mass is a relatively new practice in Ireland. The older custom was to attend the "First Light Mass" celebrated at the first light of dawn on Christmas morning. People used to go to church on Christmas Eve for confession only, a very important part of the season as a preparation for the holy events. Before leaving church after midnight mass, one traditionally wishes friends and neighbors *Nodlaig Nait Cugar!*

Sharing with the poor and unfortunate plays an important part in the holidays, as the Irish tend to be very charitable. Churches, groups, and organizations assist as carolers sing in shopping areas for the needy, and school children give Nativity plays for charity. On Christmas Day, children deliver food to the less fortunate.

The Irish shine at the art of storytelling, and following the custom of telling stories on Christmas Eve, the oldest family member gathers everyone around the hearth or table and tells the story of the first Christmas, about family tales, and about the feats of the great Irish heroes and villains.

## Christmas Food

Food plays a major part in the celebration of Christmas, and preparations are begun weeks in advance. The Christmas cake with a base of caramel to which is added dried and candied fruits, blanched almonds, citrus rind, orange-flower water, rose water, brandy, the whites of eight eggs, as well as flour, sugar, and butter. may be started as early as October to allow time for its mellowing.

The Irish used to observe Christmas as a day of simple meals with dinner consisting of fish served with white sauce and potatoes, fish stew or soup served with vegetables, or potato soup. Sometimes the father boiled and peeled the potatoes and sliced them into soup plates half-filled with spiced, warm milk. Christmas Eve dinner still remains simple in most places, but the Irish more than make up for it today on Christmas Day.

While the men are out playing, the women prepare the meal. The Christmas table is set with the best linen or lace tablecloth, polished silver, good china, and cut glass stemware. Dinner, served in the afternoon between one and three o'clock, usually consists of all or some of the following: the traditional goose or turkey with a slice of ham underneath, the traditional stuffing of potatoes heavily seasoned with black pepper, potatoes roasted or mashed and served with gravy, glazed carrots, turnips, minted peas, onions, applesauce or gooseberry sauce, whiskey, stout, and sherry. In some homes at least three Christmas puddings are made: one for Christmas, one for New Year's, and one for Twelfth Night. Mincemeat pies or tarts, sherry trifles, bread pudding with butterscotch sauce, soda scones, fairy cakes, and cookies (called biscuits) top off the meal with the usual pot of tea.

## Games and Activities

Everything closes on Christmas Day, and the men and boys have their Christmas games. Hurling, which resembles field hockey, or Gaelic football, which resembles soccer, are popular sports. In the past, hurling matches often began right outside the church gates as the men took the hurleys, or sticks, with them to church. Shooting competitions were also popular on Christmas Day, and hunting hares with greyhounds is still popular in some areas.

## St. Stephen's Day

On St. Stephen's Day, December 26, "Wren Boys" collect money for the needy. Masked and in costume, going door to door chanting rhymes and begging for money, the children carry a caged wren or a symbolic one made of straw and mounted on a stick. The tiny wren has been traditionally associated with the holy family in Bethlehem. The Wren Boys often sing:

"The Wren, the Wren, the King of all Birds,
St. Stephen's Day was caught in a furze,
Although he is small, his family is great.
Open up, lady, and give us a trate."

Mummers also perform for charity on St. Stephen's Day. They dress up and go door to door performing folk plays, always in verse. Modern mummers often belong to groups who perform plays before an audience also.

Steeple chasing, fox hunting, and greyhound racing are traditional on St. Stephen's Day as are hurling, Gaelic Football, and fishing, especially for salmon. One of the country's major dog shows is held on December 26. This is also the day when many dances take place.

## Holy Innocents Day

Holy Innocents Day on December 28 commemorates the slaughter of the male children in Bethlehem by King Herod's men when Herod learned of the birth of Jesus. In Ireland this day is thought to be filled with bad omens and referred to as "the cross day of the year" or *La Crostna na Bliana* in Gaelic. No new enterprises are begun for fear they will turn out badly.

## New Year's Eve and Day

Only fairly recently did New Year's Day become a holiday in Ireland. Young people now party on New Year's Eve. Bonfires are lit, and parades are held in the cities. Fireworks are set off, and church bells are rung.

It was always customary to eat heavy meals on this evening to ward off hunger all year. Some believed that it was necessary to eat every bit of food in the house before January 1 to ensure plenty in the coming months. Many customs to do with staving off hunger for the coming year were observed, not such a surprising thing in a country as poor as Ireland has been in the past. In some areas, the man of the house, armed with a cake or a loaf of bread, struck the inside of the front door three times saying:

"Out with misfortune, in with happiness, from tonight to this night twelve months, in the name of the Father, and of the Son, and of the Holy Ghost, Amen."

In Ireland, the first Monday of the year is Handsel Monday. Children knock on doors soliciting a handsel or small gift of money.

The Feast of Epiphany or Twelfth Night on January 6 is known as Little Christmas and marks the end of the holiday season for the Irish.

# Italy

*Buon Natale!*

Christmas really began in the beautiful, romantic European country of Italy. Christ was born in the tiny village of Bethlehem in Judea, but His birthday was first celebrated in Rome almost 300 years later when Emperor Constantine adopted the new faith of Christianity. Besides starting the celebration of Christmas, Italy's other contributions to the worldwide Christmas celebration are very important, Christmas carols, Christmas bells, and outdoor manger scenes.

The Christmas season in Italy remains a very religious holiday beginning with Novena, a nine-day period of special church services ending on Christmas Eve and lasting until Twelfth Night or Epiphany on January 6.

Italy, a land of many different regions, has Christmas customs varying as much as does the weather of the different regions. Gift giving, for example, occurs on different days in different areas. On December 6, St. Nicholas Day, good St. Nicholas, wearing his bishop's robe and mitre, visits many of the children. In Sicily, *Santa Lucia,* accompanied by a donkey carrying baskets of gifts, goes about her rounds wearing a blue, star-sprinkled cloak. Youngsters place their shoes outside the door the night before, hoping that *Santa Lucia* will fill them with gifts. They sometimes place food outside the door for her donkey.

In some regions, New Year's is a time for gifts as in ancient Rome. *La Befana,* the kindly, old witch, delivers the gifts, and even children who received gifts at Christmas receive something from *La Befana.*

During World War II, American GIs stationed in Italy introduced Santa Claus and popularized gift giving and Christmas trees. In recent years, Santa Claus has become a very popular figure, called *Babbo Natale* or Father Christmas. He has replaced *La Befana* in many parts of Italy, but *La Befana* has been delivering gifts for almost 2,000 years; thus, it is likely that she will continue to do so.

Christmas trees are popular, especially in northern Italy. A forerunner of the Christmas tree was the *ceppi* or pyramid used especially in the Florence area. *Ceppo* means tree trunk, and it may have been a substitute for the Yule log. The *ceppi* was composed of shelves of varying sizes fastened to light, wooden poles and decorated with sprigs of evergreen. Candles, pictures, and little figurines were placed on the shelves, the lowest shelf often containing, in the center, a cradle with the Infant Jesus lying in it and surrounded by shepherds, saints, and angels. The smaller shelves held presents and toys.

It's traditional to decorate Italian homes with sprigs of holly and mistletoe.

## The First Christmas Carol

The birthplace of the first, true Christmas carol is thirteenth century Italy. Among the early Franciscans, St. Francis of Assisi, who had a special devotion and affection for the mysteries of the holy childhood of Jesus, introduced the joyous idea of carols which soon spread all over Europe. St. Francis wrote a beautiful Christmas hymn in Latin called *"Psalmus in Nativitate."* There is no evidence that he composed any carols in Italian. His companions and spiritual sons, however, the first Franciscan friars, contributed a large number of lovely Italian Christmas carols.

## Manger Scene

The crib or manger scene in its present form and its use outside many churches is also credited to St. Francis of Assisi. He made the Christmas crib popular through his famous celebration at Greccio,

Italy, on Christmas Eve, 1223, which portrayed a Bethlehem scene including five people and animals.

In Italy, the Christmas celebration centers upon the crib with its figures. The most beautiful cribs are set up in churches. Often a carillon plays beautiful Christmas carols, and the lights are regulated in such a way as to enhance the crib's beauty. Contests occur among the towns' churches for the best crib scene. People, especially children, go from church to church to see the manger scenes on display.

In every Italian home, the *presepia* or miniature manger finds a place of prominence and usually remains in place from Christmas Eve to Epiphany on January 6. Long before Christmas, little clay figures are on sale in the markets and village fairs. Settings for the manger are built at home either with cardboard, moss, and bits of twig or with something a little more sophisticated. At times, the backgrounds appear very elaborate, depicting the sacred grotto, the tavern, the shepherds' huts, and glittering pools of water all set in a charming Italian landscape with angels suspended from invisible wires. The figures of the Magi join the scene at the manger on January 6.

One of the most endearing crib festivities is the famous custom of the Children's Sermon at the Church of Ara Coeli on the Capitoline Hill in Rome. The church contains a beautiful statue of the Holy Child, carved from wood, wrapped in linen, and adorned with a crown. This *Bambino* is highly venerated, and all through the Christmas season, It lies in the church crib, visited by thousands. On a little platform in front of the crib, boys and girls from the ages of five to twelve come to recite short sermons and poems in honor of the Infant Jesus. Adults crowd around and listen with rapt attention as the little ones preach to their elders.

Since 1968, the Pope, the head of the Roman Catholic Church, has presided over a special ceremony for children on the last Sunday before Christmas. Thousands of children bring their manger figures of Baby Jesus to St. Peter's Square to be blessed by the Pope. When Pope John Paul II observed his first Christmas as Pope in 1976, more than 50,000 of Rome's children came to the square. They serenaded Pope

John Paul II with carols, including a Christmas song from his native Poland.

In Rome, at sunset on Christmas Eve, cannons boom from the Castle of St. Angelo, announcing the start of the holy season. The Pope conducts midnight mass at St. Peter's, the largest Christian church in the world. It is believed that the first church bells ever used in a Christian church service were Italian, and they peeled out on a Christmas Eve over 1,600 years ago. Bishop Paulinus of Noia, in the province of Campania, is credited with starting this custom. Until that time, a man ringing a hand bell called people to mass. In Italy today, at midnight on Christmas Eve, all the country's church bells ring out the glad tidings.

The most characteristic Italian Christmas sound is not bells, but bagpipes. The bagpipers or *zampognari* are shepherds from the mountains who come down each year to perform in the Christmas markets, especially in Rome's Piazza Navona and other sites in Rome and in the regions of Calabria and Abruzzi. Modern day *zampognari* dress much as their ancestors, in shaggy sheepskin vests, leather breeches, or sheepskin leggings. Over their shoulders they wear long, woolen cloaks, and they wear white stockings bound by leather thongs. A couple of days before Christmas, in imitation of the *zampognari,* children dress as shepherds with sandals, leggings tied with crossed thongs, and shepherds' hats and go from home to home playing songs on shepherds' pipes and giving recitations. They are given coins to buy Christmas delicacies.

## Christmas Eve

On Christmas Eve, *La Viglia,* everyone attends Christmas Mass and worships before the life-sized figures of the holy family. In rural areas, people often lay humble offerings of fruits, nuts, or vegetables at the Christ Child's feet.

At Irpino, an image of the Babe is carried in solemn procession before the worshippers. Music from the flute and bagpipe, the rough, white sheepskins worn by the many participants, and the presence of shepherds from the hills all add to the rustic charm and simplicity of the Christ Child's festival.

Whenever it is possible to burn a Yule log on Christmas Eve, the custom is followed. Before the lighting, children are gathered around the fireplace and blindfolded. Each child must recite a sermon to the Christ Child. The blindfold is removed, and the child finds before him a small pile of gifts.

When the tapers are lighted before the *presepio,* children surprise the elders by reciting little verses. Italian children also like to "surprise" their parents with the traditional Christmas letter written on ornate stationery in which they promise to be good and obedient and wish Mamma and Papa a happy holiday. These letters are slipped under Papa's dinner plate and are read aloud by him amidst a lot of emotion and good feelings from the whole family.

In Cortina D'Ampezzo in the snowy north of Italy, a spectacular event takes place on Christmas Eve called *Fiaccolate degli Sciatori.* At midnight, the Alpine guides, holding flaming torches, ski down the mountainside, darting over the slopes in sweeping curves and criss-cross patterns creating a beautiful sight.

## Christmas Food

Foods vary for an Italian Christmas. The Christmas Eve meal begins around 7:00 or 8:00 P.M. and usually lasts for several hours. By ancient custom, this meal often remains meatless. Many Italians still observe a rigid twenty-four-hour fast that ends on Christmas Eve.

In Venice, Florence, and Rome, huge wholesale fish markets open their doors to the public a day or so before Christmas. One of the noisiest and most picturesque markets is Rome's *Piazza Navona* beginning around December 15. Here is purchased the *capitone,* a big, female eel which is roasted, baked, or fried and will appear on many tables on Christmas Eve. *Capitone* is also frequently eaten in Naples and the southern areas. The meal will also feature *sott'aceti,* a wide variety of vegetables preserved in vinegar and sometimes served with oil and anchovy sauce. Pasta in many shapes and sizes with *vongale* or small clams is very popular. North of Rome the traditional dish is cappelleti, little dough hats stuffed with meat or tortellini, a sort of ravioli.

On Christmas Day the main course can be anything from capons stuffed with chestnuts, stuffed turkey, or boiled chicken with mustard. Fresh pork sausage stuffed into a pig's leg and smothered with lentils is especially popular in northern and central Italy. No matter what the main course, almost all Christmas dinners start with tortellini in broth. In the south, the first course is regularly macaroni with minced meat and tomato sauce.

The most popular Christmas sweets are *panettone,*a cake filled with candied fruit, *torrone, nougat,* and *panforte* which is gingerbread made with hazelnuts, honey, and almonds. All Christmas sweets, as a rule, contain nuts, especially almonds. In rural folklore, the eating of nuts encourages good crops.

## New Year's Day

On *Capo d'Anno* or New Year's Day, there are parties and visiting. Children receive gifts of money from their parents. At Capri, groups of dancers meet in the spacious Piazza di Capri and hold contests dancing the *Capri Tarantella.* At Santa Agata dei Goti, dramatic presentations featuring the "Story of the Blue Knight" are enacted on the public piazza.

Often a special New Year's banquet is eaten on the last day of the year: raisin bread, turkey, chicken, rabbit, and spaghetti are served, and champagne corks pop at midnight.



3282-TUCK

## Epiphany

On *La Vigilia dell"Epifania* or Epiphany Eve on January 5, many Italian children receive gifts in memory of the presents the Magi brought the Christ Child. *La Befana,* the little, old woman whose name undoubtedly is abbreviated from *Epifania,* is the gift bearer at this time in many sections of Italy, particularly in the north. According to legend, *La Befana,* was sweeping the house when the Three Kings came by on their way to Bethlehem with gifts for *Gesu Bambino,* Baby Jesus. When she was asked to accompany them, she gruffly replied that she was too busy with her work. Later, when the work was done, she started out for Bethlehem, but she lost her way and couldn't find the Child for whom she still searches. Each year *La Befana* passes through Italy on her search, and she leaves pretty gifts for children who are good and bits of charcoal for the naughty children.

In Rome, the Feast of Epiphany is celebrated in the Piazza Navona where toys dangle invitingly from hundreds of brightly decorated stalls. The piazza is filled with children, mothers, fathers, and old people moving from stall to stall gossiping, bargaining, buying, and exchanging greetings. Everyone buys at least one tinhorn or trumpet or perhaps a little clay figure which is brightly painted and fitted with a shrill whistle.

At Monta, Polo, boys and men carrying a rotating, illuminated star go from house to house singing traditional songs. At Varenna, Como, men dressed like the Three Kings and their attendants go through the countryside carrying torches and giving gifts to the needy. Bonfires are lit on Epiphany Eve in many areas as people dance about the fires and predict good or bad weather for the coming year according to which way the wind is blowing.

On *Epifania* or Epiphany on January 6, a quaint, old custom called the "Clothing of the Child Jesus" still exists at Niscemi, Caltanissetta, where a poor parish child is carried to the church and there dressed to represent the Infant Jesus. A procession of priests and worshippers take the child home to the joyous accompaniment of bagpipe music, and parishioners offer all kinds of gifts.

In large cities like Rome and Milan, Epiphany is the favorite day of traffic policemen as they are showered with gifts from motorists. Mountains of gifts pile up around the police officers' stands. This day ends the Italian celebration of Christmas.

# Jamaica

Merry Christmas!

Because of the geographic and historic closeness to the United States, the Caribbean island country of Jamaica celebrates Christmas in much the same way as people do in the United States.

## Christmas Traditions

A lot of preparation is done for Christmas. At home the place is cleaned up inside and out. The lawn is manicured, and stones and trees are whitewashed (the lower portion of the trunk). An animal is killed, a pig or a goat, a few days before Christmas. Large white yams, fruits, and vegetables are picked. These are shared with the neighbors. There is a lot of baking of cakes and puddings.

Streets, homes, stores, shops, supermarkets, gas stations, just about all places decorate with lights and other festive touches. Not much is accomplished during this season, and it called the "silly season." People are filled with good cheer and jubilation.

People in Jamaica exchange Christmas cards and gifts and go caroling. Christmas trees are decorated with tinsel, ornamental balls, and cotton wool to represent snow. Santa Claus appears in department stores and on the streets. Although Jamaica has a warm climate, Santa is dressed in his usual, fur-trimmed, red suit. There are no chimneys in Jamaica, but children do hang stockings to be filled by Santa.

Most churches have carol services, cantatas, or concerts.

Schools have their programs a little earlier when school lets out for vacation. Gift exchanging occurs in schools and Sunday Schools.

Typically, Christmas Eve is filled with frenzied, last minute shopping. The main shopping streets in the urban areas are closed to traffic to allow the crowds of children and adults dressed in their Sunday best to promenade, blowing toy whistles and horns, carrying balloons, and waving "starlights." Vendors spread their wares all over the street.

On Christmas Eve, many people attend church services and candlelight masses. They often attend services again at 5:00 A.M. the next morning. Others have parties at home or at clubs. Still others spend the evening at home with the family.

## Christmas Day

The highlight of Christmas day is dinner. Turkey, goat, or ham usually supplies the main course or perhaps a large chicken for those who can't afford the others. Rice and peas cooked in coconut milk (the national dish of Jamaica), baked plantains, and a large, mixed salad accompany the main course. Dessert is Christmas black pudding, a fruitcake baked or steamed with lots of Jamaican rum. All of this is washed down with the Christmas drink known as sorrel made from the sorrel bush.

New Year's is celebrated much as in the United States with partying, eating, and celebrating, thus ending the Jamaican Christmas holiday celebration.

## *Jonkunnu*

One very "Jamaican" folk tradition that used to be observed far more at Christmas time is the appearance of *Jonkunnu* (or John Canoe), a group of masqueraders who appear in some towns at Christmas. The custom dates from the days of slavery when the bands of masqueraders were much larger than they are today. The tradition



3282-TUCK

became associated with Christmas since that was the only major holiday granted to the slaves. Today the masqueraders may include a cow or horse head, a king and a queen, a Devil, Pitch-Patchy who is an acrobat who wears tattered rags, Indians wearing costumes of mirrors and feathers, a large, pregnant woman, and often a mock police officer who keeps the motley group in line.

Musicians playing fifes, drums, and rattles often accompany the group. The characters wear masks and are played by men. They speak only in hoarse whispers to keep their identities secret. *Jonkunnu* is thought to originate from West African secret societies, and the word itself can be translated as "deadly sorcerer" or "sorcerer man."

# Japan

*Meri Kurisumasu!*

Christian missionaries brought Christmas to the exotic, far eastern island nation of Japan. The first recorded Christmas in Japan was in 1874 at the First Presbyterian Church in Tokyo where the Christmas tree was trimmed with *kanzashi,* women's ornamental hairpins, and Santa Claus wore *kamishimo,* traditional samurai clothing. The female students sang carols at this first of many Christmas celebrations in Tokyo.

After the death of Emperor Taisho on December 25, 1926, Christmas celebrations were banned because it would have been a sacrilege to have merrymaking on the anniversary of the Emperor's death. This was not the only reason for the decline of Christmas celebrations. In the 1920s and 1930s, nationalistic feelings were growing in Japan, and these feelings made celebrations of western festivals out of the question. Foreign languages and anything with a foreign flavor were removed from Japan. By the 1940s Christmas, as well as anything else western, was gone from Japan.

After World War II, the GHQ, as the American Occupational Forces were called, brought Christmas to Japan once again. For all the despairing, hopeless Japanese of the postwar period, the happy Christmas parties of the GHQ soldiers seemed like something from another world. Santa Claus and the presents brought by him gave dreams to Japanese children who had scarcely enough food to eat. The Japanese were intrigued by the American material culture; consequently, they tried to do everything in an American way in order to become a rich, strong, and independent country and to be a good member of international society. They celebrated Christmas enthusiastically, for it was a symbol of American popular culture.

Today this sort of blind Americanization has disappeared, but Christmas celebrations still exist. There may be several reasons for this. First, the world of commerce may use the holiday season for economic gains. Second, the Japanese people do not like to be different from others. Third, the time of year when Christmas takes place may have caused it to remain popular, this being the time of year when *bonenki* occurs, a celebration for closing the year as well as the time of *oseibo,* giving gifts to one's acquaintances as an expression of gratitude for their kindnesses during the year.

Probably the biggest reason for Christmas' continued popularity in Japan is the polytheistic nature of the Japanese or their belief in many gods. People go to Shinto shrines on New Year's Eve to pray for good luck. Then they listen to the Buddhist temple bells at midnight to rid one's evils of the past year. They have a Shinto wedding ceremony, and sometimes they marry in a Christian church. They have a Buddhist funeral; they take a newborn baby to a Shinto shrine for a blessing, and they celebrate Christmas. In larger cities like Tokyo, many non-Christian Japanese attend midnight masses to appreciate the beauty of the services. They accept and absorb all religions.

Christmas is now one of the most popular festivals in Japan. The word Christmas is even found on the calendars of Buddhist temples and Shinto shrines. Less than 1 percent of the Japanese population is Christian, thus making Christmas a nonreligious celebration for most people.

Adults and young people have fun at the many parties held during the week before Christmas. During the season, streets and shops in Japan are decorated with stars, synthetic snow, and decorated trees. Some common images of Christmas in Japan are Santa Claus, reindeer, Christmas trees, cakes, parties, and presents, but the Nativity scene rarely appears. Mistletoe, holly, and branches of pine are used for decorating in stores, public buildings, and homes. Many towns and villages have a community tree.

Christmas carols are heard everywhere. Japanese people send

Christmas cards, and the children write letters to Santa Claus. For many, *Hoteiosho,* an old Japanese god, stands in for Santa Claus. He is a kind, old man with a huge pack on his back, and he has an interesting characteristic; he has eyes in the back of his head!

Turkey is often eaten as the main course for Christmas dinner. Japanese Christmas cake is a sponge cake decorated with Christmas trees, flowers, and a figure of Santa Claus, all made of creamy icing.

For Christmas in Japan, celebrations are similar to those in America with many Japanese touches added, of course. Pageant plays of the Christmas story, with the characters often in Japanese dress, are popular. It is also a day when many Christians try to do something for others, especially sick people in hospitals or orphans in orphanages.

## New Year's Day

New Year's Day is the leading holiday of the year in Japan. *Oshogatsu* is the time when houses are given a thorough cleaning before they are decorated. Branches of pine are attached to the entrance gates of homes, and both pine and bamboo have a place of special importance at the family shrines as symbols of long life. Ropes of twisted rice straw hang above the gates meaning strong family ties, and when the tiny, Japanese oranges are added, they signify roundness and smoothness.

Families dress in their best clothes and pay visits to their relatives and friends. They pay tribute to their ancestors and departed family members on this day. Ceremonies are held in homes to drive out the evil spirits. Dried beans are tossed into the corner of every room to dismiss evil that is replaced with good fortune. Boys fly kites, and girls enjoy favorite games. The boys also organize small bands made up of drums, cymbals, and flutes and go about playing for the elders and anyone caring to listen. This performance is in mimicry of adults who go about as maskers, performing in a similar fashion.

Toys are used to decorate trees and later given to the children. In many ways Japanese New Year is like Christmas in the western world. Businesses are closed for three days, and it is truly a family festival. All debts are settled, and business books are closed at this time. No Japanese person wants to begin a new year owing any one anything. At midnight on New Year's Eve, the "Great Last Temple" bells sound out 108 times.

Special rice cakes called *mochi* are made for serving on New Year's Day. Foods for this day are often selected for their symbolism. Seaweed means felicity in the coming year; bamboo means long life; langoustes or lobster and red rice bring good luck. Everything is cooked separately in soy sauce and sugar and then placed in a *jubako* or a nest of boxes of tiered porcelain or lacquerware and arranged according to color, texture, and design. At every meal during the New Year's celebration, these boxes are brought out, and each person takes whatever he wishes from them.

# Jordan

*Edi Milad Saied !* or *Mboni Chrismen!*

In the Middle Eastern, predominately Sunni Muslim country of Jordan, Christians celebrate Christmas by family feasts, giving children new clothes and sweets, visiting relatives, making trips to cemeteries to remember the dead, and giving to the poor.

Western culture is beginning to influence the celebration of Christmas. *Baba Noël* who looks like Santa Claus is a familiar figure to children. Christmas trees are put up and decorated in many homes. Western carols translated into Arabic are sung in Christian churches and schools.

Some Christian schools have instituted Santa Claus or *Baba Noël* gift giving. Parents buy presents for their children, wrap the presents, and take them to the school. For a small fee, the gifts are delivered to the house on Christmas Eve and presented to the children by a students dressed up in a Santa Claus costume.

Even the smaller towns are becoming more westernized. The small Christian village of Fuheis near Amman has a large tree placed in the town square and decorated about a week before Christmas.

Many of the Orthodox Christian groups practice fasting before Christmas. The fast consists of abstinence from all animal foods including meat and dairy products. The Armenian Orthodox fast for 49 days; the Eastern (Greek) Orthodox fast for 40 days; the Syrian Orthodox fast for 10 days.

After the Armenian Orthodox Church celebrates its early Christmas Eve Mass, the choral group from the church tours the houses of all

300 families in the parish to sing Christmas carols. They do not finish until around 4:00 A.M.

The Roman Catholic women collect food and clothes for the poor living in the outlying areas. The priest visits all of his sick parishioners before Christmas. After Christmas, the priest visits the homes of all his church members and blesses their homes with holy water. People do not take down their Christmas trees until after the priest has blessed the home.

Many Muslims celebrate Christmas also. To them, Jesus is a prophet, and an entire chapter, "Sura 19" of their holy book the *Koran,* is devoted to Mary. According to the story of the birth of Jesus, Mary conceived her Son through the Holy Spirit although she was a virgin. Verses 22 through 26 of the chapter "Sura 19" state:

> "And she conceived him, and she withdrew with him to a place. And the pangs of childbirth drove her unto the trunk of the palm tree. She said: Oh, would that I had died ere this and had become a thing of naught, forgotten ! Then one cried unto her from below her, saying: Grieve not ! The Lord hath placed a rivulet beneath the tree. And shake the trunk of the palm tree toward thee, thou wilt cause ripe dates to fall upon thee. So eat and drink and be consoled."

# Lithuania

*Linksmu Kaledu!*

Lithuania, the first of the former Soviet republics to break away from Russia, has a very proud and deeply religious people. They celebrate Christmas as a day of peace, good will, and family spirit.

Lithuanians are conservative Catholics, and they observe the Advent season, the preparatory time beginning with the fourth Sunday before Christmas Eve, in a very strict manner. Partying does not exist before Christmas.

## Christmas Decorations

Christmas ornaments in Lithuania are very creative. They are formed from wheat or rye straw gathered by women and artistically made into literally hundreds of designs. Some are made of various lengths of straw strung together with needle and thread in the form of birdcages, bell towers, stars, or other geometric shapes. Fantastic birds with eggshell bodies and wings of feathers or paper are created.

The straws may be cut into small pieces and glued on their ends to paper. The ends are then split and turned back to make tiny, star-like designs or flowers. Lengths of straw may also be glued together to make three-dimensional designs. At waysides along Lithuanian roads, beautiful displays ranging from simple crosses to elaborate productions are built.

## Christmas Eve and Day

Houses are thoroughly cleaned, and family members often scrub themselves in the *pirtis* or steam bath and dress in holiday clothes.

Christmas Eve dinner or *kucia* is the highlight of the holiday. People fast until the *kucia* is served. Dinner begins after someone spots the first star of the evening. The table is spread with sweet, fresh hay as a reminder of Christ's manger and then covered with a white tablecloth reserved for this meal. A crucifix and a plate of holy wafers or *plotkeles* are placed in the center of the table. The head of the family begins the meal with a prayer of thanksgiving for all the past year's blessings and adds a wish that the family will remain intact during the coming year. He breaks and shares the wafers with each member of the family, and they, in turn, with each other.

Often meatless, the *kucia* menu consists of twelve courses representing the twelve apostles: soup, fish, vegetables, *slizikai* or *preskuciai* which are small, hard biscuits served with poppy seed and honey sauce, *kisilius* or oatmeal pudding. Eaten in leisure, the meal exudes an atmosphere of good will and peace.

The mysteriousness of the evening encourages the traditional legends and superstitions. Straws are drawn from under the tablecloth, the length of the straw determining the length of life, or for the very young, the length of time they will remain unmarried. Girls carry kindling wood into the house to count; an even number of sticks indicates marriage during the coming year. Children run frequently to the well to taste to see if the water has changed to wine. They also run to the stable to eavesdrop on the animals that are supposedly given the gift of human speech on this night.

*Piemeneliu Misios* or Shepherd's Mass held either at midnight or at dawn draws large crowds in the churches.

A Santa Claus figure called *Kalodu Senellis,* dressed much like Santa Claus, delivers gifts under the tree for children.

Christmas Day or *Kaledos* is spent at home or visiting neighbors, relatives, and friends. Before being admitted to a home, the visitors are required to sing a Christmas song.

During the Second Day of Christmas on December 26, people visit, party, and play games. Most people do not work too hard during the time between Christmas and the Feast of the Three Kings on January 6.

## New Year's and Epiphany

New Year's celebrations are similar to those the world over, with parties and carnivals. Families get together for a New Year's Eve dinner. In earlier times, young people masqueraded as Old New Year and New Year or as geese, goats, bears, or other animals and visited friends and neighbors. New Year's Day usually abounds in merrymaking and partying or participating in outdoor sports such as skating or sledding.

Three Kings Day or Epiphany on January 6 is a holy day and a legal holiday. The evening before, people make crosses and write the initials of the three Kings on their doors: K+M+B, Kasparas, Melchioras, and Baltazaras, entrusting the care of their homes to these three noble persons. Young people used to dress up like the Three Kings and visit friends and neighbors.

# Malta

*Il-Milied It-Tajjeb!*

Christmas on the Mediterranean island of Malta occurs much like that of Catholic countries elsewhere, but it does have its unique celebrations. Brightly lit shop windows, toys and sweets, Christmas trees, carol singing, and the exchange of Christmas cards are all present; since 1964 street decorations and illuminations in Valletta and other centers are displayed.

## Christmas Crafts

Christmas preparations begin with the first Sunday of Advent, the fourth Sunday before Christmas Eve. On this Sunday families begin to make the crib or manger scene for display in their homes. The Maltese Christmas centers on the *presepju* or crib scene. Cribs are found in homes, churches, friaries, and hospitals, simply everywhere. Written references of cribs go back to 1617 when the Black Friars lit up a crib using earthenware lamps burning inside a large number of paper lanterns.

On December 8, the Feast of the Immaculate Conception that celebrates the Virgin Mary's birth without sin, wheat, barley, vetches, and birdseed are cultivated to surround and decorate the crib or manger scene and Baby Jesus during the season. The sown grain is placed in the dark to grow yellowish instead of greenish, and it is watered on alternate days.

Years ago, the framework of the crib was made of stone alone or burnt cork residue. Today it is usually made of papier maché, paper soaked in carpenter's glue and molded into shape. The bed of the crib may be strewn with wild thyme, greenish-white grass, statice, moss, turf, earth, clay for a bridge or road, and pounce or yellowish stones or some other small stones for a wall. At Qormi in the 1870s, the first large-scale, mechanized Christmas crib is mentioned in a publication. This idea grew, and today in virtually every village and town in Malta and Gozo, there is a very large, mechanized manger scene. (Gozo is the second largest island in the Maltese groups of islands, Malta being the largest.) A very popular, mechanized crib that still stands today is the one of the Nuns of Jesus of Nazareth at Zejtun.

Crib making is an art, and artisans compete with each other to see who makes the most artistic crib. The figurines known in Maltese as *pasturi* are made mainly from clay, papier maché, or wax. There are two types of locally made *pasturi*: the ones in Biblical costume and those in local dress. Some figures are traditional in Malta such as "the climber" who is always placed on top of the rocky exterior of the cave looking down in; "the astonished one" is usually placed near a windmill; "the sleeper" finds himself under a tree; "the singing pair" are always accompanied by two to four musicians, figures with bagpipes, a tambourine, a mouth organ, and a *rumbaba,* a skin top with a stick in the middle. The makers of *pasturi* create other figures so that people can add to their collections, figures such as a woman with a hen or pigeon, a woman holding a basket of vegetables or a jug of water, a farmer and his wife with their tools and animals, or a fisherman. Crib making is flourishing today. A live crib at Lija and the many competitions started a revival of interest in the 1960s. There are two crib societies, one in Malta and one in Gozo. The Friends of the Crib organize a competition for the best crib, hold shows, show video films on crib making, give lectures, and offer other activities all year round. They also keep in close contact with similar societies abroad.

Children used to go to the butcher shop long before Christmas and arrange to have him save them a bull's horn. A week before Christmas, all the children would go to the school gates, playing the horns.

Certainly not to be practiced today, an interesting old custom in Gozo began on November 1 when some hunters used to set out in a



3282-TUCK

group or alone at about 7:00 P.M., betting on which one would catch the best animal. The hunters hid and waited for the cats that came out from the old cellars in Rabat, the ancient section of Gozo. They would catch the cats, put them in sacks, dehydrate them, and inflate them. A reed with holes in it was inserted into the skull. Through this reed, the player produced the various musical sounds. No musical sound could be produced if the skin had the least crack or tiniest hole through which air could escape. Some used to insert a reed pipe into their "bagpipe." Two other popular instruments were the *tanbur* or drum and the *rabbaba,* a cooking pot covered with the skin of a rabbit and held taut, in the middle of which stood a medium-sized reed tied from inside and played by means of the musician's hand being passed along it, producing a sound like "rob . . . rob . . . u . . . rob."

## Calends

The Rules or *Calends* start around December 13. Following an ancient custom that has not changed much over the years, farmers, since they have continuous contact with the weather, are mostly concerned with this series of twelve days. This superstition, beginning on December 13th and ending on December 24, has spread throughout much of Europe, although the dates may vary. It used to be said that the last twelve days before Christmas correspond exactly with the twelve months of the following year; the thirteenth would be January, and the fourteenth February until the twenty-fourth would be December. The day begins at midnight and lasts through the next twenty-four hours. Therefore, twenty-four hours should be divided between thirty or thirty-one days, depending on the month with which it corresponds. In order to be exact, the farmer is supposed to follow the weather changes very carefully throughout the day, especially slight variations of the wind, the increase or decrease of the wind's force, rainfall, sunshine, and cloudiness. Thus, the weather almanac for the coming year is created.

# Il-Tokk

On December 15, the novena, or nine days of prayer and celebration begins. People used to gather at the Cathedral at Gozo to take part in the religious celebrations each day. People would fast during these nine days, and all would meet at the Cathedral on Christmas Eve at sunset, about 9:00 P.M. A shot was fired signaling that the fast was over, and the men congregated in the center of the Cathedral and women and children at the sides. Things got out of hand when during the "Gloria" men threw nuts at the women while the children scampered down to the ground to catch the nuts. Pandemonium reigned, and often the police had to be called to intervene. After mass, eating was immediately resumed. Shopkeepers opened up their doors to sell cheesecakes, soufflés, and lots of beer. Vendors would put up displays of delicacies, especially honey ring cakes of all sizes, heart-shaped pastries with treacle, decorated with designs in icing with a figure of Baby Jesus in the center. There is a rhyme from olden days that is still heard today:

> *"Ninu, Ninu,tal-Millied,* "Ninu, Ninu, it's Christmas,
> Ommi *ghamlet il-kaghkiet,* Mother has made the rings,
> i*l-kaghkiet tal-qastanija,* the treacle (honey) rings,
> *Santa Rokku tat-tagrija;* Saint Roche and the horse races;
> *Ghaddew il-festi kollha;* this year's feasts have been celebrated;
> *Fadal biss Santa Marija."* only the feast of Saint Mary remains."

At this celebration called *Il-Tokk* in Gozo, the men of the village used to meet to play for honey ring cakes. Women made their culinary preparations beforehand. They would kill the hens, cocks, and turkeys and pluck them for cooking on Christmas Day. They would then go to each other's homes to play hazelnuts. Actually, one could see all along the stairways leading to the Cathedral all ages of people playing for Christmas nuts. This was and is a popular Christmas game in Gozo. The standard name for these Christmas nut games is *gastell* or castle. Most of these games involve tossing or flinging hazelnuts into certain target areas or certain configurations.

Another game called *ruma* involves a chocolate tied to a thread six or seven feet above the ground. Children set out at a run and jump to reach it with their mouths. Sometimes they are blindfolded, and the target they must hit with a rod is an earthenware bowl. When the bowl breaks, onlookers rush after the treats in the bowl, and the poor winner is left with nothing.

Musicians were all around the Cathedral area playing their bagpipes, drums, and *rabbaba,* having come from all the small villages. Children followed the drummer, dancing. On the way to the cathedral, they would often stop at a rich man's home and perform until thrown some coins. Some musical groups included violins, mandolins, guitars, castanets, cellos, and wind instruments.

Christmas in Malta years ago was characterized by the playing of bagpipes. They were heard everywhere, even at the midnight masses. The Maltese bagpipe called a *zagg* was a crude instrument consisting of a mouthpiece attached to a calf's, cat's, dog's, or sheep's skin which when inflated looked like a live animal. The *zagg* cannot play a tune; it has one loud drone varied by warbling notes.

## Christmas Trees

The Christmas tree, like Father Christmas, was alien to Maltese tradition, and they were both slow in gaining acceptance. It is unclear when Christmas trees became part of the Maltese celebration. There was some sort of gathering around such a tree at the Governor's Palace of San Anton in the 1860s. The idea was given a boost by the presence of wounded, convalescing British soldiers and German prisoners of war during World War I. Not until after World War II was the idea of Christmas trees in people's homes popular, as well as the figure of Father Christmas. The first real tree in Gozo was set up in 1950; since then, it has become the custom for people to borrow a tree from the Government Nursery at Rundle Garden for a nominal fee. In 1955, the government of Malta had trees planted at traffic roundabouts and other prominent places. These are brightly lighted with colored bulbs, silvery balls, and other ornaments.

## Christmas Eve

Midnight mass is a culmination of a long series of activities, and all the churches are filled to capacity. Many people from all parts of the island prefer to go to the Cathedral at Mdina, the old capital city of the Malta where the Archbishop presides over the service or to the Mosta Church. On Christmas Eve, in most towns and villages, a lay organization called M.U.S.E.U.M. or the Society of Christian Doctrine stages a procession in which children take part, carrying an image of the Baby Jesus and lighted cardboard lanterns and singing carols in Maltese. This procession was held for the first time in Malta in 1921 when the founder of M.U.S.E.U.M., Dun Gorg, was determined to instill in the people a deeper appreciation of the real meaning of Christmas. The tradition spread to Gozo during World War II. In some parishes, the procession is very elaborate. At San Lawrenz, Gozo, for example, half the village takes part, wearing costumes depicting the prophets, Mary and Joseph, and the other Nativity figures.

A boy is chosen to give a talk on the Nativity; he may or may not repeat it during the midnight mass or in some outlying church or chapel the next day. The talk is rehearsed for weeks and is often a simple retelling of the Christmas story. This tradition goes back over a hundred years.

Traditional Christmas sweets are still popular including the honey rings known as *qaghaq talqastanija, imqaret* or date-filled pastry envelopes, and *imbulijute talqastan* or boiled chestnuts.

On Christmas Eve and the days leading up to it, children go around singing carols and collecting money for charities.



3282-TUCK

## Christmas Day

Christmas Day is a time for family reunions, with married sons and daughters returning to their parents' homes. Sometimes the get-togethers are so large that Christmas lunch is held in a hotel or a restaurant. For most people, it is a five-course luncheon at home with turkey, baked macaroni or lasagna, turkey soup, cheese, and Christmas pudding. The meal lasts well into the afternoon, and in the evening Father Christmas arrives to distribute gifts at a party to which relatives and friends are invited.

Some families have started inviting a boy or girl from a local orphanage to spend Christmas Day with them. Charity plays a very important part in the Maltese celebration. Appeals by the Community Chest Fund and other organizations around Christmas time are very successful.

# Martinique

*Joyeux Noël!* (French)
Merry Christmas!

Christmas in this French West Indies, Caribbean island nation means a lot of festivities. It is usually a time of crisp, clear days coming at the end of the rains of the All Saints season. The *fleuri Noël* and currant bushes swaying in the gentle breezes spread their delicious aroma through the countryside.

Firecrackers are set off to announce the beginning of the Christmas season. Carols are often sung to the accompaniment of improvised instruments like tins and bottles beaten to the rhythms of the *biguine* or the mazurka. There is a lot of feverish activity in the preparation for Christmas, and people constantly worry that there won't be enough and that things may not be entertaining enough.

## "Feast of the Pig"

December 24 is known as the "Feast of the Pig." The pig acts truly as the life of the party, making his appearance in patés, puddings, glazed hams, stews, and nearly every dish eaten. In the sixteenth century Spaniards who had stopped to replenish their water supplies brought pigs to Martinique The pigs multiplied on the island, forming herds of wild pigs that destroyed colonial plantations in the eighteenth century. The hunt for wild pigs was very popular until recently, and some say there are still a few wild pigs left in the forests. It is only natural that the festive meals are based on pork since the pig was one of the first animals on the island. The domestic or farm-raised pigs are of a different species. Fattened up for months with the year end Christmas festivities in mind, Martinique pigs are either the pink pig raised in Europe or the country's own peculiar, black pigs which surprise many visitors.

The *filao* or artificial tree is well decorated and covered in garlands, lighting up the house where people are filled with the holiday spirit.

## Christmas Eve

On Christmas Eve under a blanket of lights, groups whispering and laughing hurry to church to attend midnight mass. After mass, the serious, religious part of Christmas gives way to joy and merrymaking, and each person returns to his warm home where there is an abundance of good cheer.

Tables are filled with blood pudding, warm plates full of stuffing, pig stew with Angolan peas, smoked ham which was soaked for five or six days in advance, pigeon peas served with stewed pork or *ragout,* "sassa" yams, and *cous-couch* which are small, delicate tasting vegetables. Shrub, a delicious liqueur made of white rum, sugar cane syrup, and the peel from locally grown oranges, is usually served with the blood pudding. There are also spicy, Creole punches and bright liqueurs with the taste of licorice, coconut, and cocoa. People eat, drink, and have a fun time. They sing and dance to the old songs with violins, accordions, and the lively cha-chas.

# Mauritius

Merry Christmas!
*Joyeux Noël !* (French)

An island nation in the southwest Indian Ocean off the coast of Africa, Mauritius was known by the Arabs in ancient times, visited by the Portuguese, and colonized by the Dutch, the French, and the English until gaining its independence in 1968. Consequently, Christmas is very international. Although the weather is very warm at Christmas, trees are still popular, reminding the people of colder places to the north. Instead of snow, there is the smell of ripe mangoes, bunches of red litchis, and blooming roses under bright, starry skies.

The crèche or Nativity scene plays an important part in the Mauritian celebration, adorning homes and churches. Christmas carols and songs may be heard everywhere; a particular favorite among non-Christians as well as Christians is *"Petit Papa Noël."* At Christmas time, there are competitions for the best carol singing choir and the most original crib or manger scene.

Advent, the four Sundays before Christmas Eve, serve as a preparation time for Christmas. Decorations are hung. A new custom that has come to Mauritius is the hanging of red and green Christmas wreaths on front doors. Other decorations are artificial snow, balloons, paper ribbons, tinsel, small toys, and stars. Christmas trees are everywhere.

People exchange Christmas cards, and *Bonhomme Noël* or *Le Père Noël* dresses in a long, red and white robe and wears a flowing woolen beard in spite of the heat. He distributes toys and gifts in the shoes that are lined up around the Christmas tree. Children believe that he comes at midnight through a window.

## Christmas Eve

Before midnight mass on Christmas Eve, there is a vigil, and the liturgy traces the story of the coming of Christ to Earth. At the closing of the mass, bells peel, and people wish each other a Merry Christmas.

The *réveillon* follows mass. This traditional meal usually features ham in slices or prepared whole and cooked slowly in beer and citronelle and finally adorned with breadcrumbs and cloves. Roast turkey is gaining popularity. Dessert may be a steamed Christmas pudding like the English or a *Bûche de Noël* or Yule log from the French. For a more humble home, a family's Christmas dinner will probably be rice and curried chicken accompanied by rum, wine, and custard pudding.

## Christmas Day

Christmas Day is a time for family reunions. Lunch lasts a long time, and in the afternoon, people often go to the beach. Firecrackers, which are usually kept until New Year's, can be heard from the Chinese quarters after midnight on Christmas Eve.

# Mexico

*Feliz Navidad!*

Christmas, *la Navidad,* in the North American country of Mexico is a time of elaborate pageantry, fireworks, feasting, and parties. Mexico celebrated its first Christmas in 1538 when Fray Pedro de Gante invited all the Indians for twenty leagues (about twenty-seven and a half miles) around Mexico City to attend. They came in droves by land and by water.

Mexico has contributed three important things to the worldwide celebration of Christmas. Poinsettias come from Mexico; turkeys were first known in Mexico; it was Cortez who first tasted chocolate in Mexico and shared it with the rest of the world.

## *Las Posadas*

Christmas celebrations begin on December 16 when *Las Posadas,* literally meaning lodging, begins, and it lasts through December 24, commemorating the events in the journey of Mary and Joseph from Nazareth to Bethlehem. Among the poor, it is customary for friends and neighbors of an area to get together to share the expense of this celebration. Christmas to Mexicans is more a community than a family event. Among the wealthier, *Las Posadas* celebrations are occasions for beautiful dances and parties from which, often, the religious element is entirely lacking. The idea of this nine day remembrance was introduced to the Indians in Mexico by Spanish missionaries in 1587.

Just after dark on December 16, ceremonies begin with a procession led by two children carrying a small, pine, decorated platform on top of which are figures of Mary riding the burro and Joseph beside her, both watched over by an angel. Sometimes Mary, Joseph, and the burro are live. Other people from the Nativity story are portrayed as well. These *Santos Peregrinos* or Holy Pilgrims carry lighted candles, the children blowing shrill whistles, as they approach the first door. They are turned away from the first house, told there is no room in the *posado* or inn. They repeat this a second time, and finally, they approach the house assigned to have the first *posada* celebration, all singing "The Liturgy of the Virgin" and asking for lodging for Mary. From within the house, the pilgrims are threatened with beatings unless they move on. Once more the group outside pleads for entrance. When the owner of the house finally learns who the guests are, he and his family throw open the door and bid them welcome. The pilgrims kneel before the *nacimiento* or manger scene and intone the litany, and the Baby Jesus is sung to sleep (although the figure of Jesus is not added to the scene until December 24) by the cradlesong "*El Rorro*" or "Babe in Arms." Ave Marias and a prayer are chanted, and then the party begins, as refreshments are served, and young and old dance. The piñata hangs by a long rope from the ceiling or a tree in the patio. One by one, the children are blindfolded, turned around and around, and instructed to strike the piñata with a long stick. When the piñata bursts, the children scramble for the treats.

These nightly celebrations continue until Christmas Eve, the ninth night, when they prepare for the Child Jesus' birth. Shortly before midnight, they sing nine Ave Marias and a little verse to the Virgin Mary that says that the desired night has come, and her confinement is approaching. Little children dressed like shepherds are placed to either side of the *nacimiento,* and the assigned godparents arrive with the Holy Infant. They place the Baby upon the manger and intone a Litany, all the people kneeling. They then sing him a lullaby. At midnight, there are fireworks, whistles, and bells.

## Piñatas

Piñatas play an important part in the Mexican Christmas celebration. They originated in Italy and are named after the *pignatta,* an ordinary, round, clay, cooking pot. In the sixteenth century, Italian royalty entertained with a game in which a pot filled with precious jewels and baubles was hung from a rope. Each person was blindfolded and tried to hit the *pignatta.* From Italy, the game spread to Spain where it was played during the Lenten season before Easter. The first Sunday in Lent was known as Piñata Sunday. Around the year 1600, Spanish colonists brought the idea to Mexico. Mexican children often sing a song as they attempt to break the piñata:

*"Ne quiero oro,* "Don't want gold,
*No quiero plata,* Don't want silver,
*Yo lo que quiero,* All I want
*Es romper la piñata."* Is to break the piñata."

The traditional method of making piñatas involves taking an ordinary, large, round clay pot called an *olla* and covering it with strips of split cane to form the shape of a star, a donkey, a dancing girl, a grotesque bird, a ship, or whatever shape is desired. Then layers of torn newspaper are pasted over the cane framework around the pot, leaving a hole at the top. Colored tissue paper ruffles, streamers, tinsel, paint, sequins, and other decorations are added. Finally, the frilly, decorated piñata is filled with candies, peanuts, sugarcane sticks, fruits, and small toys or trinkets.

Piñatas are everywhere in Mexico: in market places, on lampposts, over the middle of the streets, in schools, in churches, in hotels, and in airports. Piñata parties are held indoors and outdoors, in homes, in public squares, on beaches, in restaurants, and in nightclubs.

## Christmas Markets

The Christmas market in Mexico City delights everyone. The *puestos* or stands in the Plaza de la Republica open around December 16.

They sell woven cloth, pottery, baskets, ornaments, painted gourds, toys, and other popular art objects made by the Mexican Indians and brought in from all over the country. Having worked for weeks and months to produce their goods, the Indian families have traveled long distances from the mountain villages to the cities by truck, donkey, or on foot in order to sell their wares. During the nine days before Christmas, the little clay figures of the people and animals connected with the Nativity story are featured as well as piñatas. The market stalls are set up everywhere in Mexican cities where there is enough room to sell the Christmas toys, rag dolls, figures made from carved radishes, and other items which they make. There are stalls offering all kinds of things to eat: cheese, preserved bananas, candies, cookies made of anjonjoli seed, figs, dates, red peppers, nuts, sweetmeats, and much more.

## Christmas Colors

Colored lights shine everywhere at this season, and the colors of the Mexican flag, bright red, green, and white, are seen everywhere. As mentioned earlier, the poinsettia, the "flower of Christmas Eve," is seen all over the place. The story goes that a little boy named Pablo, eager to visit the manger scene in the village church, was upset because he had no suitable gift to give to the Christ Child. He gathered branches of green leaves from a bush that grew along the dusty road, and he took them to the church. The other children mocked him, but when they looked a second time, a brilliant red, star-shaped flower topped each branch.

## Nacimientos

*Nacimientos* or manger scenes first appeared in Mexico in the eighteenth century, and they are set up in homes on December 16. *El nacimiento* serves as the main display in Mexican homes, sometimes occupying an entire room. They are also displayed in churches, in store windows, in government and business buildings, in plazas, and in public parks. Christmas carol programs are often performed around the *nacimientos.* Many times today, Christmas trees are incorporated into the manger scene, or trees may be placed elsewhere in the house. A live tree would be an expensive purchase for most Mexican families; therefore, the tree is often an artificial one or a bare branch cut from a copal tree or a shrub. The real charm of the Mexican *nacimiento* is often its incongruity; the donkey may be larger than the manger, or there may be a Noah's ark. The Christ Child figure is not added to the scene until Christmas Eve and is often left there until February 2, Candlemas, a feast commemorating the purification of Mary and the dedication of Jesus at the temple. When the figure is taken up again, the godparents who placed the figure in the manger give a party. The Christ figure is dressed up and placed on a tray surrounded by flowers. On this occasion, it is customary to bake a tiny figure of an infant into a *rosca* or round cake. Whoever finds the infant figure must give another party.

## Christmas Eve

*Noche Buena* means Christmas Eve. After the last *Posadas* parties, the people attend the *Misa de Gallo* or Mass of the Cock. In some parts of Mexico, people have magnificent processions and present pageants representing the story of Christ's birth.

After the *Miso de Gallo,* people go home to a large dinner that may include anything from roast lamb to roast suckling pig to turkey to tortillas or tamales. The Mexican palate also enjoys vegetables, fruits, candies, hot chocolate with vanilla and cinnamon, and *bunuelos* or thin pancakes served with brown sugar.

Mexicans do not usually give or receive gifts on *Navidad* or Christmas, but gift-giving is usually confined to January 6.Gifts that are received at Christmas come from *el Niño Dios* or the Holy Child.

## Day of the Innocents

*El Dia de los Innocentes* on December 28 commemorated King Herod's slaughtering of all baby boys in his kingdom after he learned of Jesus' birth. In Mexico, the celebration of this day reminds one of April Fool's Day. Children fool people by borrowing money or some coveted trinket that they replace with a small toy, a tiny doll, or a worthless bauble. The object is accompanied by a jingle to the effect that the victim, innocent little dove, has allowed himself to be fooled in spite of knowing that nothing ever should be loaned on this day.

## Pastorelas

*Pastorelas* are a Mexican version of Europe's medieval miracle plays. Actors perform then in the afternoon or early evening of the last weeks of December. They are most often performed outdoors in a public square, in the courtyard of a church or an inn, or on someone's patio. The actors may be local people, groups of school children, or a semi-professional group of actors that travel from village to village. The *pastorela* may last half an hour to several hours or sometimes two or three days. Tepotzvelan, a town near Mexico City, is the site of Mexico's most famous *pastorela* performed each year from December 15-23.

*Pastorelas* were first introduced to Mexico in the 1500s. They are a mixture of religious teachings, Indian-Mexican folklore, and ribald comedy. The theme is the conflict between good and evil, and the plot revolves around a pilgrimage of shepherds to Bethlehem to see Jesus. They encounter all sorts of setbacks brought about by the Devil, The drama ends with the shepherds giving gifts to the Christ Child. During the performance, the bad guys are booed and hissed, and the heroes are cheered and applauded. Main characters are shepherds called Bato and Bartolo or sometimes Florindo and Blas. Other characters are the Devil, a hermit, and a couple of angels. The Devil sometimes has a buffoon assistant called Asmodeo. There are sometimes an Indian, a farmer, and others. Women often play the roles of men.

## Regional Customs

Mexico abounds with regional Christmas customs. On the east coast in Vera Cruz, they have *La Rama,* a branch decorated with paper chains, strips of colored paper, ribbons, Japanese lanterns, and small, clay figures of objects like donkeys or angels. Accompanied by musicians playing instruments made of tin cans, the branch is carried door to door. The bearers of *La Rama* sing traditional verses demanding gifts of money, fruit, or candies. If the giver is slow, the branch bearers sing, "Give me my Christ gift if you mean to give; the night is long and we have far to walk." Those givers who are quick to respond with gifts hear, "I sing for you at Christmas, not for your money but in the name of the saints in Heaven, and with as much joy as that of the Virgin Mary. The branch is leaving now, very grateful, because it was well received in this house." To people who give no gifts, the bearers sing, "The branch is leaving now without anything on because in this house they are miserable poor."

December 23 is *La Noche de los Rabanos* or The Night of the Radishes. In Oaxaca, there is a contest for the best radish carving. In the same city, there is a three-day festival honoring the Virgin of Solitude, the patron saint of Oaxaca. This begins on December 19. People eat *buenelos* or pancakes with brown sugar. Vendors sell their wares on crockery saucers that are hurled into the air, smashing to bits on the ground and bringing good luck in the coming year. On December 24, each of the city's thirty-five churches invites a lady, preferably a rich one, to be the godmother of the Infant Jesus. She donates money for lanterns and fireworks. The godmother carries the Child on a cushioned tray to the main square, and all the neighbors follow behind, proceeding to the churches.

Different regions of Mexico have traditional dances associated with the Christmas holidays such as the *Santiagos,* the *matachines* dances, and *los moros y Cristiano.* These are classical dance-dramas with elaborate costumes, and they relate the story of the battles between the Moors and the Christians in which the Moors always lose.

## Three Kings Day

On the evening of January 5, children put their shoes on balconies and place straw in them for the camels of the Three Wise Men. Weeks earlier they wrote letters to the Three Kings, told them what gifts they wanted, and informed them how good they had been.

On January 6, *Dia de los Reyes* or Three Kings Day, a special ring-shaped cake or sweet bread called *La Rosca de Reyes* or The Kings' Ring is made, and baked into the sweet bread is a small doll representing the Christ Child. Whoever finds the doll is then expected to give a party for his friends on February 2, Candlemas or *El Dia de la Candelaria.* This day signals the end of the Christmas holidays in Mexico. It is a noisy holiday with lots of revelry and fireworks.

# Myanmar (Burma)

Merry Christmas!

In the Asian country of Myanmar, Christians make up an estimated 4 to 7 percent of the population, the majority of the people being Buddhist. Burma gained its independence in 1948 from the United Kingdom, and the country has survived a tumultuous half-century. In June of 1989, the military seized control of the country and changed its name from Burma to the Union of Myanmar or Myanmar.

Christmas begins on December 24 and ends on the Feast of the Baptism of Jesus the Sunday after Epiphany. Since the Christian population is so small, in some areas there may be just one or two Christian homes; whereas, in some areas entire villages are Christian; thus, celebrations differ greatly.

Midnight mass plays an important part in the celebrating. It is a time of good will, and often people who are not even Christian attend mass.

In the month of December, almonds, walnuts, oranges, apples, and grapes are available and enjoyed as treats. Christmas cakes are often bought at the confectioners or bakers.

Most people shop for gifts on Christmas Eve, and they purchase mainly edibles. Christmas comes at harvest time in Myanmar; hence, things are a bit more prosperous. Often people buy themselves colorful clothing for the season. Rather than exchanging gifts a lot, wealthier people tend to give gifts to the needy. Students and young people, even non-Christians, often exchange gifts.

Santa Claus appears at group gatherings, wearing his usual red outfit. If he is not padded around the middle by nature, he will be artificially plump. If he does not look the part, people will believe that he is not genuine and that his gifts are not up to par. He must convince the children that he has just arrived from a far off place. Besides the usual Santa, there is a figure called the Generous Pho Pho or the Good Hearted Gentleman. He is a short, fat man with gray hair and gray beard and is dressed in red clothing also.

## Christmas Food

Christmas dinner does not usually differ from the normal daily fare except that there is more variety. Often food is prepared for a whole community, and the expenses shared by those who can afford to help. Large quantities of food are available, and relatives, friends, and neighbors join to eat the feast. The food may be just the usual rice and curry. A favorite dish is a noodle made only in Myanmar from rice flour in the form of strands and served with a special curry that is primarily gravy. It may be prepared from fish, chicken, duck, pork, or mutton. In more westernized homes, a typical Christmas dinner might be roast turkey, chicken, or duck, salad, sausage, bread and butter, and hot rum or Johnny Walker.

## Christmas Decorations

Homes are often decorated with crepe paper of different colors cut into strips and joined with glue. The strips are twisted and arranged like the spokes of a wheel of a cart. Some people purchase imported decorations used year after year. In large cities, people decorate their homes, churches, and convents with streamers, balloons, lights, and other trinkets in the western style. In smaller villages, people tend to decorate only their churches and their cribs or manger scenes with colored paper, flowers, and plants.

Artificial Christmas trees from abroad are used; sometimes people use a big branch from a live pine tree or a bamboo tree. These are decorated with toys, fairy lights, balloons, cotton, or gold and silver papers. Christmas cards are tied to the branches. Churches and convents decorate in the same way.

The manger scene has the place of importance in the decorations. Often the faithful come far distances to view the manger scene and to celebrate the season and cannot return for Epiphany on January 6 when the Three Wise Men arrive; thus, these figures are often added to the manager scene early, ignoring the fact that these Wise Men did not arrive until Epiphany. The faithful often compete with these wise visitors with their gifts to the Christ Child by dropping gifts of money, *kyats* or *pyas,* into a receptacle close by the manger scene in the church.

People who can afford to do so, send Christmas cards to their friends and relatives at home and abroad. These are often pictures with small calendars attached.

## Holiday Entertainment

Christmas plays, pageants, and concerts are performed with traditional backgrounds. Groups of carol singers are welcomed everywhere, and many non-Christians would be offended if ignored by the singers as they make their rounds. At some homes, the singers are given tea or coffee and perhaps some oranges, sweets, and cakes. Small children from ages nine to twelve go around in groups of ten or twelve, singing such favorites as "Silent Night, Holy Night" They are often given a few *pyas* for their efforts or sometimes oranges or sweets. These groups may go around as early as two or three weeks before Christmas.

On New Year's Day, Catholic children and young people go from home to home paying respect to their parents, teachers, and elders, asking forgiveness for failures, ingratitude, and mistakes committed during the past year. In Myanmar, one says Happy New Year as such: *Min Ga Lar Nik Thick Koo!*

# The Netherlands (Holland)

*Zalig Kerstfeest!*

For years and years, St. Nicholas Day on December 6 has been celebrated in a unique way in the European country of The Netherlands, also called Holland. The day belongs to young and old, to rich and poor, to Christian and Jew, without any religious overtones. In recent years, according to a book by Jan de Bas titled *Sinterklaas Can Stay*, the *Sinterklaas*, or St. Nicholas, celebration has started to fade. In 1983, seventy-seven percent of the Dutch people celebrated this holiday; in 1998, fifty-eight percent of the households joined in, according to Fritz Booy of the National St. Nicholas Committee which has been crusading against the influence of Santa Claus for years.

Fewer Dutch are willing to write the traditional *Sinterklaas* poems to one another, to wrap gifts the way in which they do, or to bother to hide the gifts and write clues as to their whereabouts, opting instead for simpler, American-style gift swapping on December 25, which used to be primarily a feast day. According to Booy, people have less time and energy. He states that people today live hard and fast, focused on themselves, while *Sinterklaas* focuses on others.

One of the main concerns about *Sinterklaas* or St. Nicholas Day has to do with *Sinterklaas'* helpers, the Moorish "Black Petes" played by white people in black faces and curly wigs. These figures are perceived as politically incorrect and perpetuating negative stereotypes.

St. Nicholas or *Sinterklaas* dresses in his bishop's regalia, wearing his red robe and elaborate mitre (hat), with crozier (staff) in hand.

*Piet* or Black Peter accompanies him, dressed in puffed velvet breeches with a plumed beret on his head, carrying a sack on his shoulder and a rod in his hand. *Sinterklass* lives in Spain and spends most of the year writing down the children's behavior in a big, red book, while *Piet* stocks up on presents for their next fifth of December visit.

Around mid-November, *Sinterklaas* mounts his white horse, and *Piet* swings the sack full of gifts over his shoulder, and the three of them board a steamship bound for Amsterdam harbor and a formal welcome by the mayor and a delegation of citizens. Thousands greet him as traffic snarls and streetcars stop. The parade begins, and first comes the motorcade of police; then a brass band is next, followed by *Sinterklaas* on horseback dressed in his bishop's finery with *Piet* walking beside him. The mayor follows along with other dignitaries. Next come the floats, local students, and more brass bands. The parade is televised, and it marks the official beginning of the St. Nicholas season.

A *Sinterklaas* present is not like a usual Christmas present. Dutch tradition dictates that these presents must be camouflaged in some imaginative way and that each gift must be accompanied by an appropriate poem. This goes hand-in-hand with the sheer fun of the *Sinterklaas* celebration. Kidding is not only permitted, but it is expected among parents, children, and teachers, between employers and employees, and among society at large, without regard for differences in age and social status.

St. Nicholas gifts are not wrapped in pretty wrapping paper, but they are concealed or disguised. Recipients must follow a trail of clues or directions all over the house to find the presents. They could be hidden in a potato bin, in a pudding, in a head of cabbage, or in a doll. People have to work to get their gifts; the present givers must work even harder to think up clues and hiding places.

The custom is to write a poem to accompany each present, and the poems are read aloud by the recipients. All gifts are supposed to come from *Sinterklaas,* so the real gift giver and poem writer is anonymous. When a person receives the gift and poem, he must say aloud, "Thank you, *Sinterklaas!*" The poem usually contains references to something that has just happened in the recipient's life such as a love interest, a recent embarrassing moment, anything to cause embarrassment, as long as it is done in good taste and good-naturedly since the poem is from *Sinterklaas.* These poems appear everywhere in The Netherlands: in the newspaper, at school, at work, on stage, even in both houses of parliament.

At supper on *Sinterklaas* Eve, the Dutch sit around a table filled with all the traditional sweets and baked goods. Large, chocolate initials serve as place settings along with the so-called "lovers," tall men and women made of *speculas,* a crisp, dark-brown pastry similar to gingerbread. A basket full of mysterious gifts stands close by, and scissors are at hand. Gifts are unwrapped, and poems are read one at a time so that all may enjoy the originality of the surprise, the embarrassment of the reader, and the efforts of the gift-giver and poet not to give himself away. The emphasis is on giving rather than receiving because so much work and thought go into it.

Early in the morning of *Sinterklaas* Day, children hurry to see what the saint has left. The night before, they leave their shoes to be filled by the saint who rides through the air on his white horse and slips down the chimney to fill the shoes. The children leave carrots or hay for the horse.

In the rural, eastern area, there is a Yuletide custom from ancient times that is still going on. It is called Midwinter Horn Blowing. It begins on the first Advent Sunday and is repeated daily until Christmas Eve. In the still dusk, farmers blow on long, slightly crooked horns made of hollowed limbs of elder trees. They hold the horns above their wells to amplify the weird sound. It is answered from farm to farm all over the place.

## Christmas Day

No sooner has St. Nicholas Day passed, than people begin to look forward to the Christmas days. Schools are closed for two or three weeks, and adults have two full days off at Christmas, December 25 and 26. Christmas is very much like Thanksgiving in the United States. It is a time of peace and goodwill, a time to spend at home with family.

Gifts weren't usually given at Christmas, but as mentioned earlier, this is beginning to change. Cooks are kept busy preparing traditional Christmas food. Carols are heard everywhere from chimes and carillons; decorations abound; towns and villages are aglow with candlelight, tinsel, greens, and trees.

The tree, often with real candles, is lit on Christmas Eve. People may attend a service afterward or in the morning of First Christmas Day, December 25.

Christmas Day dinner is served in the evening when families gather around their candlelit tables set with decorations of red, green, and white. Roast hare, venison, or goose used to be the main dishes, but today most Dutch have roast turkey. A flaming pudding or a bright red, cold pudding are traditional desserts.

On Second Christmas Day, people may attend a play, go to a concert, or dine in a restaurant. Tables must be reserved weeks in advance because dining out is so popular. In churches and auditoriums throughout the country, amateur choral and instrumental groups give their annual Christmas performances, as do many professional ensembles.

## New Year's Eve

On *Oudejaars Avand,* New Year's Eve, people attend early evening church services when ministers give a listing of the year's events and have a brief memorial for parishioners who've died during the past year. They never mention the dead by name unless they are members of the royal family. Most Dutch spend the evening at home where they play parlor games. Traditional refreshments are passed around, and a light, cold supper is served. Children stay up late, and at midnight, everyone shoots off fireworks, ships blow their whistles, church bells and carillons begin to ring and play while the Dutch clink glasses, hug, shake hands, and wish each other a Blessed Ending and a Happy New Year.

# Netherlands Antilles

Merry Christmas!

The islands of Curacao, Aruba, and Bonaire lie about thirty-five miles north of South America in the Caribbean Sea; six hundred miles further lie St. Marten, Saba, and St. Eustatius. Altogether, they form the Netherlands Antilles. Christmas celebrations tend to differ slightly from island to island.

## Curacao

In Curacao, the first important event in December was always St. Nicholas Day Eve on December 5. Children eagerly awaited gifts that were placed in their shoes, under their beds, or scattered around the house. Today St. Nicholas makes his appearance about two weeks before then, arriving right in the middle of town accompanied by his two assistants *Zwar Piet* and *Sjaak Sjoerd.*

After St. Nicholas' arrival, things calm down until about two weeks before Christmas. Then people give their homes a major overhaul inside and out: roofs are repaired; houses receive new paint and curtains; furniture receives renewing or refinishing; linoleum floors get replaced. Everywhere one smells fresh paint, varnish, and the smell of newness.

Drugstores are literally invaded by customers who wish to buy the famous *awa di laba cas,* the indispensable house cleaning potion. This is concocted by pharmacists according to old formulas and is mixed at home by the housewife with water to scrub the floors. This has become something of a ritual, a way to chase away disharmony and bring in peace. Only then can the family put the finishing touches to the home.

People purchase food in large quantities. Buses are overcrowded. All around is a general rush and bustle to acquire clothes and other personal items for the family.

Until about thirty years ago, the focal point of each house was a *pesebre* or manger scene. Children would go from house to house visiting friends and looking at each *pesebre.* In recent years, the Christmas tree has replaced the *pesebre* as the focal point in homes.

Santa Claus has not been generally accepted in Curacoa; not many people recognize this tradition. Christmas cards are sent to local friends and acquaintances and to foreign friends. Songs such as "White Christmas" and "Rudolph the Red Nose Reindeer" are heard during the week before Christmas even though the average temperature at Christmas is eighty-five degrees.

During the nine days before Christmas, the *Misa di Aurora* or Daybreak Masses are held at 5:00 A.M. This practice had tapered off somewhat, but once again the churches are full, and these services are even broadcast by a local radio station.

## Christmas Eve

On *Bispu di Pascu* or Christmas Eve, streets are teeming with people overloaded with packages and ringing with Christmas music. The *pikadonan di punta* are roving merrymakers and disciples of Bacchus who have a great time during this season.

On some street corners and in front of shops, groups of young people sing *aguinaldo* songs at top volume; these are Latin American Christmas carols imported from Venezuela. Another such import is the *Cena de Noche Buena* or late Christmas Eve dinner that includes the family circle along with close friends who gather to partake of much food and drink. Ham and *ayaca,* a kind of tamale of chicken and pork in a corn paste and wrapped in banana leaves, are the most traditional dishes.

The *Misa del Gallo* or Mass of the Cock takes place at midnight, and the morning mass is *Misa di Marduga* or Dawn Mass.

For Christmas dinner, those who can afford it have stuffed Edam cheese and stuffed turkey on the menu.

Some families organize dancing parties on Christmas Day in the evening hours.

## Boxing Day

December 26 is Boxing Day or Second Christmas Day. The celebrating continues until New Year's Day. This period is called the *tambu* season; the *tambu* is played, sung, and danced all over the island. At one time, it was prohibited, but it has recovered its rightful place in the island's folklore. People sing satirical songs at the *tambu* in which persons, situations, and happenings are criticized, praised, or ridiculed. This is not the main purpose of the *tambu.* It's an opportunity for participants to transport themselves into a frenzy of dancing, singing, hand clapping, foot stomping, and hip gyrating.

## New Year's

At about 10:00 P.M. on New Year's Eve, the jinx and evils of the past year that might still be residing in the house are chased away by the burning of *sensia,* a mixture of seven kinds of herbs with the skins of onions and garlic sometimes added. The concoction is ignited on a tin tray with charcoal and taken through every room of the house. Members of the family stand around the smoking incense, some even jump over the burning incense to assure themselves of getting rid of bad luck. Those families who possess a gold coin will pass this from hand-to-hand to invoke good luck in acquiring money.

Another New Year's Eve activity is the sweeping of the house all the way through to the front door. Once outside, the housewife re-enters her house walking backwards to fool any evil spirit that might be planning to follow her back into the house.

Some people still practice the custom of taking a bath with different herbs in order to rid themselves of bad luck, putting on a new set of clothes afterwards so as to start the New Year in an immaculate condition. The clothes must never have been worn before, and the louder the color, the better. Yellow, especially, brings good luck.

Most members of the family remain together until *Tiru tira* meaning literally "the gun is fired," at midnight. Others take a walk to be alone when the New Year begins. Some families drive around in a car so the New Year will find them together but unencumbered. Some go to the seashore and take a dip in the sea. After getting out of the water, they put on new clothes, leaving the old ones containing jinxes behind. Another custom has all the grown children returning from parties so as to be in the family circle at the New Year's entrance to receive the parents' blessing. They then return to their merrymaking. Many go to the Plaza Brion in front of the Bishop's mansion to receive a blessing. Everyone hugs and wishes each other the best for the New Year as fireworks go off at midnight along with the ships' whistles.

## Bonaire

On the island of Bonaire, the Christmas season begins with the fourth Sunday before Christmas Eve, Advent. All homes and offices are decorated with lights, festoons, Christmas trees, posters, artificial snow, colored balls, angels, and stars.

There are many seasonal performances by choirs and theater groups. Santa Claus is called *Papa Pasku* or Father Christmas. He doesn't personally distribute gifts, but they are put under the tree. The gifts are called *Regalo di Nino* or Present of the Baby Jesus.

On Bonaire, the typical Christmas foods are ham, stuffed turkey, salmon in vinegar, saltfish, pork, *sult* or pig's ears in vinegar, and syaka, a special dish made of chicken, prunes, olives, and gherkins covered in a corn meal bread and wrapped in banana leaves. Cakes are always served, especially the *tert,* a cake filled with either prunes or coconut.

## Saba

On the island of Saba, besides the usual food such as goat meat, chicken, fish, turkey, ham, pork, rice and peas, vegetables, and corn bread, they also have Saba spice, guavaberry, and lemon juice to drink. Their desserts are *mami,* a typical Saban fruit, puddings, pumpkin, sweet potatoes, black cake, fruitcake, and tarts.

Santa travels with his wife Mrs. Claus also dressed in red and white. He places gifts under the trees, and children open them on Christmas morning. At some public celebrations, Santa stands by the tree and calls the names of the children and gives them gifts donated by organizations. Adults receive their gifts the day after Christmas, with Christmas considered mainly a day for children.

Homes, schools, stores, and churches are decorated with both homemade and store-bought decorations. There are many plays, recitations, and singing of carols. Most of these are performed a few days before Christmas, since, on Christmas Eve everyone is quite busy cooking, baking, and getting gifts ready.

On both Bonaire and Saba, Christmas Eve is spent buying food, drinks, new clothes, and shoes. There are Christmas Eve parties and lots of carol singing, but people tend to celebrate Christmas within the family circle. Many people on Saba visit those in the old people's homes and hospitals on Christmas.

Midnight mass is held with an official opening of the Christmas crib or manger scene. Many who never go to church at any other time go at Christmas to reflect on their lives and examine their consciences. They also wish to forget their problems and reconcile with their fellow men.

# New Zealand

Merry Christmas!

Christmas time in the beautiful, southern hemisphere country of New Zealand occurs in the summer when children are on their long, summer vacation from school. Most adults take their annual leave or vacation time between Christmas and New Year too, and many businesses are closed. This makes Christmas a special time for several reasons: the celebration itself, the close of school for the year, and the beginning of a long vacation that lasts until February.

Families go to the beach and stay in caravans or camp in the campgrounds that are located throughout both the islands that make up New Zealand. Others make a trip to their summer cottages called "baches." Pleasant pastimes are swimming, water skiing, fishing, sailing, hiking, hunting, or just lying in the sun.

In spite of the summer weather, many of the traditions of the northern hemisphere are kept. Christmas cards often have pictures of snow scenes. Many of the Christmas carols refer to snow and frost, and many of the Christmas trees have white cotton on them to represent snow.

The pohutukawa, a tree with bright red flowers, blooms at Christmas and is sometimes referred to as the "New Zealand Christmas tree." It is becoming traditional to place a small, lighted Christmas tree on window ledges on Christmas Eve.

From mid-November, shops and offices are brightly decorated, and they overflow with gifts. Father Christmas sometimes arrives in the traditional way by sleigh or in a small airplane. In the main cities, the large department stores have special Christmas parades through the main streets. These include animated floats, bands, marching girls, and Father Christmas. The mayor officially welcomes him in front of the Town Hall. Most large department stores also have Father Christmas in the toy department so that children might visit with him.

## Christmas Eve

On Christmas Eve, the airplanes, trains, and buses are crowded with people trying to get home to spend Christmas with their families. The shops stay open later than usual to help the last minute shoppers who are crowding the streets.

Many candlelit carol services are held before the midnight church services. Santa Claus or Father Christmas is dressed in his usual red suit with fur trim in spite of the hot weather of the early summer. He arrives by sleigh, goes down the chimney, and fills the stockings or pillowcases that children have left out and leaves presents under the tree as well.

## Christmas Day

After the excitement of opening gifts is over on Christmas morning, the family may go to church or visit friends. There is sometimes community carol singing on Christmas morning. The family comes home to a traditional dinner of turkey, ham, goose, or lamb followed by a mince pie or a Christmas plum pudding, with the hidden coins in it bringing the finders good luck. Because of the heat, some families manipulate tradition a little and have a lighter dinner with fruit salad and ice cream instead of plum pudding. The New Zealand Christmas cake is usually a fruitcake decorated with marzipan and vanilla frosting, and it is eaten throughout the Christmas/New Year season. Christmas dinner is often eaten in the cool of the evening after a day's picnicking.

During the day, the English monarch's (Queen Elizabeth II) message to the British Commonwealth is broadcast on the radio and television. The Prime Minister and the Leader of the Opposition of New Zealand also give Christmas messages to the people. The rest of the day, people rest, sunbathe, or visit with friends.

Many organizations extend invitations to friendless and lonely old people for Christmas dinners; gifts are presented to them, and afterwards, singsongs often take place.

For New Zealand's aboriginal people, the Maoris, Christmas has a special significance. Maori families gather for a "hangi," the traditionally cooked feast. In the district of Rotorua on the North Island, nature provides a stove for cooking. It is not uncommon there to see the Maori people, as well as those of European descent, preparing a meal, even a Christmas dinner, by immersing food in a flax basket into a boiling mineral spring or steam heating the food in a concrete box built over a backyard steam vent in the ground.

The Christmas season in New Zealand includes a lot of sports, horse racing, cultural activities in the open air, and, in general, lots of outdoor life.

## New Year's Eve

New Year's Eve occurs much the same as in the United States, with parties or family get-togethers and a lot of well wishes at midnight. New Year's Day is rather quiet with no particular customs associated with it.



3282-TUCK

# Norway

*Gledelig Jul!*

Christmas in Scandinavian Norway is celebrated over a period of twenty-one days, from Christmas Eve on December 24 to Twentieth Day or *Tyvendedagen,* January 13.

Long before Christmas Eve, however, preparations for the important time begin. The first signs of approaching Christmas are the lighting of the Advent candles and the opening of the Advent calendar. Advent begins with the fourth Sunday before Christmas Eve. The candles are attached to a wreath of bound greenery trimmed with ribbons and other decorations. On the first Sunday, one candle is lit, on the second Sunday, two are lit, and so on. The lighting ceremony is broadcast on television for children. The Advent calendar has the first twenty-four days of December marked on little flaps. Each day, a child opens that day's flap, and behind each flap may be a Christmas scene, a symbol, a saying, or sometimes a treat.

## Holiday Preparations

Cooking plays an important part in these holiday preparations. In most homes, at least seven different kinds of cookies and the *julekak* or Christmas bread, are always baked.

In the country, the family pig and calf are slaughtered, and the meat becomes all kinds of delicacies such as pork and veal sausages that when sliced reveal various decorative patterns of stars, spirals, or geometric designs. The *lutefisk* or Christmas cod is dried slowly and then soaked in lye until it swells to a trembling, jelly-like mass. A special Christmas beer, *juleol,* is brewed.

To clean the household thoroughly is a Norwegian custom. Everything gets scrubbed; brasses and copper are polished; curtains are washed and rehung, and enough wood is chopped to last the holidays.

The *julebord* or Yule table is featured in many large restaurants beginning in early December. This is an enormous smorgasbord featuring a gigantic display of seasonal food from oysters, lobsters, and herring to every conceivable kind of meat, poultry, and game. The guests absolutely gorge themselves, and this event has come under lots of criticism for its extravagance and because most people become tired of the holiday dishes before Christmas even arrives.

Quite a few charitable events occur in Norway prior to Christmas. The proceeds usually go towards food, clothes, fuel, and gifts for the less fortunate at the holiday season. Choirs and entertainers visit hospitals and old people's homes.

A recent custom is that of placing lighted candles on graves in cemeteries.

## Christmas Decorations

Norwegian towns and cities are brightly decorated and lighted. The streets are crowded with shoppers and filled with Christmas music, colorful window displays, and on many street corners *Julesvenn* or Santa Claus.

Christmas trees appear everywhere, and they are lighted in ceremonies where the people join hands and surround the trees. Some make the annual trip to the woods to select a Christmas tree for the home, a tradition that has only existed for a little over a hundred years. Norway today presents huge Christmas trees to foreign cities, and the lighting of the Norway spruce is a festive occasion, such as the impressive ceremony at Trafalgar Square in London. Even the great Norwegian ships display a towering, lighted spruce tree above the decks of the ships.

Christmas trees in Norway are decorated with many handmade ornaments of straw, wood shavings, colored paper, gilded walnuts, stuffed red hearts, or other figures made of red felt, such as cones and birds. Tinsel and glass ornaments are often used. Few people in Norway use colored lights on the trees at home. They use only white lights, and some still use white candles. Parents usually decorate Christmas trees behind closed doors of the living room, while the children are ready to burst with excitement outside the door.

For decorating the home, people tend to use things provided by nature: holly, boughs of pine or spruce, flowers, and fruit. In the fall, families go to the woods to collect moss, rocks, twigs, plants, cones, and straw, anything that together with a candle or a ribbon would make an attractive decoration. Handmade decorations such as embroidered or appliquéd bell pulls, wall hangings, or table runners with Christmas motifs are made of burlap or coarse linen with felt or wool yarns. The old fashioned Christmas colors of red, green, deep blue, purple, and gold are the main colors used in decorating and accented by shining silver, copper, and brass used to create the holiday mood. The star of Bethlehem symbol is seen everywhere in Norway and is usually placed on top of the Christmas tree or displayed in windows. Behind the curtains, red and white ceramic, three-armed candleholders representing the Three Kings hold flickering candles.

Pigs are strongly associated with Christmas in Norway. Pigs appear over and over again in holiday decorations. Small, wooden pigs hang from the tree, and presents are wrapped in paper covered with dancing pigs dressed in red caps and mittens. Another important Christmas symbol is the frisky goat, the *julebukk,* that was originally the symbolic pet of the powerful Norse god Thor. Craftsmen make the *julebukk* of straw for the holidays.

Animals are well taken care of during the holidays. A sheaf of oats, the *julenek,* is placed in the yard on a pole or on top of the house or an outbuilding, furnishing holiday cheer for the birds. Generally the pole where the sheaf is placed is made from a spruce tree with little tufts of branches left at the top so that, while eating, the birds may have a firm foothold as well as protection from the wind and snow. Farmers give their animals extra feedings, and nobody hunts or harms wild animals or birds during the holiday season. Another custom has farm families making a trip to the barn with a bowl of porridge for the *nisse,* a gnome who, according to tradition, is the protector of the farm. The *Julenisse* appears many places during the season as a Christmas motif.

## Christmas Eve

Christmas Eve shines as the highlight of the Norwegian Christmas. Shops and restaurants close early that day; movies and theaters are closed; radio and television programs concentrate exclusively on special Christmas programs. Families gather for carol singing, lighting the Christmas tree, exchanging gifts, and eating their traditional Christmas meal. Christmas officially begins with the ringing of the church bells at 5:00 P.M. when the peace of Christmas settles over the land.

Families often partake of traditional *molje,* a rich liquid in which the Christmas meats have been cooked. Served hot with flat, hard bread one dips into the broth, it serves as a beautiful introduction to other culinary delights. In some rural areas, everyone puts on the national costume, while in the cities, formal dress is usually worn. The Christmas celebration begins with the father's reading of the Christmas story from the Bible. The meal may be eaten before or after the opening of gifts. Finally, the door to the living room is opened, and everyone stands in awe of the tree under which lie the beautifully decorated presents. Then follows a Norwegian ritual known as "walking around the Christmas tree." Everybody joins hands to form a ring, and they walk around the tree while singing carols. Often there is a Yule log lighted, and the gifts are distributed. Santa Claus, Father Christmas, or *Julesvenn,* all very close relatives, looking and acting very much alike, brings the gifts.



3282-TUCK

## Christmas Fare

The traditional Norwegian Christmas meal usually includes hot and cold appetizers, *lutefisk* or cod treated in a lye solution and then boiled, pork ribs, boiled potatoes, and sauerkraut. Sweets and *risengrynsgrotor* or rice porridge are served. The porridge is made with a single almond in it, and whoever finds it will be the first to marry in the New Year. *Julekake,* a sweet coffee bread, is another favorite.

## Christmas Day

First Christmas Day, December 25, remains devoted to religious services and to the family. In earlier times, there was an early morning church service followed by a big breakfast at home. Now the service starts later. The traditional Christmas Day meal often has pork as the main dish. Children sometimes spend the afternoon trying out new skis, skates, or sleds.

Second Christmas Day, December 26, is like a normal Sunday. Friends and relatives visit, eat, drink, and have parties.

Festivities continue through January 13. Throughout this season, breakfast is a happy and large meal. Long tables, decorated in holiday motif, groan under thirty or forty different kinds of delicious, hot and cold dishes. *Aquavit,* a liqueur made from potatoes, and other strong drinks accompany the food. While the rest of the days of December are officially working days, many take them off, and those who remain at work keep shorter working hours.

More and more Norwegians are choosing to escape the long, cold, dark winter days of Norway and head south to the warmer climate of southern Europe for the holidays, but the majority still adhere to the traditional Norwegian Christmas.

## New Year's Day

On New Year's Eve, *Nyttarsaften,* young people dressed in fantastic costumes and masks go visiting in groups. At every house at which they stop, they have refreshments and dancing. Often the night's festivities end with breakfast at the home of a friend or neighbor.

On New Year's Day, *Nyttarsdag,* people attend morning church services. The rest of the day is generally spent quietly at home. Dinner includes cold meats, sausages, and appetizers and roast pork, roast goose, and numerous cakes and sweets. Strong holiday beer and hearty good wishes are popular as each bids the other good luck and cheer for the coming year. In the afternoon, people make formal New Year's calls. Family parties, dinners, and dances characterize the second day of the New Year. Many organizations hold their annual festivities at this time.

## Twentieth Day

*Tyvendedagen* or the Twentieth Day after Christmas is January 13; this marks the end of Yuletide. Trees are taken down and generally chopped up and burned in the fireplace. This is also the feast day of St. Canute, so there is a saying that goes "twentieth-day Canute drives away Christmas."

## Legends

The Norwegian *nisse* goes back to pagan times. His protection of the farm can be traced back to the first man, *Haugkallen,* who some time in the far distant past first cleared the land. This man was buried in a burial mound, and at Yuletide, "the feast for the dead," food and drink were brought to the mound for him, and he was believed to come out to eat and drink. During the centuries, the popular image of this much-respected and feared ghost changed into the less dangerous, but still at times, destructive leprechaun-like *nisse* of Norwegian fairy tales. Somehow, the *nisse* has gotten intermingled with the popular image of Santa Claus to create the *Julenisse.*

Years ago, the dead were believed to travel about in great crowds during the Yule season. People vacated their beds, and even their homes, for the sake of these ghosts known as *julereien.* They not only ate and drank people's food and drink, but also farmers had to made sure that tools were not left carelessly about, as they would disappear.

The custom of sleeping on straw goes back to the Middle Ages. The beds had to be left for the ghosts, so the people slept on the straw. Magic qualities were attached to the straw. The future could be predicted from the grains that fell off the straw. A grain found by some person's place at the table was an omen that he was to die during the coming year. Dreams one had while sleeping on straw were supposed to come true. Straw crosses were made and hung above doors for protection. Straws were used to cure sick cattle and scattered in the fields in the spring to ensure a good harvest. This is called *julebalm,* and it continued until the nineteenth century. Traces of it still remain. Straw crosses and mobiles are still hung from the ceiling or put on the Christmas tree. Later, many people left food for the *julereien* on Christmas night, or for the entire holiday season.

# Peru

*Feliz Navidad!*

Religious celebrations and family get-togethers depict Christmas in the South American country of Peru. Because Peru is divided into three distinct geographical regions, each with its different weather, vegetation, and way of life, Christmas celebrations differ with each area.

On the coast with its summer weather and in the tropical jungles, the celebrations include outdoor parties, while the sierra section of the country with its cold, rain, and snow requires indoor parties and festivities.

In spite of the differences caused by the geography and climate, there are marked similarities in all areas in keeping Christmas traditions. A good example is the *nacimiento* or Nativity scene, the main theme around which the Peruvian Christmas celebration revolves. Built in a special room of the house, these scenes can sometimes grow to be as big as an entire wall. Not only does it depict the Nativity scene, but also a group of mountains on which the landscape of Bethlehem is represented. Shepherds, sheep, and other Bethlehem figures appear. It is also not unusual to find an electric train or an astronaut next to a camel caravan. These scenes or objects from today's world show that the Christmas message is for all times and places.

Store ads for Christmas purchases begin to appear in the newspapers as early as October. Outdoor markets become very crowded before Christmas with Indian toys, trinkets, and delicacies spread out on mats on the ground. Great masses of greenery are brought down from the mountains.

3282-TUCK

One finds decorated Christmas trees in squares, in parks, and in commercial buildings. Most people do not have Christmas trees in their homes, but those who do, usually decorate them with Peruvian handicrafts.

Children write the Christ Child letters asking for special presents, and toys for the young are placed beside their beds so that they may find these toys from the Christ Child when they awaken on Christmas morning.

Smaller towns keep the traditions better than the cities. Groups of singers and dancers perform before the *nacimiento* during the midnight mass. Some days before, people create *Las Posadas;* groups that go around the town from house to house, representing the search of Mary and Joseph for a place to stay in Bethlehem. Each evening during *Las Posadas* there is a small party with the final, large party on Christmas Eve.

## Christmas Eve

Christmas Eve features singing and dancing in the streets and setting off firecrackers; this begins in the afternoon. Food plays a very important part in the celebration, and delicious smells fill every room of the house as well as the streets where such delicacies as *anticuchos,* delicious chunks of marinated beef heart threaded on bamboo spears, are sold. These are followed by *picarones,* delicate, puffy, fried pastries dipped into a syrup.

On Christmas Eve, the whole family attends midnight mass. When the midnight bell strikes, all is quiet. People drop to their knees in prayer, and when they rise at the last stroke of the bells, they wish each other "*Noche Buena.*" After mass, they return home to a splendid dinner and lots of good talking. Children are not usually present at this meal, having gone to bed to dream of wonderful gifts.

*Cabrito* or goat is often served, or sometimes a relished dish of *pichon,* pigeon or squab, is consumed. Tamales are prepared from an excellent, white corn soaked, cooked, peeled, cooked again, ground, and kneaded into a *masa* or dough used for tamales that are stuffed with pork or hot peppers and spicy annatto seeds. The tamales are wrapped in *plantana* or banana leaves. *Quino,* a protein-rich grain from the Andes Mountains is also a Christmas staple.

Another Peruvian Christmas treat is a dish called *pachamancha* consisting of pork, lamb, chicken, and potatoes wrapped in banana leaves and cooked over heated stones. A recipe for a powerful drink made of corn and raw sugar, fermented like beer but tasting more like cider, has been passed down from the time of the Incas, and the drink is served during the holidays.

## Christmas Day

The children, having been absent from the dinner on Christmas Eve, take part in the Christmas Day luncheon. The "visits" start on Christmas and continue until January 6, Epiphany. These visits are tours through churches and friends' homes to admire everyone's *nacimientos.* In each house, children are given traditional candy and refreshments.

## Day of the Kings

In some of the smaller towns on January 6, the Day of the Kings, statues of the Christ Child and the Madonna are carried through the streets to a platform in the town square. When the statues are in place, the Magi or Three Wise Men appear to pay tribute to Jesus. The kings depict a Spanish conquistador, an Inca, and an Ethiopian, each one honoring Jesus with a speech.

# Native Art

For centuries, Cusco, the ancient Incan capital city of Peru, has contributed richly to the Christmas art of the world. In recent years, the work of the Quecha Indians has attracted the attention of collectors who marvel at the quaint, naïve charm of this pre-Columbian folk art. Of special interest are the manger or *nacimiento* figures made in a variety of sizes for churches and homes, particularly the Madonnas and the Wise Men that are cherished for their charm. Not only the techniques used, but also the facial expressions and the manner of molding the figures date back to the sixteenth century. Plaster, fabrics of various kinds, crude clay, and wood are the raw materials these primitive craftsmen use to make the figures. The figure of Jesus has the appearance of a member of the royal Spanish family of the sixteenth century and appears very elaborately dressed and rather grownup.

# Philippines

*Maligayang Pasko!*

Christmas in the Pacific Ocean island nation of the Philippines lasts twenty-two days, from December 16 through January 6, and is filled with colorful, romantic traditions coming from pagan rites blended with religious rituals.

For nine days, from December 16 through December 24, a series of *Misa de Gallos* are said before the crack of dawn. *Misa de Gallo* means Mass of the Cock and refers to a very early, morning mass held about the same time the rooster crows. Bells and bands can be heard before the masses, and the people set out in the early morning in shawls and sweaters, their way lit by the paper lanterns that decorate windows, porches, and garden gates.

The *belen* or Nativity scene, the focal point of the church, has a special place beside the altar. The *belen* is often the work of a Filipino folk artist and is, indeed, a work of art.

After each *Misa de Gallo,* the congregation streams out of the church toward homes, fields, or offices after lingering to look at the *belen* set up on a decorated stage at the town square. The Nativity scene has a Filipino setting, and the figures wear beautiful, native costumes of banana and pineapple fibers and exquisite hand embroidery. Mary wears a Maria Clara or *mestiza* dress; Joseph wears a hand-embroidered *barong-tagalog* made of pineapple fibers. The Three Kings dress elaborately, while the rest of the figures wear simpler, country costumes. The plaza around the *belen* is set up for the carnival that night. Often, after the morning mass, city people will go to a restaurant for an elegant breakfast, while people living in smaller towns go to the *tiendos,* humble, makeshift stalls of bamboo poles with roofs of coconut leaves and banana leaf covered tables for counters. Here they buy native rice and coconut cakes and drink ginger tea served for free by the *tienda* keepers. These rice and coconut cakes and pastries are usually served in fragrant banana leaves or hollow bamboo tubes and are baked in open earthen and tin ovens.

The main symbol of the Filipino Christmas is the Star of Bethlehem. The traditional *parol,* a star-shaped lantern held together by strips of bamboo and made of colorful paper and cellophane, is everywhere at Christmas, in homes, offices, churches, display windows, and markets. The love of lanterns at Christmas is due to the oriental influence as is their love for festivals and the lights that go with them.

The Christmas tree, a relatively recent feature of the Filipino Christmas, is topped with you guessed it, a Star of Bethlehem.

## Christmas Music

Music plays a very important role in the Filipino Christmas. Church choirs sing the lovely *villancicos* or glad songs of Christmas. In the town's plaza, bands play not only holiday songs, but also military sounding music and old favorites like waltzes.

Beginning December 16, carolers and *cumbancheros,* local roving troubadours, make their rounds. The caroling is sometimes combined with dances in costumes and masks. Some carolers called *ati-ati* smear their faces with soot, paints, and dyes. They go about the streets dressed in costumes, singing carols, and dancing to the music of a harmonica, a drum, or a piece of tinkling metal. In the town of Buhi, a snake-like ring dance accompanies the carols.

From early December on in the Visayan area, performers called *daigon* or roving carolers enhance their singing with dances and comedy skits, the program usually lasting about three hours. The *daigon* performers greatly modify the holy couple's search for a room at an inn and turn the whole thing into a variety show by mixing in comedy skits and song-and-dance numbers.

In many areas, groups of young men, women, and children serenade the neighborhood with guitars and *babdyruasm,* stringed instruments native to the Philippines. Groups of children in their best get together to make their rounds, singing to the accompaniment of their homemade instruments which range from plastic and pebble rattles, empty tin cans, thin bamboo sticks, hollow bamboo tubes, flattened bottle caps ringed by wires, and maracas, hollow, coconut shells containing mongo beans and having bamboo stick handles, to more sophisticated ukuleles and guitars or even accordions and harmonicas. They all play a combination of the old, traditional Christmas songs and the beautiful, unique Christmas songs of the Philippines.

## Pageants and Parades

The community pageant is held in many areas. A few hours before midnight on Christmas Eve, two persons playing the roles of Mary and Joseph set off from the church, while people carrying lighted candles follow, singing to the local band's music. A platform carried on people's shoulders and bearing life-size images of Mary, Joseph, and the town's patron saint accompanies. They go door to door exchanging a dialogue in song; the couple requests a room, and the owner of the house explains that there is no room. Just before midnight mass, Mary sings of her weariness, and Joseph sings of his attempt to comfort her. The procession makes its way back to the church, and the couple take their places in the tableau. At the stroke of midnight, firecrackers explode, and fireworks are lit in the churchyard while the bells peal, and the choir sings.

In a town in the Aklan area, people gather about the town square to build a huge bonfire on Christmas Eve. They form a big circle around the fire while singing incantations. The priest remains alone in the church, performing a ritual of purification in which he washes a plate engraved with the images of Mary and Baby Jesus. In another town in the same area, a bonfire is created in the town square to which the priest and his helpers come. As the church bells toll, the priest pours some water over the flames in a purification ceremony and blesses the people.

All over the Philippines, lantern parades take place on Christmas Eve. They have become a serious competition that encourages people to express their creativity, with some of the lanterns as large as the size of a house; these must be carried on trucks and lighted by generators.

After the celebrating, there is a midnight mass called *Misa de Aguinaldo* or Mass of God's Gift. The service, which is the climactic point of the religious Christmas celebration, begins a few minutes before midnight so that the "Gloria" will be chanted exactly at the stroke of midnight. A figure of an angel travels on a wire from the altar to a place just above the Nativity scene to shower the Infant Jesus in the manger with flowers. At the same time, a star slides from the choir loft through the aisle to rest just above the manger while the church bells peal and the choir sings. Outside, firecrackers and fireworks explode, while inside the many star lanterns that decorate the church dance and sway to the pealing of the bells and the singing. People take turns kissing the feet of Jesus' image as the choir continues its song to the rhythm of tambourines and castanets.

After the *Misa de Aguinaldo,* the family gathers for *noche buena* or midnight supper. The humble meal may consist of *tsokolate,* a native chocolate drink, brown bread, and bananas. The wealthier may dine on all kinds of native and imported foods and drinks such as fruit and rum cakes, varieties of rice, coconut and flour sweets, cakes and puddings, nuts, fruits like apples, grapes, bananas, pineapples, and oranges, meat rolled and grated with eggs and raisins, roast pig, ham dripping with pineapple juice, cheese, and imported wines.

## Christmas Day

Christmas Day is called *Pasko ng mga Bata* or Children's Christmas. Filipino children do not look under the Christmas tree for their presents, for their parents have already given them their gifts days before Christmas. The children rise, quickly eat breakfast, go to mass, and dressed in their best, they set out with family or friends for the customary season's greeting, the *pagmamano,* a salute in which the child kisses the hand of the elder person or raises it to his forehead. The godparents, relatives, and friends present the children with gifts of cash. These visits strengthen the bonds between the generations.

## Holy Innocents Day

Holy Innocents Day on December 28 commemorates the slaughter of many innocent, male children at the hands of King Herod and the flight the holy family made to escape from Herod. Filipinos regard the day as an occasion of cheer, a remembrance of how the couple managed to save the Child Jesus from Herod through "trickery" against Herod and his henchmen. The day is a Christian version of Halloween or April Fools Day.

## New Year's Day

More rounds of festivities welcome the New Year. As midnight nears on New Year's Eve, firecrackers and whistle bombs burst, and everyone tries to make as loud a noise as possible to drive away the evil spirits and to welcome the good ones.

## Epiphany

Twelfth Night or Epiphany on January 6 is called the Elders' Christmas. Some pageants are performed reenacting the trip of the Three Wise Men to visit the Infant Jesus. On the island of Marinduque, three men clothed in royal garments ride horses and gallop around the



3282-TUCK

town accompanied by the townsfolk in native costume. The local band plays, and the pageant ends when King Herod wrecks his palace, set on a decorated stage, in a fit of anger when he learns about the birth of Jesus.

# Poland

W*esolych Swiat Bozego Narodzenia!*

Christmas, next to Easter, is the most festive holiday in the hard-working, stout hearted, European country of Poland. Very much a family affair, the Polish Christmas abounds with traditions, often dating back many centuries.

Like many other European children, Polish youngsters often receive gifts on the Feast of St. Nicholas on December 6. They also receive small gifts at Christmas, and they often write letters to the Three Wise Men and place the letters on the windowsill for easy access.

With the usual snow and its effect on confining people to their homes, attention centers on the home and preparations for the Christmas season. Walls are whitewashed; linens are washed and ironed; holiday china and glassware are polished; repairs are made; knives, scissors, and axes are sharpened.

## Christmas Tree

As the Advent season, the pre-Christmas season that begins the fourth Sunday before December 24, progresses, market squares throughout Poland fill with the fragrance of evergreens. The first mention of the Christmas tree in Poland was in 1720 when Father Anthony Zapcinski wrote about the green branches decorated with candles and toys that were beginning to appear in Warsaw and other Polish cities. These first trees were called maiden branches or *panna rozga* and were decorated with gilded confections, walnuts, apples, miniature dolls, animals, and colored candies.

The present day Christmas tree, the *choinka,* was slow to catch on in the small villages and rural areas. They clung to the tradition of having a handmade mobile or chandelier known as *pajaki* or spiders that were hung from the ceiling. These *pajaki* are still in use in some locations in addition to the *choinka.* Villagers received their inspiration for the *pajaki* from the church chandeliers The *pajaki* resembles an intricate spider web rather than spiders. At first, materials were recycled from the harvest festival. Wreaths were covered with apples, and nuts and *sweaty* or designs made from unleavened wafers made of grains. Later, the wreaths were enlarged, using clay for the center and adding feathers, colored tissues in the shapes of stars, crosses and flowers, and straw chains. The *pajaki* is usually hung from the ceiling in the middle of the room or above the dinner table.

Today the *choinka* or Christmas tree occupies a place of honor in a room by itself and is often lighted with candles and decorated with colorful glass balls, sweets, paper toys, nuts, apples, and homemade ornaments from eggshells, bits of colored paper, straw, painted and lacquered peas, beans, corn, and other odds and ends. In 1922, Marya Geerson Dabrowska wrote *Choinka Polska* or *The Polish Christmas Tree* in which she expressed her disapproval of the trend towards gaudy, commercial decorations for the *choinka.* She advocated returning to the beautiful folk art of making the decorations in homes. Her ideas were adopted, and today great care is taken to create these beautiful gems. Eggshells make lovely ornaments, and one of the most popular eggshell ornaments is the little pitcher, decorated with a base, spout, and handle of paper, bordered with a folk art edging. The egg may become the face of a Polish historical figure, an angel, or a clown. Birds are frequently made, with the eggshell for the body. Many times the Christmas market square shops offer for sale some Christmas decorations made by students.

The motif or the symbol of the star dominates the Polish Christmas season. Christmas Day is referred to as *Gwia zo'ka* or the Little Star. The Star Man visits children on Christmas Eve, and caroling groups often carry a large, lighted, rotating star. Decorative stars are made from straw or duck or goose feathers glued together with clay or candle wax. Often stars are made from wooden chips and shavings and hung above church altars.

Many years ago, the fir tree was often placed in an area called *Bozy Rog* or God's Corner where two benches were placed. The favorite holy pictures were hung there, and the worthiest guests sat there. Branches trimmed from the tree were placed behind pictures, above windows, and were made into small crosses and placed above the door. Some of these crosses were placed above the barn door to protect the animals.

Years ago and in some rural areas today, sheaves of last year's harvest grains were braided and would ensure plenty of bread, nuts, and children for the family. After Christmas Eve supper sometimes, some nuts, a loaf of bread, and a child or two were bound with the sheaves. The binding was then cut, and everything that had been bound, the apples, nuts, a loaf of bread, and the children, all fell to the floor with many thuds and cries and laughter. After supper, these sheaves were often taken to the orchard and tied to the trees to ensure a plentiful crop.

In southern Poland in days past, it was customary to trim only the top of the tree and to hang it upside down from the ceiling. This *podlaznik* was trimmed with candy, apples, nuts, and toys. It was lowered so the children might get to the treats. In Carpathian villages, small Christmas trees are nailed over the doorway, and they may be found along roadsides also.

## The Crèche

In Krakow, there is the tradition of building beautiful crèches or manger scenes. The little figures are set in scenery resembling the architecture of Krakow, most especially the beautiful Gothic Church of the Holy Virgin. Before World War II, bricklayers usually made these manger scenes, but today they are the work of hobbyists, requiring a lot of talent, skill, and time. Every year on a Sunday between December 3 and 10, a competition is held at the Krakow Market Square for the most beautiful crèche. The competing crèches are then displayed at the Historical Museum of Krakow.

Many Polish families have family shrines where holy figures are displayed, and the family prays. Often there is a holiday display arranged in front of the shrine. There may be candles and special pastries for the season or a Nativity scene assembled by young members of the family and placed in a box. Boys and girls like to carry it in processions and to display it to their friends.

## Christmas Dramas

A custom peculiar to Poland is the performance called *Herody*, a mystery play depicting the story of King Herod, who upon hearing the news of Jesus' birth, orders that all newborn male infants in his country should be slain. In the play, justice reigns. The Devil takes King Herod to Hell after Death beheads the king. This performance occurs each year at the famous *Zywieckie Gody* Festival in Zywiec.

Since the eighteenth century, staging folk plays of the Nativity with puppets has become popular. The story of Herod appears in these puppet plays also. The puppets represent an angel, the Devil, a witch, a Jew, a gypsy, and a Pole. These puppet shows are performed in the regions of Zywiec, Rzeszow, Lublin, and Krakow.

## Oplatek

*Oplatek* or Christmas wafers play an important part in the Polish Christmas. The *oplatek* comes from Latin and means sacred bread. Preparation of these wafers dates back to the tenth century. The choicest wheat grains were chosen, and water or milk was added. The dough was placed between two iron plates similar to a waffle iron and baked for a few minutes. The beautiful figures carved into the iron plates ranged from the Nativity scene to rural scenes of everyday Poland.

These designs became very intricate, and people began to make ornaments of these wafers using circles, half circles, and quarter circles interlocked to form wings, crosses, stars, and finally a three dimensional sphere called the world or *swiat.* Often an opening was left in the center, and a small ball of quarter circles was inserted. Sometimes they added a figure of Jesus holding the cross in the center representing His rule over the universe. The *oplatek* has an almost mystical significance for Polish people. The breaking and sharing of these wafers introduces the celebration of Christmas for the family. These wafers are sent to absent family members and close friends. They are the treasured link bringing fond memories of Poland to Poles all over the world.

## Christmas Eve

*Willa* or Christmas Eve is believed to be full of magic, mystery, and omens of the coming year. Many spirits visit; animals receive the gift of human speech; future prosperity and good health are ensured, and whatever happens on *Willa* will happen in the future year. Consequently, people arise early on this day, for this will determine whether one will be alert or lazy in the coming year. Fishermen arise early to catch as many varieties of fish as possible to ensure good fishing in the coming year. A dry crust of bread and a coin are placed in cold water used to wash one's hands to ensure plenty of food and strength for the coming year. Animals are treated with great respect on *Willa* and given extra food and leftover *oplatek* and are believed to speak in human tongues around midnight.

Hay and oats symbolizing prosperity and fertility are placed under the tablecloth on the dinner table. At dinner everyone pulls out a blade of hay to foretell his future. A long blade means a long life, and a split or wiry blade means an interesting but complicated future.

Polish people fast all day on *Willa* until the first star of the evening is spotted, and then the festivities begin. The *Willa* supper is the highlight of the Polish Christmas celebration. There should be an even number of guests at the table; the number thirteen is particularly to be avoided. An odd number of guests is thought to signify the death, in the coming year, of one of the diners. A place is often set for the unexpected guest.

The most important part of the *Willa* supper is the breaking and sharing of the *optalek* or Christmas wafer. The host and hostess face one another, each holding an *oplatek,* breaking them to share with each other. They embrace and express their love by wishing that each other's deepest yearning might be fulfilled. They then break and share the wafers with everyone, beginning with the oldest down to the youngest, wishing each other good health, happiness, and an untroubled life. The hostess expresses also that she would share her bread with those present if they should ever be in need as she would be willing to take from them should the need arise.

Supper varies from region to region, but the menu for the meal is traditional and unchanging in each area. It must contain all of nature's elements that produce food except the fat and meat of animals since they are considered to be like humans at Christmas. There are usually twelve courses, as many as there were apostles. The first course is usually a soup, the most popular a borscht or clear, beet soup with *uszka,* a kind of ravioli filled with mushrooms and called "little ears." Other soups might be mushroom, fish, or pea soup. Then comes the fish: pike with saffron, carp with raisins and honey, and herring. This may be followed by such fare as noodles with poppy seeds, buckwheat groats, peas, dumplings filled with sauerkraut and mushrooms, *bigos* or a stew without meat, rice with plums, beans in sour sauce, cabbage with mushrooms, and prune stew. A special Christmas Eve dessert called *kutia* is made of crushed wheat grains mixed with wild bee honey, poppy seeds, currants, and nuts. *Piernik* or ginger cake often is served with a fruit compote of apples, pears, peaches, plums, and cherries. Oriental sweets and fruits, poppy seed cake, streusels, candies, and nuts are also served accompanied by *krupnik,* a holiday drink made of brandy, honey, spices, and alcohol.

The Christmas lights on the tree are lit. Christmas carols are sung, and gifts are distributed. In some areas, the Star Man arrives. He may be the village priest or a friend in disguise, and he questions the children on their religious knowledge. The children are given small gifts that they believe are sent by the good "Star of Heaven" but carried to them by the Three Wise Men who accompany the Star Man. The Wise Men are often young men of the village and are also referred to as Star Boys. In some rural areas, other young people dressed as characters from the Nativity, animals, or folklore characters accompany the Star Boys. They go from house-to-house singing carols.

The family gathers around the tree and sings traditional carols called *kolendy.* The oldest Polish Christmas carols are contained in a hymnal from the first part of the fifteenth century. The flourishing of carol singing took place in the Baroque period.

At midnight, ringing bells herald *Pasterka* or Shepherds' Mass that opens with the ancient carol "The Lord Is Born." Churches are decorated with beautiful crèches that remain on display until February 2, Candlemas. Years ago in some provinces like the Poznan area, young men made stars out of strong, colored paper and attached them to their hats as they went to *Pasterka.* Householders took bundles of straw to the services to be blessed.

In earlier times, *Pasterka* was a crowded, merry, noisy service. In some villages, organists trained the young people to make the sounds of birds and animals at designated times. The priest often verbally bestowed gifts on his parishioners, such as a pair of horses for a man who perpetually arrived late for Sunday mass. Many a young person, relieved that the solemnity of Advent was over, was prone to playing practical jokes on his fellow parishioners. He might tie together the shoelaces of two people standing or kneeling side-by-side, or he might put ink in the holy water and watch as people crossed themselves with the inky water.

## Christmas Day

Christmas Day is a day spent with family and friends. Menial work of any kind is not done, so often the family prepares the food for the day beforehand. Meat is the featured course, with Polish hams and sausages very popular.

In the countryside on Christmas Day, groups of boys and girls go round the villages dressed in traditional costumes of an angel, Devil, King, and *Turon*, a kind of dragon. They present miracle and mystery plays based on Biblical stories. There are many chases, wrestling, and rhymed couplets, and the performance always ends with the beheading of Herod. This goes on daily until New Year's.

## St. Stephen's Day

On December 26, St. Stephen's Day, an official holiday, people usually visit friends and relatives. Going from house to house singing carols is gradually disappearing, but in some regions such as Zywiec or Lublin, it still survives. Groups of children go door-to-door carrying a large, colorful, revolving star lit from the inside. They may carry a crèche with miniature figures. They wish people good health, prosperity, and good crops. Sometimes the "goat," a boy wearing a sheepskin inside out and holding a goat's head on a pole accompanies them. The goat's head has a movable lower jaw that is pulled up and down with a string.

## New Year's Eve

New Year's Eve in the cities is celebrated by formal balls and dances, many having long histories such as the Warsaw Philharmonic Society Ball. In the countryside, in days past, people committed unpunished pranks such as disassembling someone's wagon and reassembling it on his roof or smearing windows with tar. These were forgiven, for they were believed to be ousting the old, passing year. In rural areas, New Year's today is celebrated much as a family time.

## Epiphany

On Three Kings Day or Epiphany on January 6, many villagers mark their doors with the initials of the Three Wise Men and the date, believing that this will protect their homes from harm.

# Portugal

*Boas Festas!*

In the western European country of Portugal since ancient times, an important part of the Christmas celebration has been the setting up of the Nativity scene. Children prepare a table or other suitable place, and they gather all kinds of materials from mirrors to moss to stones from which they create a proper setting for the traditional clay figures.

The Christmas tree, usually imported from northern European countries, has become popular, and streets, shops, and homes are decorated very elaborately with lights and traditional Christmas symbols.

## Christmas Eve

The children eagerly await the arrival of *Pai Natal,* the Portuguese version of Father Christmas or Santa Claus. Families traditionally attend the *Missa do Galo,* the midnight mass on Christmas Eve. Years ago, carolers strolled through the streets singing, but this custom seems to be fading.

*Consoada* is the family meal eaten on Christmas Eve. It consists of cod or another fish called *bacalhau* that is poached and accompanied by boiled potatoes and cabbage. Dessert is usually *filhoses,* a fried dough served with syrup and *rabanadas,*a sort of French toast.

On Christmas Day or *Dia de Natal,* the main dish is usually stuffed turkey. This day is usually one filled with family gatherings.

## New Year's Day

On *Vespera de Anno Novo* or New Year's Eve, the devout attend religious services. Groups of children go from house to house singing *janeiras* or ancient New Year's songs. The singers are masked and often address the master or mistress of the house with praise if they are generous or with insults if they have been stingy with the traditional gifts of wine, apples, nuts, sausages, or coins. In some places, people go to the housetops at midnight and "blow away the old year" with trumpets and some appropriate verses. Tradition dictates that when the clock strikes twelve, everyone eats one grape for each striking of the clock to ensure having money in the coming year.

## New Year's Day

*Anno Novo* or New Year's Day begins with special services in the churches. Friends and relatives visit house-to-house greeting one another with *"Feliz Ano Novo."* In some areas, the village band goes through the streets playing. Whenever the musicians happen to pass a member's house, they stop and play a special selection.

Some believe that a person will act during the next twelve months as he behaves on the first day of the year. For this reason, youngsters carefully watch their manners, and older people likewise conduct themselves very carefully.

## Day of the Kings

*Dia Dos Reis* or Day of the Kings on January 6 is the last day of the Christmas season. People add the figures of the Three Kings to the Nativity scenes on this day since this is the day they supposedly arrived to visit the Infant Jesus. Epiphany plays are sometimes given, and bands of carolers go about singing greetings and begging for gifts, for, they, like the kings of old, are weary and have come from afar.

In some areas, family groups visit one another from house to house. The guests stand at the door and beg admittance to sing to the Christ Child. After receiving a hearty welcome and after singing carols in honor of the Infant Jesus, guests are entertained with wines and sweets.

Gifts are exchanged on this day also. This is a great festival day for children. Many mothers give the children a special party and include a *bolo-Rei* or special Epiphany cake. Within the ring-shaped pastry are hidden all kinds of fortune telling trinkets and a single, dried lima bean. The child who finds the bean is crowned king or queen of the party and promises to make the cake for his friends next year.

# Puerto Rico

*Felices Pascuas!*

Christmas is celebrated on the American protectorate, Caribbean island of Puerto Rico for many days. The celebration begins on *Noche Buena* or Christmas Eve and ends on January 12.

Much like a Latin American fiesta, groups of *trullas* or carol singers still travel the countryside, in some parts on horseback, singing traditional songs known as *aguinaldos* and *villancicos,* Spanish Christmas carols. The singers sometimes receive money for this, but are more likely to receive food and drink. It's not unusual for a family to go into debt to provide a bountiful feast since this is such an important part of the Christmas celebration. As they travel from farm to farm, their numbers increase, so that by early morning, one may find the population of a whole mountainside singing happily under the roof of one small, but hospitable home.

## Christmas Eve

Christmas Eve is a time of great feasting. The big meal usually takes place before midnight mass. In the churches, the *nacimiento* or manger scene is displayed for the midnight mass. Homes are lighted and decorated. People dress in their best clothes. In the homes of the more affluent, whole, roasted pigs will be served barbecue style. People who cannot afford this have at least *arroz con pollo,* a dish of rice and chicken. This is a time of family reunions. Families spend the evening singing and having a merry time before mass.

In Puerto Rico children say that Santa Claus comes flying through the air like a bird. The children make little boxes that they place in the courtyard or on the roof, and Santa Claus drops the gifts into them as he flies by at night. According to custom, he does not come on Christmas Eve alone, but he may come every night or two during the week. This makes for a lot of excitement, and each morning the children run out eagerly to see if Santa has left anything more in their boxes during the night.

## Three Kings Day

The major part of the season is Three Kings Day or Epiphany on January 6. The kings go house to house delivering presents to children who have put grass and cups of water for the camels under their beds or on the roofs.

Open house is held January 6, 7, and 8. Men go house to house playing guitars. Early in the morning, visitors begin to arrive, and the hostess is expected to greet them with an impromptu song composed to apply to each individual.

Children flock each year to the Church of San Jose to watch the animated *nacimiento.* The church has an altar and crucifix dating back to the sixteenth century. The *nacimiento* depicts a complete community with villagers engaged in their work or riding in miniature trains that move back and forth through the village. All of this has for its centerpiece the 2,000-year-old manger scene.

# Romania

*Sarbatori Vesele!*

As in many other countries under Communist rule for many years, in the European country of Romania, the celebration of Christmas gradually faded, and the celebration of New Year's Day became more popular. Winter festivals were organized in many towns to keep alive the traditional customs. The best known one is in the town of Sighetu Marmatiei at the end of December.

Romania is no longer under Communist rule, and Christian customs are returning to this country. Christmas is a time for family and friends to get together during this snowy holiday.

## Ignatius

On December 20, St. Ignatius Day, a custom is observed concerning the favorite food of the season, pig. A slaughtered pig is brought into the house. Straws are put into his snout, and then the pig is covered with burning straw and singed. The pig is thoroughly cleaned and covered with a piece of cloth for about ten minutes. The housewife incenses the pig, and the husband makes the sign of the cross on the pig's head, saying to all the family gathered around, "Let's eat the pig!"

After the pig is cooked and cut, there is a feast called The Pig's Funeral Feast. Friends, family, and neighbors attend the feast and eat bacon skin and small pieces of fried pork with glasses of wine or plum brandy.



3282-TUCK

## The *Turta*

The *turta* or Christmas cake used to be made more frequently than it is now, but it is still made by some on December 23. It has countless layers of dry, paper-thin dough prepared with crushed walnuts, honey, melted sugar, or sometimes with the juice of pounded hemp seed. According to tradition, the leaves of the *turta* represent the Christ Child's swaddling clothes. In some places, the making of this cake has a curious rite used to cause one's fruit trees to bear fruit. The housewife plunges her hands into the dough pan, and then, with fingers covered with dough, she follows her husband to the orchard and stands before first one, then another of the fruit trees. The farmer carries an axe and threatens to cut down the trees because "they are useless and bear not fruit." The wife intervenes and pleads for each tree in turn. Surely, she declares, next summer the trees will bear as much fruit as the dough that sticks to her fingers.

From dawn until night, boys run about from house to house shouting, "Good morning to Uncle Eve, *Mos Ajun.*" They sing *colinde* or long recitations about Christmas, the sun, the moon and stars, the master and mistress of the house and their unique interests and foibles. The lads receive apples, dried fruits, cakes, and coins in exchange for the greetings.

## Christmas Eve

Father Christmas brings the tree on Christmas Eve. Children place their shoes at the door for him to put presents in. In times past, and in some places now, on the morning of December 24, the village priest, accompanied by the sacristan and a lad carrying a kettle of holy water, makes the rounds of the parishioners' homes. The priest dips into the water with a bunch of sweet basil, sprinkles the house, and blesses it. Then the housewife drops a coin into the kettle, gives the priest a present of hemp, and invites him to sit down and partake of wine and Christmas food.

Gifts used to be exchanged more on New Year's Day. These gifts were usually placed near the Christmas tree.

## Nativity Plays

Throughout the season, dramatic performances of Christ's birth were and are enacted in many towns and villages. In Valachia these are known as *Vicleim,* and in Moldavia and Transylvania they are called *Irozi.* Usually, the actors number ten or more and include Herod, the Three Kings, a clown, a comical old man, and other traditional characters.

Popular plays, satirical in character, and puppet shows are given from village to village.

## Caroling

Carols play an important part in the Romanian Christmas, and on Christmas Eve crowds of young and old go from house to house singing carols, songs that are sung only once a year on Christmas Eve. One such song goes like this:

"Do you receive the pretty star,
Pretty and so very bright?
It has appeared on the earth
Just like God thought it would be right,
And it could be seen on high
Just like we did in the sky."

These carols can be sung outside under windows or inside houses around the table piled high with gifts for the children. On the table might be fancy breads, apples, walnuts, sausages, wine, and plum brandy. The carols are dedicated to the family, and there are special carols for the village VIPs, for shepherds, for ploughmen, and for the hunters and fishermen.

The carolers often stroll through the streets and carry a tall star made of board and paper with watercolor painted Biblical scenes on the star. Sometimes tinkling bells are added, and a candle illuminates the star from within.

As their mascots for the caroling, the groups have either a person dressed as *Duba,* the stag, or *Turca,* the goat. Girls bring something to adorn the mascot; and any girl who does not bring a waistband, kerchief, or shawl is not admitted to the feast of the goat or to the dances during the holidays. Those who refuse to receive the carolers and to offer them gifts are likewise punished. All of these are also said to be unable to marry for the coming year.

## Christmas Day

The principal food at Christmas dinner used to be the roast pig. Recently, turkey has taken over. Other foods might be jellied pig's feet or borscht, a beet soup. A dish made especially for Christmas and New Year's is *issarwale,* pickled cabbage leaves filled with ground pork. The favored drink is plum brandy, often served hot with added pepper, cinnamon, and sugar. Cheese and apple pies are also served.

## New Year's Eve

On New Year's Eve before dusk, groups of men used to start out with the *plugusor* or plough to greet the people and to wish them a Happy New Year. A plough was adorned with green leaves and flowers and either carried by the young people or drawn by oxen with gold-colored horns. They stopped at every house and dug a new furrow in the yard while a young man recited traditional lines to a *doina* tune, wishing the people of the house good health and good crops in the year to come.

In the land of Bukovina in the village of Suceava as well as in other areas of Moldavia, one tradition concerned a *buhai*, a bull made from a small, bottomless barrel covered with animal skin through which a tuft of horsehair is passed. When drawn through, it made the skin vibrate, thus imitating the bellowing of a bull. Sometimes the greeting for either of these traditions, the plough or the bull, was accompanied by a play using goat masks. The play was silent, and it developed against a musical background, a tune played on the flute by a member of a folk music band, accompanied by hollering. There may also be greetings with *caiuti,* small horses, or *ursi,* bears, in masked processions which played humorous, satirical scenes or peasant plays known as *Jieni* after the name of a famous outlaw of olden days. Contests of the greeting groups and festivals of folk theater and masks peculiar to the winter holidays were held in various areas.

# Russia

*Rodzhestvom Kritovom!*

*Sviatki* or Christmas in Old Russia was from December 25 to January 7. In present day Russia it is from January 7 to January 19. Most of the world in 1917 changed to the Gregorian calendar, but the Russian Orthodox Church kept the old Julian calendar that was thirteen days behind the Gregorian calendar. So, after the 1917 Russian Revolution, Christmas was officially celebrated on January 7.

In 1917 the religious festival of Christmas or *Sviatki* was banned by the Russian government in keeping with the Communist dislike and distrust of religions and replaced Christmas with Winter Festival that lasts from December 30 to January 10.

## Christmas in Old Russia

*Sviatki* in pre-1917 Russia was a time of family reunions, a sumptuous holiday dinner, children's parties, masquerades, fancy balls, decorated trees, the exchange of gifts, and magical rituals. These rituals were performed to bring good health and good fortune, to ward off evil spirits, and to predict the future. Some were very lighthearted, and some were darker, seeking omens or signs.

Christmas was a very religious holiday, second only to Easter. There were church services three times a day for six weeks preceding the holiday, and on Christmas Eve there was a long midnight mass. During the forty-day period of Advent, the season beginning the fourth Sunday before Christmas Eve, no meat was served, and on Christmas Eve no food was eaten until the arrival of the first evening star. For this dinner, fish was served along with borscht or beet soup, cabbage, onions, potatoes, stuffed cabbage leaves, and for dessert *kissel,* a custard like dish made of berries.

Christmas dinner was served on a table with a layer of straw beneath the cloth, symbolizing Christ's bed, the manger. The blessed wafer of peace and goodwill was divided among family and friends before the meal. Dinner was twelve courses in honor of each of the twelve apostles. Dinner could be duck, ham, goose, pig, pig's head, and borscht.

In some areas, after Christmas dinner, family members paraded around the neighborhood attired in costumes and singing *kolyadki* or Christmas carols. December 26 was the day when men went visiting, and December 27 the woman paid their visits.

In Old Russia, children were told that St. Nicholas placed wheat cakes on the windowsill for them on Christmas Eve, and these had to be eaten on Christmas Day, but it was *Babushkato* who brought them presents. She was the woman who was too busy to accompany the Three Wise Men to Bethlehem to see the Christ Child when they asked her. Later, sorry that she had refused them, she set out to find Bethlehem, but she got lost. She has traveled ever since, rewarding good children with presents in Russia.

Mummers were quite popular then, dressing up in costumes and clowning round, going from house to house with their plays of bears, horses, goats, Turks, tavern keepers, and other dubious characters, all done in good fun and high spirits.

## New Year in Communist Russia

As mentioned earlier, in 1917 after the Russian Revolution, the Communists suppressed Christianity and Christmas, and this lasted for over seventy years. The Festival of Winter celebrated on New Year's replaced Christmas. School was let out for a two-week vacation.

In 1935 Joseph Stalin, then head of the Soviet Union, lifted the ban on Christmas trees and decreed that they were now "New Year's

Trees." He also declared *Novyi God* or New Year's a national family holiday. Dinner became a New Year's dinner, and Grandfather Frost took over as the gift-giving figure.

Grandfather Frost or *D'yed Moroz* lived deep in the woods of Russia and rode into town in a sleigh. He went from house to house delivering gifts. He was not as jolly as Santa Claus, and he gave only to good children, ignoring the naughty. He wore a red coat and hat trimmed in white fur and a long, white beard and looked something like a wizard.

*Snegurochka* or the Snow Maiden became a popular figure of the New Year's celebrations also. She is the granddaughter of Grandfather Frost. She often accompanies him in parades and at parties. She has blond braids and wears either a long, blue robe or a short, fur-trimmed coat and a white fur hat. The New Year's Boys also accompany Grandfather Frost and the Snow Maiden. She is sometimes accompanied by young girls dressed as snowflakes with long, white robes and shiny headdresses.

On New Year's Eve, gifts were opened, and families sat down to their New Year's feast. There were widespread food shortages during this period, so people often pooled their resources or used connections to get the needed treats such as smoked fish or roasted meats, rare, fresh fruits and vegetables, and cakes and sweets. *Baba,* a type of coffee cake was popular as was the bread *karavay,* made from wheat or rye flour and at times as large as a table.

The government sponsored numerous children's plays, parades, and other festivities, all designed to welcome the New Year. New theatrical productions were presented as well as old, traditional dramas. Operas were given, and dance programs appeared on television. There was even a grand children's party that took place inside the walls of the Kremlin itself. The Palace of Congresses, the government center, was transformed into a fairy world with a seventy-five foot tall New Year's tree decorated in a very lavish manner. Over 50,000 tickets were sold for this annually. Children received presents, and Grandfather Frost arrived on a Sputnik-drawn sleigh or some other high tech vehicle. He was accompanied by lots of attendants including the Snow Maiden, snow bunnies, clowns, and New Year's Boys dressed in peasant tunics, baggy pants, and boots, and girls in old-time pinafores. Folk dancing was part of the program along with magicians, acrobats, and clowns.

Older students and adults attended dances and parties at their schools, clubs, theaters, union halls, farm collectives, factories, and many other places. New Year's trees appeared everywhere along with festive lights and other decorations.

Christmas was not totally suppressed in the Soviet Union. It was still observed in the small number of churches that still existed. It lost a lot of its power since it came after New Year's, on January 7 and the lavish, government-approved celebrations.

## Christmas in Russia Today

In 1991 Russia had the first official Christmas in seventy-four years! To most people this was an eventful time since Christmas had been forbidden for so long a time. The revolutionary changes that have occurred in Russia in recent years have been radical. The personal freedoms allowed today are immense after all of the years of Communist rule and because of the drastic changes in the 1980s under Mikhail S. Gorbachev and his policy of *glasnost* or openness. He also instituted a program of economic reform, *perestroika,* to reverse the damages done during the Communist regime.

Russia has had serious economic problems since the reforms, but Christians may now celebrate their faith openly since the government's change of position on religion. The Russian government now believes that embracing religious values will strengthen the country. It is thought that there are now over 40,000,000 Christians in Russia today. Crowds are filling the churches. The Russian Orthodox Church is the largest religious institution in Russia.

As with other Eastern traditions, the Russian Christmas is on the old calendar again, falling on January 7.

The Christmas celebration begins in November when forty days of fasting begins in preparation for Christmas. Russian people abstain from any animal products, except seafood, and any dairy products. Such things as chocolate are also avoided.

On Christmas Eve, Russian people go to church for the Christmas Mass. A beautiful tradition called *Krestny Khod* has been resurrected from pre-Communist days; it is the religious procession on Christmas Eve. This custom, dating back over a thousand years, means "walking with the cross." After Christmas services are over, people parade around their churches, carrying religious flags and icons. After completing the journey, people reenter the church to sing Christmas carols or hymns before going home to Christmas dinner.

Many of the sumptuous Christmas dinners of the past no longer take place. Most people have feasted during the New Year's celebrations and have a quiet dinner for Christmas. Everyday food is usually served, but a Christmas candle is set on the table.

On Christmas morning they go to church again for the Christmas Liturgy. After church, people gather at one relative's home to be together. On the whole, Christmas is a family time of religious observations. The family gives gifts and has Christmas lunch, the main Christmas meal. All day children will go from door to door caroling, singing especially the song "Thy Nativity" or "Your Birth."

Homes are decorated with trees, and pine is placed on front doors and in the home also.

Christmas is celebrated for six days, and the Christmas trees are taken down after the feast day of the Baptism of Christ.

## Christmas Music

The Russian Orthodox Church is known for its beautiful sacred music. Christmas services reflect this as months and months of practice produces outstanding music. Christmas Eve services are now televised in Russia, a fact unheard of a few years ago. The Patriarch or Head of the Russian Orthodox Church may now be seen leading the service, a moving event for many Russians who remember the years and years of suppression.

One of Russia's greatest contributions to the worldwide celebration of Christmas is the beautiful ballet "The Nutcracker," by Peter Ilyich Tchaikovsky performed all over the world during the holiday season.

It is expected that more and more of the pre-Communist traditions may gradually be started again for the Russian Christmas.

## Today's Winter Festivals

Russia's Winter Festivals are still celebrated with much enthusiasm. There is still a huge New Year's tree in Manezh Square in front of the Kremlin; decorations are still everywhere, and New Year's greeting are plentiful. Fireworks still fill the air while people gather to ring in the New Year. Russian television televises the New Year's activities in Red Square.

Psychics and astrologers predict the country's events for the New Year, and the events of the past year are remembered.

Children still receive a visit from Grandfather Frost on New Year's Eve or New Year's Day. One of the men in the family, a friend or neighbor, or someone who has been hired, often students, visit as the beloved Grandfather Frost, and this is often the highlight of the year for Russian children. It is slowly beginning to change, with some children receiving gifts on Christmas Eve, but as long as Christmas comes after New Year's in Russia, Christmas will most likely remain more of a religious celebration, with the party atmosphere shown at New Year's.

# Rwanda

*Umunsi Mwiza!* or *Noheli Nziza!*

Rwanda is a civil war torn, African country about the size of the state of Maryland. Fierce clashes and large-scale ethnic cleansing have occurred between the two ethnic groups called the Hutus and the Tutsis in recent years; consequently, there is a lot of instability.

About 65 percent of Rwandans are Christian, and many of these are deeply religious. Pope John Paul II ended his 1990 tour of Africa with a visit to Rwanda.

At Christmas, the beautiful church services are especially moving as entire families, dressed up in their finery, climb or descend the hills on the way to mass. At the Roman Catholic cathedral in Butare, the clergy, led by the Bishop, don magnificent ceremonial vestments, as the people join the choir in beautiful Christmas hymns, accompanied by a traditional orchestra.

The celebration of Christmas usually lasts from Christmas Eve through December 26. The Santa Claus figure is virtually unknown in Rwanda except by those people who have close European connections. Christmas trees are not usually put up either. Christmas is very much a family occasion.

There is no typical Christmas menu, but Rwandans eat plenty of meat, especially goat meat with either rice or cassava paste, and they drink sorghum beer or banana beer. Rwandans do not usually eat desserts.

# Scotland

Merry Christmas!

In the highlands and lowlands of Scotland, New Year's Day or Hogmanay is celebrated with more eagerness than is Christmas. During the Reformation, Protestant reformers attacked the Christmas traditions, and the Scots took it to heart and cut back on the celebrating. Today Christmas is celebrated very quietly within the family, with the major focus on the children. Trees are decorated, presents are given, especially to children, and people attend church services, but the celebration is not as exuberant or colorful as it is in other western countries.

Several customs were associated with Christmas in Scotland years ago. A waxing moon was always luckier than a waning one at Christmas. Housewives dared not leave any chores undone. No one must go to bed before midnight on Christmas Eve, nor was the fire allowed to go out on this night for fear that the elves might come down the chimney and dance in the ashes. A bonfire, dancing, and bagpipe playing were entertainments before eating Christmas dinner.

## Daft Days

St. John's Day on December 27 is the day when Daft Days Yule bread, a thin, oatmeal bread with the sign of the cross marked on it, is made. The Daft Days are the days between Christmas and Hogmanay and are probably called that to emphasize the difference between them and the rest of the year.

## Hogmanay Traditions

Throughout the Middle Ages, Scotland and France were closely linked by the "Auld Alliance," and the Scottish word Hogmanay comes from an old French phrase exclaimed on New Year's Day which means "To the mistletoe the New Year." Another explanation of the word's origins is that in the highlands of Scotland, men used to perform an unusual rite. One of the men covered himself with a cow's hide from a cow that had been slaughtered that winter and ran around the village chased by other villagers who hit the cowhide with sticks. As the men circled the houses, they demanded to be let in. Doors would open, and the men were given something to drink. The group's leader would give the head of each household the "breast stripe" of a deer, goat, or sheep wrapped around the point of a stick. The "breast stripe" is a piece of skin that had been removed from the animal without a knife. The head of the family would then put the piece of wood with the skin wrapped around it into the fire, and the family would pass it around breathing in deeply so as to suck the smoke right down in their lungs. This smoking stick, called a Hogmanay, was a talisman against evil spirits.

Another theory of the origin of the word Hogmanay is that it was a name given to a cake made of cheese and oats that was presented to children on New Year's Eve. Children marched up and down the streets all wrapped in one sheet like a Chinese dragon. They called out for Hogmanay at each door and recited the following:

"Rise guid wife, and shak' your feathers,
Dinna think that we are beggars;
We're only bairnies come to play,
Rise up an' gie's our hogmanay
Hogmanay, troll-lol, troll-lol-lay!"

A time filled with interesting customs from the past, one of the most interesting Hogmanay ceremonies performed is the Burning of the Clavie. Seamen and coopers turn an ancient tar-barrel into a wheel, and a herring cask is broken up into staves and joined to the wheel. A piece of burning peat is put into the machine, and the Clavie-bearer takes the burning wheel on his shoulders and carries it to every boat in dock to bring them luck. If the carrier should stumble, it is considered to be a great calamity. Another person takes charge of the Clavie at a place where two streets meet and makes a circuit of the town. It is then carried to a small hill where a kind of altar called a Doorie is built. There, when the Clavie becomes a mass of flames, it is lifted down and thrown down the hill. People all around snatch at the embers and preserve them for the coming year. This custom takes place primarily at Burghead on the Moray Firth.

The Strathdown Highlanders used to bring home great loads of juniper that were kindled on New Year's Day in the different rooms with all the openings being closed so that the smoke might produce a thorough fumigating. This was done to humans, horses, and other animals.

Another interesting custom involves the first person who enters the house after the clock strikes midnight on New Year's Eve or Hogmanay. As people stand around the fire with "a tot of het pint" in their hands, a knock comes at the door that opens quietly, and a tall, dark, handsome man enters. In one hand he has a small branch, and in the other he carries a piece of mistletoe. The stranger walks to the fireplace, puts his branch into the flames, and places the mistletoe on the mantelpiece. Finally he wishes everyone a Happy New Year. In return he is given wine or whiskey and a piece of cake. Called "first-footing," this was once a popular custom in England as well as in Scotland, but today it occurs mainly in Scotland. There are many peculiar beliefs connected with "first-footing." The "first-footer" determines the household's fortunes for the coming year; women are considered to be bad luck if they should be the first to enter; therefore, families often rig the sequence of events rather than let a woman ruin the family's fortunes. In England a red-haired person is considered very lucky, while a fair-haired person is unlucky in Northumberland, England. On the Isle of Man, flat-footed "first-footers" are considered unlucky; they should have insteps sufficiently arched so that "water runs underneath."

Most Scots are very sensitive to a large number of such personal peculiarities in their "first-footers." The lame, the blind in one eye, the splayed feet person whose feet both point out to the sides, or one whose eyebrows meet in the middle all are suspected of having the Evil Eye. The "first-footer" must not be mean nor carry a knife or anything else sharp. The worst possible "first-footer" would be a decrepit old woman cursing or a one-eyed, immoral old crone with very bushy black eyebrows which meet in the middle who is standing on the door-step with her very flat feet at ninety degree angles to each other and waving a knife!

If one were unlucky enough to be 'first-footed" by one of these unfortunate persons, bad luck could still be held off; one might sprinkle salt on the fire or speak to the undesirable persons before he or she speaks to you. One might make the sign of the cross or throw some burning embers up the chimney. Once the unlucky one has gone, one might still save oneself from the bad luck by putting a red ember into a bowl of water.

Sometimes instead of a branch and mistletoe, the "first-footer" might bring salt and coal, symbolizing life, hospitality, and warmth. In fishing communities, the "first-footer" might carry a herring. If the "first-footer" is a male, he expects to kiss all of the females under the mistletoe. Sometimes he carries a lump of coal and says, "Lang may you lum reek," meaning long may your chimney smoke.

It's also traditional on Hogmanay to visit all your friends, but this needs to be coordinated, obviously, or you will spend Hogmanay on the street because all your friends are at your front door cursing you for not being home, and you'll be doing the same.

Hogmanay has always been very much a communal celebration. As the bells strike midnight, the lid comes off all over Scotland. There is a lot of kissing, shouting, handshaking, drinking of toasts, dancing, music, and at a traditional meeting place like the market square cross or the churchyard, bonfires are lit, torches are waved, and tar barrels are burned.

In northern fishing villages, old boats were ceremoniously set on fire on Hogmanay. Still today, in the Shetland Isles, toward the end of January, a boat is still burned commemorating "Up-Helly-Aa." which is Norse for the end of the holiday, the end of the Viking Yuletide.

Inside homes, Hogmanay is a time for putting everything in

order before the New Year has arrived. The house is swept; clothes are mended; clocks are wound; musical instruments are tuned; crooked pictures are straightened; silver brass and pewter are polished, and beds are made up with clean sheets. All debts are supposed to be paid, and everything borrowed must be returned. Fire is piled high in the hearth, and the higher the flame, the better the luck to come. Stray dogs hanging around must be sent away as they bring bad luck.

Often at the stroke of midnight, the head of the house opens the door wide until the last stroke of the church bell has died away, letting the Old Year out and the New Year in. Windows are also opened, and household bells are rung, trays are banged, and pots are clanged. This loud noise sends any evil influence lurking in the corners of the rooms rushing out of the house. Afterwards, the windows are shut to stop the spirits from slipping back again. "Auld Lang Syne" is then sung, and more "het pint" drunk.

## Hogmanay Food

Special Hogmanay food is prepared: oatcakes, cheeses, shortbread, black buns, treacle bannocks, and ankersocks. Black bun is a rich cake made with dried fruit, almonds, spices, and brandy baked in a pastry. Angersocks are gingerbread loaves made with rye flour. The traditional drink is "het pint," a warm, mild ale spiced with nutmeg and laced with whiskey. This is carried into the streets in copper kettles so that the revelers can drink a toast to the New Year. In Aberdeen the toasting drink is "sowens," a gruel made from the insides of bran and oats and sweetened with honey or treacle and laced with whiskey. "First-footers" would often, in years past, carry buckets of "sowens" that they splashed about the door jambs of those they "first-footed."

Candlemas, the feast of the purification of Mary and the dedication of Jesus, on February 2 and Christmas are linked in an old Scottish weather saying:

"If Candlemas Day be bright and fair

The half of winter is to come and mair.
If Candlemas be wet and foul,
The half of winter's gone at Yule."

# Somalia

*Cid wanaagsan iyo sanad cusub oo fiican!*

Somalia, a small, northeastern African country is one of the poorest and least developed countries in the world. The population is 99 percent Muslim; thus, Christmas is not celebrated much at all.

In Mogadishu, the capital city, the church has Christmas Midnight Mass. Almost every year a *Sacree Representation,* a sacred play, is produced portraying the events of the original Christmas.

Usually foreigners who are Christian celebrate Christmas in a very private way. The different nationalities of the perhaps 3,000 Christians influence the celebrations. Most of these people eat traditional Christmas foods of their nationalities.

Christmas Eve is usually spent with friends playing, eating, and enjoying each other's company while awaiting the highlight, the midnight mass. Christmas Day is usually spent at home, sleeping more than usual and in the afternoon visiting friends.

Homes and churches are decorated with whatever is available. Some people even have a plastic Christmas tree. Christmas cards aren't usually available, but people send other kinds of cards to friends and relatives.

# South Africa

Merry Christmas!
*Geseende Kerfees!* (Afrikaans)
*Ngikufisela ukhisimuzi omuhle!* (Zulu)

South Africa is a multi-ethnic, multi-cultural country: native Africans, Afrikaners originally from Holland, English, Indians, and many others. Customs observed in celebrating Christmas may vary slightly, but people tend to celebrate Christmas in much the same manner as people in Europe or the United States.

Christmas celebrations are usually concentrated around Christmas Eve, Christmas, and Boxing Day. Christmas has a somewhat more somber tone than in many other countries. The holiday finds people traveling many miles to be with family during this time.

Even though Christmas occurs during the sweltering summer days, the idea of the traditional, snowy, European Christmas is still idealized. Anyone who can afford it evacuates the inner parts of the country's sweltering summer heat and takes to the seashores. Flights to the coasts are fully booked until mid-January. Johannesburg offices are virtually deserted except for complaining secretaries.

Stores are decorated as early as November. Many shops in an exclusive northern suburban shopping mall of Johannesburg have displays such as female mannequins dressed in beachwear cavorting through the snow and an ice-laden Christmas tree growing on the beach or male mannequins in cool safari suits with helmets as protection against the hot African sun. They are dusted with snow while nearby is a snow-flecked fir tree. In the downtown shopping areas, it is even hotter, and tiny parks are packed with people seeking relief from the heat. Ice cream vendors do a brisk business. Shoppers loaded down with parcels and bags move slowly through the streets.

Groups of children and families sometimes go around on the evening of the twenty-fourth and sing carols throughout the neighborhood. They usually walk from house to house or sit on the back of a truck and drive slowly through the town. In the cities, a custom dating from the British colonial days and originating in Australia, is still observed. Large groups of people come together in a park or open area; candles are sold to the people who sing carols. This usually occurs about two weeks before Christmas and is called "carols by candlelight."

In some parts of the country, Christmas bands are popular. They are all males and usually originate from churches or from father to son. There are about fifteen to thirty members ranging in age. The band raises money to purchase uniform suits, and they travel through neighborhoods playing Christmas songs for friends and dignitaries several days before Christmas. Their appearance is eagerly awaited.

Christmas decorations tend to be more subdued than in other countries. There are usually no candles in the windows or decorations on doors. Christmas tree decorations are similar to other countries, but perhaps not as extravagant or glittery. Children often make the tree decorations.

People send Christmas cards. Presents are placed under the Christmas tree. The family gathers, and at the midnight hour the father will conduct a short service with readings from the Bible and prayers. Some carols are sung, and then the presents are opened.

Father Christmas appears in stores before Christmas to listen to children's requests for presents. Many families do not include him in the celebration, preferring to bring their children up in a more realistic and humble way with the true message of Christmas.

On Christmas morning, churches often feature a special choir performance. Different groups in the congregation may have additional celebrations like an "oldtime" dinner or a Christmas pageant presented by the children.

The Christmas dinner is usually after morning church service. It often consists of traditional homemade chicken pie, roasted leg of mutton, golden sweet potatoes, cauliflower with cheese sauce, and an assortment of other vegetables. A dessert such as *souskluitjies* or dumplings may be served. Christmas puddings or trifles are often served. Cookies, macaroons, tartlets, and cold ginger beer are common as is watermelon in the afternoon.

Christmas Day is spent quietly and usually with the family at home. After the morning church service and the big dinner, everyone lies down for a nap. Coffee is served, and often everyone will go to the beach in the late afternoon or visit friends. Young people may go around to visit relatives.

Jews and Muslims living in South Africa often wish their Christian friends a very happy holiday. In some places that must remain open, such as hospitals, Jewish or Muslim people will work so that their Christian friends may celebrate the holiday. This favor is returned during holidays of the Jewish and Muslim faiths.

# Spain

*Feliz Navidad!*

The southwestern European country of Spain has a nickname; it is the Land of Festivals, the biggest and most elaborate being Christmas.

## Feast of the Immaculate Conception

The Spanish observe The Feast of the Immaculate Conception beginning on December 8 for an entire week as a fitting prelude to Christmas. Since the Virgin Mary is the patron of Spain, a predominately Roman Catholic country, this special day dedicated to her and the week following are observed on a most elaborate scale. This festival commemorates the fact that Mary is the only human being ever born without sin because she had been chosen to be the Mother of God. In the northern regions of the country, the balconies of houses are decorated with flowers, carpets, and flags, and candles are burned all night in the windows on the eve of the feast.

In the cathedral in the city of Seville, a most unusual ceremony known as the "Dance of the Six" takes place. Since the dance in its various forms is so much a part of the life and spirit of the Spanish people, it is easy to understand why dances are performed as part of an act of worship. The dance is usually performed following Vespers at Easter, on Corpus Christi, and at the Feast of the Immaculate Conception. Ten boys dressed in pale blue satin trimmed in lace, wearing brimmed hats and plumes, sing and dance a beautiful, enchanting liturgical dance.

## Christmas Markets

Christmas markets appear everywhere in Spain, with streets and plazas lined with stalls heaped high with oranges, melons, lemons, flowers of all colors, ribbons, Christmas ornaments, children's toys, and piles of Christmas sweets like *turron* or marzipan. City streets are brilliantly lighted for the season and flooded with laughter, music, and jostling, good-natured men and women. Everywhere eager children run from booth to booth. Gypsies often sell Christmas trees at the markets. As it gets dark, tiny oil lamps are lighted in every house, and among all devout Catholics, the image of the Virgin Mary is illuminated with a taper.

## *Nacimientos*

The Nativity scene called the *nacimiento* or *belenes* holds the place of honor in Spanish homes. Some are made of cardboard and others of plaster. The scene is lighted with candles, and the children dance around it to the music of tambourines and joyously sing the Nativity songs. Included in the scene is the home of Herod at a distance and the wise men far off. Most manger scenes have a small stream where women kneel as they tend to the family laundry, so typical of the scene one might find in rural Spain. In addition to the innkeeper and numerous animals, there are often figures of well-known *toreros* or bullfighters and politicians.

In Catalonia, a hollow tree trunk or Yule log occupies an important place in the family celebration. Called a *tio,* the burlap-covered log is hung up and trimmed with gifts for the children. Inside the trunk are crammed more gifts that tumble forth when the youngsters excitedly beat it with sticks.

In often snowy, northern Spain, many decorate their homes for the holidays with mistletoe and holly, while those in the warmer, southern areas use geraniums and heliotrope. Rural celebrations tend to be more religious than urban ones. One occasionally sees a Santa Claus figure in the cities before Christmas.

Christmas cards are sent, and they usually depict reproductions of paintings of the Nativity or The Three Kings. In some areas, businesses present cards to their customers, wishing them a happy holiday season. Large, commercial organizations like banks send extravagant baskets full of liquor, fruit, and sweets to their important clients.

Another uniquely Spanish custom is the granting of amnesty to military and political prisoners and criminals. On Christmas Eve or a little before then, prison officials accompanied by lawyers, make the rounds of the wards and pardon those with offenses which are not so serious.

## Christmas Eve

*Noche Buena* or Christmas Eve usually is a family affair. It actually begins in the afternoon when towns are bustling with throngs of buyers selecting turkeys, wines, cheese, olives, and assorted fish. Children roam from place to place singing carols and playing instruments such as the *zambomba* made of a flowerpot over which a bladder is drawn like a drum, and through the center of the bladder is a stick that is moved up and down producing a drumming sound.

As evening approaches, crowds diminish, and the Christmas meal is served. A number of courses include cheese, *cardo* that is an edible type of thistle, a salad of red cabbage, a fish dish, usually baked flounder or bream, turkey or capon, and fruit and *turrons.* Each province has its own specialties.

In Sorfa, giant bonfires play an important role on Christmas Eve. Oak barrels, dry grape vines, and logs of juniper add flame and fragrance to the big pyre that burns in each town's main plaza at 7:00 P.M.

At midnight the clocks strike, church bells peal, and everybody goes to *Misa del Gallo,* the Mass of the Cock, the midnight mass. The faithful crowd the churches to take part in a ceremony commemorating Christ's birth. At the height of the service, the priest draws a curtain, revealing the Christ Child in all His glory. The mass differs from region to region. In Segovia, the shepherds attend the *Misa del Gallo* in costumes adorned with jingling sheep bells. Before the traditional Nativity scene, they begin the adoration with joyful leaps into the air. They then do a complicated dance known as the *vuelta de caracol.* In Burgos, the Christmas Eve activities take place outdoors even if it is cold.

Gift-giving is becoming more popular on Christmas Eve, especially in the cities.

## Christmas Day

Christmas Day or *Navidad* finds everyone attending church services where joyous music is played and sung. Patrons receive calls or holiday reminders from washerwomen, postmen, baker's boys, garbage men, and so on who have rendered services during the year. Family servants, as well, receive presents of money. In some areas, the priests and doctors receive gifts, and the wealthier send food and other gifts to less fortunate neighbors.

After the Christmas luncheon, the day is spent in merrymaking, strolling through the streets and plazas, and greeting friends. The luncheon usually includes *puchero olla,* a dish made from chicken, beef, mutton, pigs' feet, bacon, and garlic and served with turkey, goose, fruits and nuts of all kinds, and a rich almond-flavored cake.

Among the traditions during the season in Cadiz, children observe the old rite of swinging at Christmas. Swings are set up in courtyards, and throughout the holidays until Carnival, the three days preceding Ash Wednesday, young people gather in the evening to swing to the accompaniment of song and laughter. The custom of Christmas swinging probably originated in a very old, magical rite, once intended to help the sun in its gradual upward course to the highest point in the summer sky.

## New Year's Eve

*Noche Vieja* or New Year's Eve is a happy time. The *tertulia* or New Year's Eve party is a happy affair for young people who have an unusual way of matching couples for the coming year. This is called the "Urn of Fate," and names of men and women guests are written on slips of paper that are numbered in pairs and then drawn by lot. The man and woman who draw the same number become partners not only for the evening but also for the entire year. Custom demands that the man send the woman flowers or sweets the day after the party, and he is to be her escort to social functions for the next twelve months.

In Madrid, the people go to *Puerta del Sol* in front of the Department of the Interior Building, and when the clock on top of the building strikes midnight, the people swallow twelve grapes, one with each stroke of the hour.

The pig is believed to bring good luck for the New Year because a pig roots in a forward direction. It is considered bad luck to eat turkey, goose, or other fowl on New Year's Eve because fowls scratch backwards.

## New Year's Day

New Year's Day is called *Ano Nuevo.* According to old superstitions, the luck of the entire year depends upon the first day. A gold coin in the pocket means plenty of gold during the next twelve months, while empty pockets predict a lean year ahead. Eating a good meal and drinking good wine symbolize an abundance of good food and drink the whole year. Meeting a beggar is considered bad luck, while coming face to face with a rich man is a good sign. After attending New Year's church services, people go home to enjoy family reunions, feasting, and holiday cheer.

In the Pyrenees, there are usually carnivals on New Year's Day. They tend to be rowdy, festive occasions with lots of singing and dancing in the streets. Mummers' plays are popular where people wear masks of animal heads, particularly bears, and perform humorous skits.

Trials of strength are popular in the Basque country. In the northwest, they select a King of the Wrens similar to a custom in Ireland and England. They hunt a wren and return to the village with it fixed to a long pole. They parade through the streets in triumph.

## Holy Innocents Day

Holy Innocents Day, December 28, commemorates King Herod's ordering the killing of the innocent baby boys after he learned of Christ's birth. Boys light bonfires at the town gateways and select a mayor who enforces law and order by requiring citizens to clean the streets. Fines are imposed for various alleged offenses in order to collect money for the expenses of the celebration.

## *Cabalgata*

On January 5, the *Cabalgata* or Christmas parade takes place. The parade makes its way down the largest and most beautiful avenue in Madrid where miles of white lights on evergreens light the way. Until recently, the Three Kings came mounted on camels, but they now arrive in luxury convertibles instead. The three camels still take part, laden with colorful gifts.

## Epiphany

Epiphany, The Day of the Kings, or *Dia de los Reyes Magos* on January 6 is a very big day in Spain. Little children eagerly anticipate Epiphany Eve when, they are told, the Three Kings travel through Spain with gifts of sweets and goodies for all the good boys and girls. At night children stuff their shoes with straw and place them on the balconies. By morning the Magis' horses or camels have eaten the straw, and in its place the Kings leave toys, cookies, and all kinds of sweetmeats.

It is very traditional to eat a kind of fruitcake called *roscon.* It is delicious eaten plain or with whipped cream and is often eaten for breakfast, lunch, and in the afternoon as a snack. Anyone who discovers a toy in his or her *roscon* will have good luck in the New Year.



3282-TUCK

# Sri Lanka

*Subha Aluth Awrudhak Vewa!*(Singhalese)
*Nathar Puthu Varuda Valthukkal!* (Tamil)

In the Indian Ocean country of Sri Lanka, formerly known as Ceylon, 8 percent of the population is Christian, and the celebration of Christmas has many western customs. Even non-Christians consider this a sacred day honoring the birth of a religious leader.

Advent, the four Sundays before Christmas Eve, is the time of preparation for Christmas, with most of the preparing done the week before Christmas. In some areas, people stop work on Christmas Eve and do not resume until New Year's Day. Schools are out for vacation, and the weather is warm.

Homes and churches are decorated with buntings, stars, bells, artificial holly leaves, and pine branches. Stores decorate, giving themselves a winter look by using cotton wool to represent snow.

Christmas trees are seen usually only in homes, and they are kept up until after New Year's. They are decorated in western fashion with balloons, buntings, and stars.

Christmas cards are exchanged; most cards are the typical European ones, but there are some with local scenes also.

There is a Santa Claus figure called *Natal Seeya* or Christmas Grandpapa. He dresses in the usual red outfit trimmed in fur, and he carries his gifts in a sack on his back.

Christmas plays are popular. Crib or manger scenes are a common sight in Christian homes. Christmas Eve is strictly a religious time as people attend confession and midnight mass where western carols are usually sung. Christmas Day is spent visiting friends and family. Lunch is usually rice and curry with ice cream, puddings, and bananas served after the meal. Oil cakes or *kevun* are also served.

# St. Vincent & The Grenadines

Merry Christmas!

St. Vincent & The Grenadines is composed of thirty-two islands and is a part of the beautiful Windward Islands in the Caribbean. The celebration of Christmas usually begins nine days before Christmas and ends on January 6, Epiphany.

## Nine Mornings

A special way of greeting Christmas in St. Vincent & The Grenadines is the custom started in the 1920s by the Dominican Order of the Catholic Church called the Nine Mornings. This is a novena, a mass held nine days before Christmas in the early morning hours, usually around 5:00 A.M. After mass, the early worshippers wander home, greeting their friends with holiday blessings and doing a bit of window-shopping.

The tradition expands each year. The "Bom Drum" bands, young musicians playing goatskin drums and wooden flutes, began to accompany the people on their walks home. Over the years, the number of walkers grew, and the steel drum band was added. Street dancing also became part of the celebration, giving the whole tradition a carnival-like atmosphere. Street vendors sell drinks, made from ginger and sorrel as well as holiday cakes and sweets. Singers stroll through the streets singing carols too.

The most recent addition to this tradition are the dances held in Kingstown's dance halls on each of the nine mornings before December 25, except Sundays. The music starts at 1:00 A.M.

People decorate their homes, offices, churches, and stores with streamers, balloons, angels, and other Christmas symbols. Christmas trees are popular. There is a large, decorated tree put up in the center of Kingstown, the capital city. Local trees are used as Christmas trees, as there is a government ban on imported trees.

## Serenading

Serenading is a popular tradition at the holiday season. Small children go from house to house singing in groups. They sing carols and recite lines pertaining to Christmas. They are given a small token of money and perhaps some cake and juice. They take the money, divide it up, and buy gifts for themselves.

String band musicians (guitar, cuatro, and mouth organ) serenade from house to house also, singing and playing folk music and Christmas songs. A small token of money is given to them, and the proceeds from this go toward organizing their Christmas parties.

Christmas choirs go from house to house. These groups, usually sponsored by clubs such as the Rotary, notify people of their coming in advance, and they are invited into homes and served snacks and drinks. The tokens given to these groups go to charity.

A rhyme that is popular in the Grenadines at Christmas goes as follows:

"Ladies and Gentlemen of this magnificent residence,
We have just come to put you in remembrance of Christmas.
Christmas comes but once a year,
And everyone must have their share.
Sit down in your rocking chair,
And drink a glass of ginger beer."

Churches or local playgroups present holiday plays. People send Christmas cards. Santa Claus makes an appearance in St. Vincent &



3282-TUCK

The Grenadines, dressed in his red suit, and distributes gifts at gatherings of the Red Cross, Lions, Rotary, and other like organizations.

## Christmas Day

Christmas is very much a family time; members of a family congregate at one member's house, bringing different dishes and spending the day going through old photo albums, renewing promises, and planning the family's future. The dinner usually consists of baked ham, stuffed, baked turkey, roast beef or pork, and stewed mutton accompanied by green peas and rice, local vegetable pies, and side dishes of yams, potatoes, tannias, breadfruit, stewed green peas, plantains, and fresh, local salads. Dessert may be black fruitcake and puddings with locally made drinks such as ginger beer, sorrel, and mauby. The rest of the day is spent listening to music, playing games, and more eating and drinking.

# Sudan

*Wilujeng Natal!* or *I'D Miilad Said ous Sana Saida!*

Only 5 percent of the population of this northeastern African country is Christian. The Sudan is the largest country in Africa and one of the most troubled. The country is an Islamic controlled military junta republic. This radical Islamic regime has caused the deaths of over 2,000,000 of its people through calculated starvation and slaughter. Slavery is another atrocity that is widespread in this country.

Christmas customs are pretty much confined to church celebrations. There are many lively hymns in the tribal languages of Dinka, Nuer, Shilluk, Zande, Naban, Tira, and Baria. Drums of various sizes accompany the singing.

Most people are poor in the Sudan, but on Christmas Day they dress up in new clothes and have a meal with plenty of meat and gravy. There are no special decorations, no Christmas cards, no Christmas trees, and no Santa Claus. After Christmas, the people organize dancing parties in the various tribal styles and costumes.

# Suriname

*Zalig Kerstfeest!* (Dutch)
*Wang swietie Kresnetie!* (Sranangtongo or Creole)

The former Dutch colony of Suriname became independent in 1975. Located in the northeastern part of South America, this country's Christmas celebration is a combination of Dutch and native customs. The population of Suriname is made up of native Indians and descendants of African slaves. There are East Indian immigrants, Indonesian and Chinese immigrants, and the educated, more sophisticated descendants of slaves, the Creolen who live in the capital of Paramaribo and surrounding cities along the Suriname River.

Advent, the period beginning with the fourth Sunday before Christmas Eve, is observed as a time of preparation for Christmas.

As in many European countries, St. Nicholas Day is celebrated on December 6. When Suriname was under Dutch control, St. Nicholas, who comes the night of December 5 to bring presents to good boys and girls, was a white man and his assistants were black. He arrived by ship on a white horse. After 1975 when Suriname gained its independence, St. Nicholas changed into a black man by the name of *Goedoe Pa* or Dearest Daddy. His servants remained black, and instead of hay and carrots in their shoes, children now left homemade cookies and milk for the horse and the servants.

Christmas is celebrated for two days, December 25 and 26. The first day is reserved for the family with the traditional Christmas dinner, visits to church, and the exchange of gifts. Christmas is much more elaborate than it is in Holland; it is more like an American celebration. The second day on December 26, called *Tweede Kerstdag,* is a national holiday, and the day is one of fun, parties, more food, dancing, and dressing up.

Homes, stores, and shop windows are brightly decorated. Some shopping streets and Christmas trees along these streets are illuminated with colored lights. Beautifully decorated trees and manger scenes or cribs are in most homes.

There are many vocal and instrumental concerts in churches and cultural centers, and military and police bands present concerts in places like hospital yards. A few days before Christmas, there is a large gathering on the grassy Independence Square in front of the Government Palace in Paramaribo under the supervision of the Committee of Christian Churches. People sing Christmas carols, prayers are offered, and a priest or other clergyman gives a talk on Christmas.

Midnight mass on Christmas Eve and Christmas Day services are an important part of the celebration. People send Christmas cards to each other. There are no special foods served for Christmas dinner, but many people prefer a dish called *POM* prepared with grated xanthosoma, chicken, butter, salt, spices and herbs. It is served with rice, vegetables, and greens.

Between Christmas and New Year's, there is a lot of partying and celebrating throughout the country. New Year's Eve sees a lot of fireworks, firecrackers, and very lively festivities and all night parties.

# Swaziland

*Khisimusi Iomuhle!* (siSwati)

The smallest country in the southern hemisphere, the tiny southeastern African country of Swaziland is surrounded on three sides by South Africa and on the eastern side by Mozambique. This beautiful, oval shaped country is slightly smaller than New Jersey; the official language is siSwati, a Bantu language, and English is used for government business.

Swaziland is a very religious country that is about 60 percent Christian. The celebration of Christmas begins on Christmas Eve and ends on Boxing Day on December 26. Church services are at midnight and again on Christmas Day at 6:00 A.M., 8:00 A.M., 10:00 A.M., and 11:00 A.M. Christmas is a time when Swazis thank God, known as *Mvelincanati,* for their having survived the past year and ask Him to give them a good New Year.

Father Christmas is called *Babe Khisimusi.* He appears in towns and churches and dresses the same as Santa Claus. In rural areas, parents represent *Babe Khisimusi* by buying presents and hiding them until children awaken on Christmas morning. There is usually a special place chosen to put the presents since most homes do not have chimneys. Some parents in rural areas cannot afford presents, so they try to provide special dishes for Christmas lunch or dinner as a way of celebrating.

Broiled, baked, or steamed chicken or grilled beef or goat accompanied by rice or porridge, greens, carrots, potatoes, shallots, and beets are often served. In the more affluent areas, trifle, a dessert made from cake, Jello, fruit, and custard is prepared.

Christmas plays are performed in churches and schools.

New Year's is celebrated with much feasting and partying.

# Sweden

*God Jul!*

The beautiful Scandinavian country of Sweden has contributed many delightful traditions to the worldwide celebration of Christmas. Christmas is the biggest and longest holiday of the year, the height of the season being Christmas Eve followed by Christmas Day and Boxing Day.

## Advent

The holiday celebrations begin with the Advent season, the four Sundays prior to Christmas Eve. Church attendance swells as people come to sing the well-known Yuletide songs. The first Sunday in Advent is the day when communities decorate their streets and squares with wreaths, garlands, lights, and Christmas trees.

A four-pronged candelabra is used for the Advent candles. The first Sunday, one candle is lit; the second Sunday, two candles are lit, and so on. Advent calendars are also popular in Sweden. An Advent calendar has the first twenty-four days of December on little flaps. Behind each flap or window is a picture, a saying, or sometimes even a treat. These wonderful calendars that help children mark each day until Christmas didn't appear in Sweden until the 1930s. Radio and television stations broadcast daily Advent programs for children.

During Advent, many people hang luminous stars of paper, straw, or perforated metal in their windows. These stars were introduced from Germany around 1910. Candelabra are another popular window decoration.

Swedes like to decorate with candlesticks, table runners, and wall hangings. There are many Christmas symbols used in decorating: Father Christmas figures, angels, straw figures, and straw animals. Christmas trees are decorated with stars, sunbursts, and snowflakes made of straw. Christmas flowers are mostly red: poinsettias, tulips, begonias, and also the pink, white, and pale blue, pungently fragrant Swedish favorite, the hyacinth.

## St. Lucia Day

*Luciadagen* or St. Lucia's Day is celebrated on December 13. Many legends surround St. Lucia, a medieval saint who went about carrying food and drink to the hungry folk in her area. According to tradition, this date on the medieval calendar marked the longest night of the year. It was thus a time when man and beast needed extra nourishment. Originally, only men celebrated this festival with much food and drink. Lucy means light, and this is undoubtedly why lighted candles and lanterns have been associated with this saint who was condemned to death at the stake as a Christian in fourth century, pagan Sicily. Many legends surround St. Lucia. One states that when Lucia was being burned at the stake, the flames would not go near her body when the wood was lighted, and she was killed by the thrust of a sword. Another legend says that St. Agatha, an earlier Sicilian martyr, comforted Lucia in a vision with the words, "Lucia, thou art indeed a light." Another says when Lucia and her mother were converted to Christianity they began to minister to the poor. Because of the fear of discovery, they used to go about at night, and in order to free their hands and in order to see the way, Lucia placed a candle on her head. Just before she was to marry, Lucia gave her entire dowry to a poverty-stricken village, and her fiancé reported her. Many people claimed to see the saint after her death.

St. Lucia wears a white dress, crimson sash, and traditional lingon leaf crown adorned with lighted candles. Lucia morning is celebrated in nearly every Swedish home. The eldest daughter usually portrays Lucia who brings a tray of coffee, saffron rolls, and ginger biscuits to family members still in bed. Every community, office, school, or club chooses a Lucia also. Girls and boys dressed in white, the girls with glitter in their hair and boys with tall, paper, coned hats with stars on them accompany her. They sing traditional Lucia carols.

## Christmas Fairs

The Christmas market in Stortorget Square, the medieval section of Stockholm, is an old-fashioned Christmas fair with booths filled with every possible handmade item fashioned from wood, metal, straw, or textiles as well as homemade candy in bright wrappers. In the center of the historic square rises a tall Christmas tree decorated with large lanterns containing real candles inside.

Christmas crafts are also displayed at the fair held at Skanse, Stockholm's famous outdoor museum, folk-park, and zoological garden. Tree ornaments such as little straw goats, picturesque candelabra known as applesticks, quaint and brightly colored Dalecarlian wooden horses, rustic doilies, hand-woven baskets, and other trinkets are sold.

The making of *pepparkakor,* spicy gingerbread cookies, is very traditional in Sweden. They are often baked from a special family recipe, or you can buy ready-made dough in stores. Even little children help by making gingerbread stars, hearts, men, goats, and all the other traditional designs. Gingerbread houses are also built.

## Christmas Eve

Christmas Eve or *Julafton,* the highlight of the season, is a day when no work should be done other than tending to the livestock. By this day, housewives have to have the house spotlessly clean. The farmer must have his tools indoors in their proper places, or the wandering shoemaker from Jerusalem might pause to rest on them and bewitch them.

A tradition before the main meal called "dipping in the kettle" is popular. The assembled family and guests dip bits of bread into the broth left over after boiling the ham. Traditionally, this bread is eaten for good luck before the feast begins. Toasts are drunk with *glogg,* a concoction of wine, rum, spices, and herbs. It is lighted and poured over lumps of sugar.

The Christmas feast is a smorgasbord made up of traditional dishes such as boiled or baked ham accompanied by some kind of boiled cabbage, jellied pig's feet, herring salad with pickled beetroot, Swedish meatballs, brawn, liver pate, and *lutfisk,* a dish made from fish called ling (that is dried, soaked in lye, and then boiled and served with a cream sauce), mustard, boiled potatoes, and green peas. Another popular dish is *potatiskorf,* a sausage made of potato, pork, beef, and herbs packed into casings. Other treats might be roast goose and prunes, lingonberries stewed in sugar, and rice pudding or porridge called *grot* that often contains a hidden almond whose finder will marry during the coming year. Some porridge is left outside for the *tomte* or Christmas gnome who lives under the floorboard of the house or barn. His job is to look after the family and their livestock. Toward the end of the last century, a Swedish artist began producing greeting cards illustrated with these gnomes, and they were a huge success. The *tomte* has assumed a role similar to Santa Claus, as he comes with presents. In many homes, someone disguised as a *tomte* with a back sack of presents over his or her shoulder, appears on the doorstep on Christmas Eve.

## Christmas Day

Swedes attend church in the small hours of Christmas morning. In former days, it was customary to race in sleds or horse-drawn wagons home from the services. The winner was believed to have the best harvest in the coming year. Today Christmas Day is spent quietly with the family. Parties and get-togethers usually happen from Boxing Day to St. Knut's Day on January 13.

## New Year's

Unlike many countries, Sweden celebrates *Nyarsdagen,* or New Year's Day, very quietly. On New Year's Eve, a few friends may be invited over, or many greet the coming year in front of their television sets. Since the early 1900s, Stockholmers have gathered at Skansen at midnight to hear a reading of the English poet Alfred Lord Tennyson's poem "Ring Out the Old, Ring in the New." When radio became popular in the 1920s, this reading was broadcast throughout the country, a tradition now carried on by television. This may be the reason why most Swedes stay at home on New Year's Eve. Restaurants are fully booked, and some people let off fireworks, but more often, a quiet evening at home prevails.

There are many legends connected with the celebration of New Year's. A Swedish custom that most likely came from Germany is predicting the fortunes of the coming year by melting lead and pouring it into a bowl of cold water. The shape of the resulting lead clump predicts future events. In former days, one would go out into the frozen fields or roads in the dark and stand and listen. If you thought you heard the sound of a scythe cutting grass, it meant a good harvest for the coming year, but if you heard the clang of sword against sword, a war might be close.

## Twelfth Night

January 6 is *Trettondedag Jul,* Twelfth Night, or Epiphany, the day the Magi arrived to see Jesus. In earlier days Twelfth Night pageants telling the Christmas story were commonplace as was the custom of *Stjarngossar* or Star Boys. Wearing white robes with cone-shaped hats, bearing pompoms and symbols of moons and stars, these Star Boys carried white paper stars attached to long poles. Candles illuminated the stars from within. The character of Judas, wearing a huge, false nose and carrying a moneybag jingling with thirty pieces of silver, often accompanied the boys. These customs live on in some communities.

## St. Knut's Day

*Tjugondag Knut* or St. Knut's Day falls on January 13 and brings the Yuletide season to a close. According to legend, St. Knut's Day comes from Canute the Great's laws written between 1017 and 1036. They commanded that there be much feasting between Christmas and Epiphany. This day commemorates the generous spirit of the saint.

Because of his pious nature, his generosity to the poor and the churches, and his building of a magnificent cathedral, he was made a saint and became the patron saint of brotherhoods or unions. People part with their Christmas trees if they have not already done so. All decorations are put away. This is the time for a final party, especially for children. Friends and classmates are sometimes invited over to help dismantle the tree and to eat cakes and candies and play games. When the tree is taken down, all the edible decorations are devoured, and the group lifts the tree and literally tosses it out of the house while singing:

"Christmas has come to an end,
And the tree must go.
But next year once again
We shall see our dear old friend
For he has promised us so."

In the past, this day was an occasion for masquerading. Men and boys dressed as "Old Knut" would prowl about playing practical jokes and doing general mischief. In some parts of the country, this day is the occasion for regular carnivals, especially in the province of Uppland just north of Stockholm.

# Switzerland

*Froeliche Weihnachten!* (German)
*Joyeux Noël!* (French)
*Buon Natale!* (Italian)
*Bun Nadel!* (Romantsch)

Christmas in the glorious, mountainous European country of Switzerland is definitely colored by the customs of the four linguistic regions, German, French, Italian, and Romantsch or Swiss. These different language regions reflect themselves in their cultural differences. The largest linguistic region is German, and many of the customs reflect this fact.

## Advent

Christmas begins with Advent, the four Sundays before Christmas Eve. Families buy or make a pine wreath that is decorated with four large candles. On the first Sunday, the first candle is lit; on the second Sunday, two candles are lit, and so on. Some families read the Christmas story during these times when the candles are lit, and others may listen to music.

Children enjoy the Advent calendar with its twenty-four doors representing the first twenty-four days of December. Each day a child opens a door and discovers a Christmas scene, saying, symbol, or perhaps a surprise such as a piece of candy or a small toy. Often mothers create their own Advent calendars using cookies fastened to a ribbon or using small matchboxes filled with surprises.



3282-TUCK

Switzerland is well known for Christmas cookies called *aenischrabeli* that are baked during Advent. Coming in many shapes, these cookies don't contain butter; therefore, they can be made early, and people like to eat them when they are hard by dipping them into coffee. *Zuri tirggel, basler brunsli,* and *berner lackerli* are other popular cookies made during the Christmas season.

Christmas is very much a family affair, and each family has its own special traditions, its own favorite Christmas food, and its own special Christmas crafts.

## Santa Claus Day

December 6 is St. Nicholas Day, but in many places in Switzerland it is *Samichlaustag* or Santa Claus Day, a day usually celebrated in the family as a children's holiday. Some towns, villages, or churches offer a special service on this day. They will supply a *Samichlaus* who will visit your house. Many fathers or uncles dress the part and play *Samichlaus.* He often visits schools too. In some high schools, a student dresses the part and chides some teachers. Young children are told that *Samichlaus* will visit them, and if they have been good, he will bring them nuts and fruit, but if they have been bad, he will bring them a switch, or he may carry them off in his big bag. Often *Samichlaus* has a companion called *Schmutzli* who is dark-faced and wears a green robe. He threatens the children with the bag. To appease *Samichlaus,* a small child will recite a poem such as this:

"*Santi Nigginaggi* "Santa Claus
h*inder em Ofe Stagg I,* I'm hidden behind the woodstove;
gi*mmer Nuss und Bire* give me nuts and pears
o*nd kumm I wider fire!*" then I'll come out again.

A very important part of the December 6 tradition is the *Grittibanz,* a little bread figure made from eggbread dough. The figure looks a little like a clown, his face and outfit marked with raisins and almonds. Most Swiss bakeries sell them on December 6, but many families make their own. Eating *Grittibanz* for breakfast in December is very popular. In some households it is *Samichlaus* who brings the *Grittibanz.*

Many villages have public festivals on December 5 or 6. In Kussnacht am Rigi, they have the *Klausjagen* that ends in a spectacular procession of people carrying fancy, handmade mitres (bishops' hats) lit from inside. Young men carry bullwhips that they use in a rhythmic fashion, and others carry cowbells, swinging them. In the middle of the procession is *Samichlaus,* accompanied by one or more *Schmutzlis* and a donkey, handing out cookies and nuts. Similar processions occur in other places.

Weeks before Christmas, children write their wish lists for the *Christkindl* or Christ Child and place them in front of their windows or stick them in envelopes for their parents to mail.

## Christmas Eve and Day

Christmas Eve is the time when *Christkindl* will bring the presents. Parents send their children to their rooms or ban them from the room where the tree is being put up. The parents then decorate the tree that usually has real candles. Glass ornaments in different colors, aluminum decorations, apples, chocolates wrapped in silver foil, and many other things are used in the decorating.

While the children are in their rooms, the *Christkindl* may bring the presents, but in the area of Hallwil in the canton of Lucerne, *Christkindl* is a young girl in white who wears a sparkling crown on her veiled head and is accompanied by white-robed children, lighted lanterns, and baskets of gifts. Youngsters await the sound of tinkling bells announcing her arrival at the door. As soon as the *Christkindl* enters the house, the tree candles are lit. She shakes everyone's hand before leaving.

In the French-speaking region of Switzerland, *Père Noël* has a jovial red face and a white beard. He wears a long, fur-trimmed robe and marches through the villages with his wife Lucy who has two long braids and a lace bodice and a bright, silk apron. She wears a round, fur cap and distributes gifts to the girls as *Père Noël* gives them to the boys.

The family gathers round the tree to sing carols or to listen to a recording of Christmas carols before opening the presents. Often the Christmas story is read. After gift opening, the many cookies baked weeks before are brought out. There may be a special drink for the children and wine for adults. Some companies market sparkling grape juice for this occasion so that the children may have a fancy drink also.

Particularly in Roman Catholic families, Christmas Eve ends with attendance at midnight mass. In some areas, all of the people from the different churches meet in one church for a Christmas Eve service.

In the canton of Valais, ringing the church bells on Christmas Eve has developed into a competition with each community in the valley attempting to "outring" each other to show that it has the most beautiful bells.

Christmas Day is a family day, often including attendance at a church service. Some areas of the country will have a dinner of smoked Christmas ham, others venison, and others some other fancy meat.

On December 26, St. Stephen's Day, there are many public festivals. In many places, the festivities for New Year's begin, bringing the old year to a close.

Among the people of the mountain regions, the week between Christmas and New Year's is a visiting week, and it is a common sight to see two or three generations from the same house, all equipped with skis and bound for a social evening at a neighbor's house.

## New Year's Eve

New Year's Eve has a variety of customs also. Children stay up until midnight to toast the New Year with their parents. Many families try to make this a family-centered evening with games for everybody or an evening of reminiscing about the past year by looking at family albums, films, or videos. Many of the unmarried or childless go to parties or dancing. Many families take a brief skiing holiday over New Year's.

## Three Kings Day

Three Kings Day on January 6 concludes the twelve days of Christmas, and this holiday is celebrated mainly within the family also. The center of attention this day is the *Dreikonigskuchen* or Three King's cake, a sweet, yeast dough with raisins. In the cake is a little, plastic figurine or an almond. Whoever gets the piece of cake with the figure or the almond is king or queen for the day. The cake comes with a big, paper crown, and the king or queen wears it and is excused from his or her chores for the day.

# Turkey

*Mutlu Noeller! or Noel'iniz kutlu olsun!*

Turkey is at the crossroads of Europe and Asia. The population is 99 percent Islamic and 1percent Christian and Jew. The Christian community in Turkey consists of approximately 100,000 Orthodox Christians of the Greek and Armenian rites.

Probably the most significant contribution to the worldwide celebration of Christmas from Turkey is in the person of St. Nicholas, from whom the modern image of Santa Claus was fashioned. This fourth-century saint was born in Lycia and became Bishop of Myra. Many miracles have been attributed to his intercession, and he is the patron saint of sailors, travelers, bakers, merchants, and especially children.

In Europe, many people observe December 6, the day St. Nicholas died. In Germany, Switzerland, The Netherlands, and Belgium, men dress in bishops' robes and pose as St. Nicholas, visiting children, examining them on their prayers, urging them to be good, and giving them gifts. The saint's role as gift-giver probably comes from the legend that tells of St. Nicholas giving gold to each of three sisters who did not have dowries and could not get married without dowries. He either dropped bags of coins down the chimney or tossed them in through the window of the girls' home, and the "gifts from heaven" allowed them to marry.

In Germany and Protestant northern Europe, St. Nicholas evolved into Father Christmas. The Dutch brought St. Nicholas to America. The English who had settled in America transformed the saint into the kind, jolly Santa Claus who is known and loved today. The Dutch name for St. Nicholas, *Sinterklaas,* changed into Santa Claus.

Tradition holds that the apostle John brought the Virgin Mary to live in Turkey after the death of Jesus, and they remained there the rest of Mary's life. St. Paul was born in Turkey and wrote his *Epistles* there.

Christmas is celebrated in Turkey much as in the rest of the world. The season begins with Advent and ends with Epiphany. Christmas is not a legal holiday, but Christians do not go to work on this day.

Church services are held, filled with traditional Christmas music, an abundance of candles, and burning incense. In Constantinople, the baptism of Christ is celebrated at Christmas. The head of the church throws a small, wooden cross out to the Bosporous Sea, and three boys swim out after it. The boy who gets the cross is blessed by the priest and is given a present. He takes the cross from door to door and receives many gifts that people give him in gratitude for being permitted to see his sacred object, the rescued cross.

Christmas dinner is a typical Turkish festive dinner of lamb, turkey, or fish served as the main course. Desserts are heavy and sweet, like baklava. Turks are known for being coffee drinkers, and during Christmas, coffee is served with sweetmeats, fruit, and sometimes meat and sour cream that most Turks relish.

Santa Claus is called *Noël Baba* meaning Father Christmas. Christmas trees are used, even among non-Christians. They are most prevalent in large cities.

# United States of America

Merry Christmas!

To write of Christmas in the United States is a difficult undertaking; this country, like Australia and Canada, is truly a melting pot of ethnic and cultural backgrounds.

America's first clearly recorded Yuletide ceremony took place on Virginia soil in 1608 when Captain John Smith and his fellow Virginians had the first real Christmas feast, a gift from the Indians.

Early Europeans who had migrated to America were divided sharply into pro and anti Christmas according to their attitude toward the Reformation. The people who cherished Christmas in their homelands were the English, Dutch, and Germans, members of the Lutheran, Moravian, Episcopalian, and Reformed Churches. Methodists, Baptists, Presbyterians, Quakers, and smaller sects opposed the recognition of Christmas. Many of the first settlers clung closely to tradition, but succeeding generations were eager to cast off the old, and Christmas became one of the symbols of "Americanization." Every nationality that came to the United States added something to the joyous celebration of an American Christmas.

Colonial Christmas was celebrated during the period of December 15 through January 6. Christmas was actually January 5 until 1750. Colonial Christmas was usually not the gift-giving kind. Children got a few toys, but not until the 1800s did Southerners take part at all in exchanging presents.

The first three states to recognize Christmas as a legal holiday were Louisiana and Arkansas in 1831 and Alabama in 1836.

Christmas's particular characteristics today go back to the time of author Charles Dickens in Britain and Washington Irving in America. Victorians instilled the belief that Christmas is a time for families and for the indulgence of children. They also built into the festival nostalgia for Christmases past.

## A "Typical" Christmas

A "typical" American celebrating Christmas might observe much of the following in his or her observance of the holiday.

## Macy's Parade

Macy's Thanksgiving Day Parade in New York heralds the "official" start of the Christmas season in America. Shopping "officially" begins at malls, discount stores, large chain stores, local boutiques, and just about every possible type of commercial establishment. Actually, many stores have had decorations and specials for the holidays for sale for several weeks before this.

## Advent

Advent, the season beginning the fourth Sunday before Christmas Eve, is observed by many, particularly Roman Catholics, Episcopalians, and Lutherans. The Advent calendar showing the first twenty-four days of December is hung. Each day a child opens a door on the calendar, revealing a picture, a saying, or sometimes even a treat such as candy or a small toy. An Advent wreath is either purchased or made. It has four candles on it, usually three purple and one pink. The first Sunday, a candle is lit; the second Sunday, two candles are lit, and so on. A special devotion and Bible reading often accompany the lighting of the candles.

## Christmas Cards and Charities

An important task at the beginning of the season is the addressing of Christmas cards; this is a very popular part of the holiday. An average of ten times as many cards are purchased per person in America as in England. Families and friends are scattered over this vast nation, and the nostalgia of the holidays causes people to want to communicate with loved ones. UNICEF or the United Nations International Children's Emergency Fund sells Christmas cards, the proceeds going to the purchase of rehydration salts and immunizations for children in Third World countries. Many other charities and health support groups such as the American Diabetes Association offer holiday cards for sale. School groups and churches sell cards as well. President David D. Eisenhower sent the first official, presidential Christmas card in 1953. President Eisenhower also broadcast a Christmas message from America's first orbital satellite, the Atlas, on December 19, 1958. The United States Post Office has issued Christmas stamps since 1962.

Christmas seals are used to decorate cards and presents. Emily Bissel, State Secretary of the Delaware Red Cross, in 1907 issued the first Christmas seal in the United States to raise funds to fight tuberculosis.

Charity is an important part of Christmas in the United States. There are over 785,000 public charities in this country and many, many private ones. The Salvation Army collects money outside stores and other buildings during the season. They supply the underprivileged with food and other items for the holidays. The United States Marine Corps has sponsored Toys for Tots for many years. They collect new toys that are distributed to children who might not otherwise receive gifts. In many churches, there are gift trees from which people take an ornament; on the ornament is the name or age and sex of a person who could benefit from some appropriate presents. People bring presents back to the church with the identifying ornament attached. Church groups, schools, and organizations collect food, gifts, and money for the poor.

## Gift-Giving

Gifts are a very important part of the American Christmas. Families, friends, school children, and co-workers exchange gifts. The idea of having a "secret pal" is very popular in schools or businesses. Companies often give Christmas gifts or bonuses to their employees. People give gifts to those who perform services for them during the year such as hairdressers, newspaper delivery people, and clergy. Gifts are wrapped with brightly colored paper and ribbon often purchased from a PTA or other school group's fall money-making project. In recent years, the Internet has become a rich source for holiday shopping, and over 6,500 different Christmas catalogs are prepared for at-home shoppers in the United States, with sales topping forty billion dollars.

Many believe that American Christmases have become too extravagant. The Society to Curtail Ridiculous, Outrageous and Ostentatious Gift Exchanges (SCROOGE) centered in Charlottesville, Virginia, believes that people should never spend more that 1 percent of their annual income on Christmas and never use their credit cards. Another group that believes that we need to simplify Christmas is Alternatives for Simple Living in Sioux City, Iowa.

There is the dilemma of when to open gifts. Most children open theirs on Christmas morning, many times at a very early hour. Some adults open gifts on Christmas morning along with the children or after the children, while others choose to open gifts on Christmas Eve so that the morning may be devoted to the children's gift opening.

## Santa Claus

Santa Claus in his red suit and with his white beard and twinkling eyes begins to appear everywhere. He arrives in towns by various methods: by boat in Maui, Hawaii, by sleigh, helicopter, car, airplane, and horse. Children wait in lines at malls, stores, schools, or nurseries across the country to have their pictures taken as they sit on Santa's knee to tell him what they would like to receive for Christmas. He is often seen ringing bells on the street, trying to collect money for charities, at parties, at performances in churches, in schools, at town halls, or in people's homes.

One of the most important of the American contributions to the worldwide celebration of Christmas is today's Santa Claus figure. St. Nicholas or *Sinterklaas* came over with the Dutch to New Amsterdam and delivered gifts to children on December 5. He wore his vestments and mitre (bishop's hat), and carried his crozier (staff). Knecht Ruprecht, his assistant, who carried a sack into which he would put bad boys, accompanied him. He also carried a handful of rods that he would shake menacingly. Over the years his image gradually became what it is today, and due to calendar changes, he now delivers presents on Christmas Eve, December 24. His appearance and demeanor are the creation of Thomas Nast, the cartoonist who first drew him in 1863 and of the writings of Washington Irving in his *Sketch Book* and Dr. Clement C. Moore in his poem "A Visit from St. Nicholas" often called 'The Night Before Christmas" that was published anonymously in 1823 in the Troy, New York newspaper the *Sentinel.*

Western Temporary Services claims to be the largest source of trained Santas in the country. At the University of Santa Claus, they have trained over 3,000 Santas.

Children write letters to Santa Claus. They may write to Santa in care of Det 2, 11$^{th}$ WS, Elison Air Force Base, Alaska 99702. For over thirty years, these men at this Air Force Weather Squadron have been performing this service. A child writes a letter to Santa; the parent intercepts the letter and writes a reply; the parent then sends the letter of reply plus a stamped envelope to these Air Force men, and the men send the reply back to the child. The letters must reach Alaska by December 10.

Another Santa service offers a reply for $2.00 plus a return envelope. The child sends the letter to Santa Claus House, Santaland, North Pole, Alaska 99705. They will write the reply.

Some children just write to Santa, North Pole. For over fifty years, the U.S. Post Office has had Operation Santa Claus. They collect all of the letters and give them to volunteers who answer them.

Via the Internet, children write to Santa in various ways. There are web sites for this run by older classes in schools who write replies to the younger children via the Internet. There are quite a few web sites for children to contact Santa and get a reply.

Judge John H. Hatcher of the West Virginia Supreme Court brought the law to the defense of Santa Claus with his opinion "Ex parte Santa Claus" in 1927:

> "Let legislators outlaw the law of evolution if they must, let the Constitution be amended till it looks like a patch-work quilt; but rob not childhood of its most intriguing—Santa Claus. Let him be to succeeding generations as he has been to us—a joyous faith of childhood, a pleasant indulgence of parenthood and a happy memory of old age."

On September 21, 1897, in the New York *Sun,* there was an editorial by Francis P. Church addressed to a little, eight-year-old girl named Virginia who had written to the paper saying that some of her friends said that Santa Claus did not exist. She wanted to know if, indeed, Santa did exist. Church's answer is as follows:

"Virginia, your little friends are wrong. They have been affected by the skepticism of a skeptical age. They do not believe except they see. They think that nothing can be which is not comprehensible by their little minds.

All minds, Virginia, whether they be men's or children's, are little. In this great universe of ours man is a mere insect, an ant, in his intellect, as compared with the boundless world about him, as measured by the intelligence capable of grasping the whole of truth and knowledge.

Yes, Virginia, there is a SANTA CLAUS. He exists as certainly as love and generosity and devotion exist, and you know that they abound and give to your life its highest beauty and joy. Alas! How dreary would be the world if there were no SANTA CLAUS! It would be dreary as if there were no Virginias. There would be no child-like faith then, no poetry, no romance to make tolerable this existence. We should have no enjoyment, except in sense and light. The eternal light with which childhood fills the world would be extinguished.



3282-TUCK

Not believe in SANTA CLAUS! You might as well not believe in fairies! You might get your papa to hire men to watch in all the chimneys on Christmas Eve to catch SANTA CLAUS, but even if they did not see SANTA CLAUS coming down, what would that prove? Nobody sees SANTA CLAUS. The most real things in the world are those that neither children nor men can see. Did you ever see fairies dancing on the lawn? Of course, not, but that's no proof that they are not there. Nobody can conceive or imagine all the wonders there are unseen and unseeable in the world.

You tear apart a baby's rattle and see what makes the noise inside, but there is a veil covering the unseen world which not the strongest man, nor even the united strength of all the strongest men that ever lived, could tear apart.

Only faith, fancy, poetry, love, romance, can push aside that curtain and view and picture the supernal beauty and glory beyond. Is it all real? Ah, Virginia, in all this world there is nothing else real and abiding.

No SANTA CLAUS! Thank GOD he lives, and he lives forever. A thousand years from now, Virginia, nay, ten times ten thousand years from now, he will continue to make glad the heart of childhood."

## Holiday Performances

Rehearsals begin for the many Christmas pageants, plays, concerts, and a myriad of other performances given for the holidays. Some of the more popular are Handel's "Messiah," Menotti's "Amahl and the Night Visitors," Dickens "A Christmas Carol," or Robinson's "The Best Christmas Pageant Ever." These may be at schools, churches, community halls, little theaters, or even at Rockefeller Center, Carnegie Hall, or the Kennedy Center.

## Popular Christmas Music

Americans love the old European carols, oratorios, and hymns of Christmas, but there are many popular songs that Americans enjoy that are very American:

"Here Comes Santa Claus Right Down Santa Claus Lane"
"All I Want for Christmas Is My Two Front Teeth"
"Winter Wonderland"
"I Saw Mommy Kissing Santa Claus"
"Rudolph the Red-Nosed Reindeer"
"It's Beginning to Look a Lot Like Christmas"
"Jingle Bell Rock"
"Santa Claus Is Coming to Town"
"Silver Bells"
"White Christmas"

Those are but a few of the popular songs. There are some Christmas carols that are American contributions to the worldwide celebration of Christmas also:

'It Came Upon the Midnight Clear"
"Joy to the World"
"O Little Town of Bethlehem"
"We Three King of Orient Are"
"O Holy Night"

## Holiday Television Shows

The following television shows are eagerly looked forward to each year:

"Rudolph the Red-Nosed Reindeer"
"Frosty the Snowman"
"The Grinch Who Stole Christmas"
"Charlie Brown's Christmas"
"The Night Before Christmas"
"Little Drummer Boy"

"The House Without a Christmas Tree"
"The Gathering"
"The Homecoming"
"Emmet Otter's Jug Band Christmas"
Specials from people like Andy Williams, Perry Como, Bing Crosby, the Osmonds, and Kathie Lee Gifford

## Christmas Movies

Many American movies have become Christmas classics, such as:
"Holiday Inn"
"White Christmas"
"Miracle on 34th Street"
"Going My Way"
"The Bells of St. Mary's"
"Santa Claus. The Movie"
"It's a Wonderful Life"

## Christmas in Uniform

Comedian and entertainer Bob Hope became an important part of the American Christmas when he started his Christmas show on the road in 1941 to entertain military troops abroad and at home. He usually took a big band, some gorgeous starlets, fellow entertainers, and lots and lots of humor. For the many, many years that Bob Hope did this show, Christmas wasn't Christmas without watching Mr. Hope and his troops on television each year.

## Christmas Trees

Christmas trees appear everywhere, sometimes beginning long before the official opening of the holiday season, especially in stores.

The Christmas tree is put up in a place of importance in the home. Some people cut their own trees in the wild, while others purchase them. They range from small, tabletop, artificial trees to fresh evergreens of an infinite variety and size. Many people collect decorations through the years, and their trees are ones of nostalgia and quaintness. Others prefer "designer" trees such as a country tree with calico and wooden decorations or one with velvet, shiny, or extravagant decorations. There are trees of one color scheme or ones created by a decorator and delivered to the door.

Trees are usually topped with an angel, a star, or a Santa Claus. In 1918 the first commercially made Christmas ornaments went on sale, and since then Christmas tree decorations have been very creative and varied. Many people take their trees down after New Year's Day, while others wait until the end of the Twelve Days of Christmas on January 6. People who purchased live trees plant them; others have their trees recycled; others take them down and store them in a box until the next year.

German Hessian soldiers introduced Christmas trees to Americans during the Revolutionary War. The first Christmas tree was set up in the White House in 1856 by Franklin Pierce. Calvin Coolidge lit the first national Christmas tree on the White House lawn, a custom repeated each year since..

The idea of a public or community tree started in the United States when, in 1909 in Pasadena, California, an illuminated tree was placed atop Mount Wilson. A sixty-foot tall tree was placed in Madison Square Garden in New York City in 1919. Many communities, town, and cities have their own public trees, usually located in a central place to be enjoyed by all. These are often the scenes of Christmas events such as concerts or other performances. Many "living Christmas trees" in communities and churches feature singers arranged on risers in the shape of a Christmas tree. In 1926, one of the oldest living things in the world, a giant Sequoia tree standing in King's Canyon National Park near Sanger, California, was named the "Nation's Christmas Tree." The tree stands 267 feet tall with a circumference of 107 feet. It is believed to be



3282-TUCK

about 4,000 years old. It is, of course, too large to decorate, but a wreath is laid at its base where Christmas services are held.

## Christmas Decorations

Lights have always played an important part in the American Christmas. At first, candles were used. The first electrically lit Christmas tree was seen in New York City in the home of Edward Johnson, a colleague of Thomas Edison's in 1882. We went from tiny, pointed tip bulbs to elongated bulbs to lights of figures like Popeye and Dick Tracy to flashing lights to bubble lights to midget, flashing lights. Many people decorate the outsides of their homes in extravagant displays of lights featuring Biblical figures, cartoon figures, etc. People outline their homes with bright lights. Streets are decorated with greenery, wooden decorations, and bright lights. In recent years, a new tradition has begun across the country; one of the most extravagant is the Winter Festival of Lights at Oglebay Park in Wheeling, West Virginia. Each year beginning in November, the beautiful, 1,460 acre municipal park boasts light displays of over one million lights. People come from all over to drive slowly through the park and to view the displays, admiring the many scenes.

Homes, churches, streets, schools, offices, and stores are decorated for the holiday season. Greenery of every kind is used along with ribbons, ornaments, candles, fruit, and decorative objects of all kinds.

In 1825, a Charleston, South Carolina diplomat, Joel Roberts Poinsett, became intrigued with some brilliant red flowers found all over the Mexican countryside. He cultivated cuttings at his home in Charleston. Thus began the worldwide use of the poinsettia as the Christmas flower.

## Christmas Stockings

As Christmas draws near, people hang stockings above a fireplace or at some other convenient place. Some use everyday socks, while other have ornate, handmade stockings. In Washington Irving's *Knickerbocker History of New York,* written in 1809, there is the first mention of the hanging of Christmas stockings in America. In 1810, an engraving by prominent New York artist Alexander Anderson shows a fireplace with two oversized stockings at each side, one stuffed with toys, oranges and sugarplums, the other with sticks. Above the mantel are pictures of a little girl with lots of toys and a sad little boy with a stick in his buttonhole. Stockings were the sole repository for gifts for quite a few years, but then Christmas trees became popular, and gifts were also placed under the trees.

People often stuff stockings with amusing gifts or ones selected for a person's special interests such as his hobbies. Miniatures are often placed in stockings.

## Christmas Food

Food plays an important part in the celebration of Christmas. It would be ludicrous to attempt to select a "typical" Christmas dinner for the entire United States. It would be safe to say that fruitcake fits into most people's Christmas somehow. Turkey or ham usually makes up the meat course. Goose, duck, or lamb is sometimes served. There is usually a stuffing, a variety of vegetables according to one's taste and location, and for dessert there might be cake, plum pudding, pies, and much more. The variety is as large as is the country.

## Unique Customs

Medieval mumming still exists in Alabama, Maryland, Kentucky, and West Virginia and features men in masks and costumes serenading, skylarking, going from house to house, or marching in the streets.

The first Mummers Parade on New Year's Day in Philadelphia was in 1901 and has continued yearly.

Colonial Williamsburg, Virginia, has a big Christmas celebration. Services are held in Baruton Parish Church; crafters sings Christmas carols; a pre-Christmas mistletoe dance is held. There are concerts and the firing of Christmas guns, visits to plantations, and reenactments of Colonial sports such as bowling, cudgeling, fencing, foot races, wrestling, juggling, hoop races, and acrobatics. There is also a Yule log ceremony and a lighting of the community tree.

At the Moravian development of Old Salem in Winston Salem, North Carolina, love feasts are held Christmas Eve afternoon. At these ceremonies, women serve buns and coffee to all and then pass out candles that are placed in the windows with prayers that the Christ Child will enter. Later on, adults have their own leave feast with more buns and coffee. This Moravian town is often called "The Christmas City." They produce beeswax, homemade candles with rufflled holders or "petticoats." Moravian many-pointed stars are everywhere, lighted with candles or electric lights.

For almost fifty years, the Santa Claus Express train has run from Pikeville, Kentucky to Kingsport, Tennessee. Whole families camp in poplar forests by the tracks the Friday night before Thanksgiving weekend. When the engineer spots people, he slows down, and Santa and his helpers throw candies and toys out on the track to the children who run along behind the train with paper bags in hand. These mostly Kingsport businessmen deliver over twelve tons of candy and gifts in the 110 minute run.

Christmas boat parades take place in places like Ft. Lauderdale, Florida and Charleston, South Carolina.

Chicago hosts a month long celebration of Christmas Around the World in which many ethnic groups provide the food, dance, music, crafts, and pageantry of each country.

## Place Names

The American love of the Christmas celebration is reflected in the following geographical names:

Christmas, Gila County, Arizona
Christmas, Orange County, Florida
Christmas, Lawrence County, Kentucky
Christmas, Bolivar County, Mississippi
Christmas, Roane County, Tennessee
Santa Claus, Indiana
Christmas Village, Oregon

## New Year's Eve

The celebration of New Year's in the United States is filled with parties, dances, family get-togethers, firecrackers and fireworks, watching the ball lower exactly at midnight in Times Square in New York City, and the song "Auld Lang Syne." Special foods are often eaten for good luck in the New Year such as red rice and beans or other regional favorites. Most people take down the holiday decorations on New Year's Day, while some leave them up until the twelfth day of Christmas, January 6.



282-TUCK

# Wales

*Nadolig Lawen!* (Welsh)
Merry Christmas!

Christmas in the beautiful hills and valleys of Wales, located in the western part of the British Isles on the Irish Sea, is filled with fascinating legends and beautiful music.

Each year *Eisteddfoddes* a contest for poems and music written in Welsh, takes place when people gather to sing carols, thousands of voices led by dozens of trained, caroling choirs. Contests are held to find the best music for the words of a song. The winner's chorus will sing the song that year. If it's good, it will be adopted and will be sung the next year by all of the carolers.

## Old Customs

As mentioned, carol singing has been popular in Wales for generations. At *Plygain,* the early Christmas morning church service named for the crowing of the rooster, begins at 3:00 A.M. or 4:00 A.M. It was common for young men to accompany the rector to the service using lighted torches. After the service, the procession again led the rector back to the rectory. To bide their time until church began, young people would make treacle toffee and decorate their houses with freshly gathered mistletoe and holly. The mistletoe was considered magical and served as a protector of the house. The holly, a symbol of eternal life, was displayed along with ivy, rosemary, and bay leaves. The young people danced to the music of a harp helping them to revel before the serious Christmas morning church service.

Churches were lighted with as many as several hundred candles brought by the parishioners to recreate the ancient Festival of Light. The service may have lasted until 8:00 A.M or 9:00 A.M. This custom has managed to survive in some areas; in other areas because of its simplicity and beauty, it is being revived.

Years ago, a plough was brought into the house and placed under the table to announce the beginning of Christmas and the ceasing of work. The plough was wetted down with beer to show that even though the plough wasn't being used for a short while, its services were not forgotten and should be rewarded. The rest of the day was spent in feasting and merrymaking, in rough and tumble games of football or squirrel and rabbit hunting.

The unique custom called "Grey Mary" or "Mari Lwyd" originated in southern Wales. "Mari Lwyd" was the name given to a horse which was supposedly turned out of its stable to make room for the holy family, and the horse has been looking for shelter ever since.

To represent "Mari Lwyd," a horse's skull was mounted on the end of a five-foot long pole that was covered by a big sheet. Bits of black cloth in the shape of ears were sewn onto the head, and the skull itself was decorated with ribbons. Pieces of glass were placed in the eye sockets. A man stood beneath the sheet and worked the horse's jawbone so that it made a snapping sound.

A procession formed at one end of the town with "Mari Lwyd" at the front. When they reached a house, they stopped, banged on the door with a stick, and sang verses of a song that those inside had to answer. When the people became too tired to continue or forgot the words, the "Mari Lwyd" went around biting people. If you were held captive, the only means of release was to pay a fine. This custom has almost disappeared, but still may be seen in a few places.

A similar practice called *Hodening* used to be played by children during the Christmas season. A carved, wooden horse's head with big eyes and snaggleteeth was attached to a stick with which the head was carried. Fastened to the head of the "horse" was a sheet that covered two boys who formed the animal's body. Groups of revelers would walk the streets at night trying to frighten people. Often the children were invited in for cakes and cider. *Hodening* originated in medieval Christmas miracle plays in which there was usually a prankish character riding a hobbyhorse.

## New Year's

Before dawn on New Year's Day, children used to make it a practice to carry about a jug of water that had been freshly drawn from a nearby well. Carrying a sprig of boxwood or some other kind of evergreen, they roamed the village, singing and sprinkling everyone they met, wishing them the best of the season. In paying their respects to those who were not yet awake, they knocked on doors to rouse friends and neighbors and serenaded them with the verses of an ancient song known as the "newe water" carol.

Stray dogs are a threat on New Year's Eve. The *Cwn Annwm* are spirit hounds passing through the air in pursuit of victims. Their howling is regarded as an omen of death. These dogs have been described in various ways: small dogs as white as drifted snow with tiny ears rose-colored on the insides and eyes glittering like the moonbeams; black and very ugly dogs with huge, red spots; red dogs with large, black patches like splashes of ink. The worst are blood red in color and dripping with gore, while their eyes look like liquid fire. Still others are reported to be liver colored, all spots and spangles of red and white.

Christmas in Wales today is less like the older customs or beliefs and more like that observed by the British. The Christmas dinner is usually turkey or ham with Christmas pudding or Christmas cake for dessert. People listen to the British monarch's (Queen Elizabeth II) message to the Commonwealth. In general, Christmas is a family celebration with the usual exchange of greetings, Father Christmas, performances, gifts, and music, music, music.

One of the most important of Welsh contributions to the worldwide celebration of Christmas is the short story "A Child's Christmas in Wales" by the Welsh writer Dylan Thomas. It is often dramatized.

# Selected Bibliography


*An African Christmas.* Amecea Pastoral Institute. Eldoret, Kenya: GABA Pub, 1983.

Anderson, Leone Castell. *Christmas Handbook.* Elgin, Illinois: Child's World, 1984.

Anderson, Leigh Michelle. The Country That Stole Christmas. *The Japan Times.* 23 December 1987, 16.

Askim, Ole. Yuletide with Old Roots: Norwegian Christmas Traditions. *The Norseman No. 6.*, 1971.

*Austria Folk Customs.* Vienna: Federal Chancery. Federal Press Service, 1985.

Badger, Lorraine. *Christmas Tree Ornaments.* New York: Sedgewick Press, 1985.

Barber, Mary, and Flora McPherson. *Christmas in Canada.* Toronto: Dent, 1959.

Bird, Malcolm, and Alan Dart. *The Christmas Handbook.* Woodbury, New York: Barron's, 1986.

Brady, Agnes M., and Margarite Márquez de Moats. *La Navidad: Christmas in Spain and Latin America.* Lincolnwood, Illinois: National Textbook, 1986

Bucher, Richard P. *The Origin and Meaning of the Christmas Tree.* 29 July 2000. *<http://www. Ultranet.com/~tlclcms/chrtree.htm>*

Burnett, Ermin, and Roger Burnett. *Christmas in the Virgin Islands.* British Virgin Islands, 1983.

Bjaaland, Pat. Christmas in Norway. *The Norseman No. 6.,* 1985.

Campbell, Margaret. *Other Yuletides, Other Lands.* El Monte, California, 1948

Charlmers, Irena, and Friends. *The Great American Christmas Almanac.* New York: Viking, 1988.

*Christmas Around the World.* 25 Aug. 2000 *<http://the-north-pole.com>*

*Christmas Around the World: A Celebration.* Poole, Dorset, England: New Orchard Editions, 1985.

*The Christmas Book: a Treasury of the Sights, Sounds, Crafts, Tastes, and Joys of the Season.* Ortho Books, 1987.

*Christmas in Brazil.* Chicago: World Book, 1991.

*Christmas in Canada.* Chicago: World Book, 1994.

*Christmas in Denmark.* Chicago: World Book, 1986.

*Christmas in Hungary.* 11 July 2000< *http://www.geocities.com/Wellesley/3656/ch>*

*Christmas in Iceland.* 2 Aug 2000 <*http://www.eve.org/christmas/Iceland.htm*>

*Christmas in Ireland.* Chicago: World Book, 1985.

*Christmas in Italy.* Chicago: World Book, 1996.

*Christmas in Latin America.* Washington: Pan American Union, 1968.

*Christmas in New England.* Chicago: World Book, 1984.

*Christmas in Russia.* Chicago: World Book, 1992.

*Christmas in Spain.* Chicago: World Book, 1996.

*Christmas in the Big Igloo: True Tales from the Canadian Arctic.* Yellowknife, Northwest Territories,Canada: Outcrop, 1983.

*Christmas in the Holy Land.* Chicago: World Book, 1987.

*Christmas in Today's Germany.* Chicago: World Book, 1993.

*Christmas in Zion.* Minneapolis: Association of American Laestadian Congregations, 1984.

Conway, Judith. *Manos: South American Crafts for Children.* Chicago: Follett, 1978.

*Cooking With Ease in English and Portuguese.* Rio de Janeiro, Brazil: The Woman's Auxiliary to the Stranger's Hospital, 1970.

Count, Earl W. *4,000 Years of Christmas.* Berkeley, California: Ulysses Press, 1997.

Crawford, Anne. An Arctic Christmas. *Canadian Geographic.* December 1988-January 1989, 24-9.

Dempsey, Hugh A. *Christmas in the West.* Saskatoon, Saskatchewan: Western Producers Prairie Books, 1982.

Drehman, Vera. *Holiday Ornaments from Paper Scraps.* New York: Hearthside, 1970.

Ebanks, Alan. Once upon a Cayman Christmas. *Newstar The News Magazine of the Cayman Islands.* December 1987, 25-28.

Edwards, Gillian Mary. *Hogmanay and Tiffany: The Names of Feasts and Fasts.* London: Bles, 1970.

*A Family Christmas.* Pleasantville, New York: The Reader's Digest Association, 1984.

Foley, Daniel J. *Christmas the World Over; How the Season of Joy and Goodwill Is Observed and Enjoyed by People Here and Everywhere.* Philadelphia: Chilton, 1963.

Fowler, Virginia. *Christmas Crafts & Customs Around the World.* Englewood Cliffs, New Jersey: Prentice-Hall, 1984.

Gardner, Horace J. *Let's Celebrate Christmas; Parties, Plays, Legends, Carols, Poetry, Stories.* New York: A.S. Barnes, 1940.

Golby, J.M., and A.W. Purdue. *The Making of the Modern Christmas.* Athens, Georgia: University of Georgia Press, 1986.

Gulevich, Tanya. *Encyclopedia of Christmas.* Detroit: Omnigraphics, 2000.

Hamar, Haraldur J. Christmas in Iceland: The Long Family Affair That Keeps Winter at At Bay. *Iceland Review.* April 1979,14-18.

Harvey, Roland. *Roland Harvey's New Book of Christmas.* Hawthorne, Victoria, Australia: The Five Mile Press, 1986.

Henderson, Yorke. *Parents' Magazine's Christmas Holiday Book: The Story of* Christmas with a Treasury of Favorite Reading, Music, Cookery, and Holiday *Activities.* New York: Parents, 1972.

Henriksen, Vera. *Christmas in Norway.* Oslo: Royal Norwegian Ministry of Foreign Affairs, 1986.

Hewison, Robert. Pantomania: From the Million Pound Show to the Family Outing. *The Sunday Times.* 6 December 1987, 61.

Hole, Christina. *Christmas and Its Customs, a Brief Study.* New York: M. Rarrows, 1958.

A Home in Nome *Alaska.* December 1987, 14.

Hooper, Van. *Christmas Around the World.* Milwaukee: Ideals, 1958.

House, Charles. *The World at Christmas.* New York: Bruce, 1969

Hrnièko, and Jidita Jechová. Christmas with Its Thousand Smells. *Welcome to CzechoslavakiaTourist Review No. 4.* Vinohradská, 1987.

Ickis, Maraguerite. *The Book of Christmas.* New York: Dodd Mead, 1960.

*The Irish Christmas Book.* Dover, New Hampshire: Blackstaff Press, 1985

*Joy Through the World.* Produced in Cooperation with the U.S. Committee for UNICEF. New York: Dodd, Mead, 1985.

"Junkaroo": A Booklet of the Exhibition Held at the Art Gallery, Jumbey Village 13 *February–3 March 1978.* Bahamas: Minister of Education and Culture, 1978.

Kainen, Ruth Cole. *America's Christmas Heritage.* New York: Funk & Wagnalls, 1969.

Kalman, Bobbie, and Lisa Smith. *We Celebrate Christmas.* New York: Crabtree, 1985.

Kane, Harnett T. *The Southern Christmas Book: The Full Story from Earliest Times to Present: People, Customs, Conviviality, Carols, Cooking.* New York: McKay, 1958.

Kay, Sophie. *Menus from Around the World.* Milwaukee: Ideals, 1976.

Kelley, Emily. *Christmas Around the World.* Minneapolis: Carolrhoda, 1986.

Kerina, Jane. *African Crafts.* New York: Lion Press, 1970.

Kraus, Barbara, comp. *The Cookbook of the United Nations.* New York: Simon & Schuster, 1970.

Lankford, Mary D. *Christmas Around the World.* New York: Morrow Junior Books, 1995.

Lawhead, Alice Slaikeu. *The Christmas Book.* Westchester, Illinois: Crossway Books, 1985.

Lehane, Brendan, and Editors of Time-Life. *The Book of Christmas.* Alexandria, Virginia: Time-Life, 1986.

Megas, George A. *Greek Calendar Customs.* Athens, 1958.

*A Merry Christmas in Over 300 Languages.* 15 July 2000 <*http://www.flw.com/merry.*>

Metcalfe, Edna, comp. *The Trees of Christmas.* Nashville: Abingdon, 1969.

Miles, Clement A. *Christmas Customs and Traditions: Their History and Significance.* New York: Dover, 1976.

Montpetit, Raymond. *Le Temps des Fêtes au Quebec.* Montreal: Les Éditions de L'Homme, 1978.

Morimoto Etsuko. Background of Japanized Christmas Celebrations. *The Japan Times.* 23 December 1987.

Muir, Frank, and Jamie Muir. *A Treasury of Christmas.* London: Robson Books, 1981.

Munro, Roxie. *Christmastime in New York City.* New York: Dodd, Mead, 1987.

Newman, Thelma R. *Contemporary African Arts and Crafts.* New York: Crown, 1974.

Ortiz, Elisabeth Lambert. *The Complete Book of Caribbean Cooking.* New York: M. Evans, 1973.

Perry, Margaret Curtis. *Christmas Magic: The Art of Making Decorations and Ornaments.* Garden City, New Jersey: Doubleday, 1964.

Pettit, Florence. *Christmas All Around the House: Traditional Decorations You Can Make.* New York: Crowell, 1976.

Prosperous Christmas Precedes A New Year. *The Cayman Pilot*. 23 December 1983, 1.

Purdy, Susan. *Christmas Cooking Around the World.* New York: Franklin Watts, 1983.

*Christmas Decorations for You To Make.* Philadelphia: Lippincott, 1965.

Rand, Christopher. *Christmas in Bethlehem and Holy Week at Mount Athos.* Oxford: Oxford University. Press, 1963.

Ray, John Bernard. *Christmas Holidays Around the World.* New York: Comeet Press, 1959.

Ridley, Jacqueline, ed. *Christmas.* Poole, Dorset, England: Blandford, 1978.

Ruland, Josef. *Christmas in Germany.* Bonn: Hohwachat, 1978.

Sandler, Bea. *The African Cookbook.* New York: World, 1970.

Sansom, William. *A Book of Christmas.* New York: McGraw-Hill, 1968

*Santa's Net Around the World.* 21 Aug. 2000 *<http://www.santas.net.com>*

Sheraton, Mimi. *Visions of Sugarplums: A Cookbook of Cakes, Cookies, Candies, and Confections from All the Countries That Celebrate Christmas.* New York: Random House, c1968.

Shull, Brian. *The National Trust Guide to Traditional Customs of Britain.* Exeter: Webb & Bower, 1985.

Sider, Gerald M. *Mumming in Outport Newfoundland.* Toronto: New Hogtown Press, 1977.

Silverthorne, Elizabeth. *Christmas in Texas.* College Station, Texas: Texas A & M, 1990.

Snyder, Phillip V. *The Christmas Tree Book: The History of the Christmas Tree and Antique Christmas Tree Ornaments.* New York: Viking, 1976.

*December 25th: The Joys of Christmas Past.* New York: Dodd, Mead, 1985.

Stevens, Patricia Bunning. *Merry Christmas! A History of the Holiday.* New York: Macmillan, 1979.

Tamayo, Juan O. "Happy Holidays? Not Likely for Most Cubans" Knight-Ridder: Tribune News Service. 23 December, 1995.

Telemaque, Eleanor Wong. *Haiti Through Its Holidays.* New York: Blyden, 1980.

Tests of Courage *Alaska.* December, 1988, 28.

Tonn, Maryjane Hooper. *Christmas Around the World.* Milwaukee: Ideals, 1974.

*Treasured Polish Customs and Traditions: Carols, Decorations, and a Christmas Play.* Minneapolis: Polante, n.d.

Tucker, Kristin M., and Rebecca Lowe Warren. *Celebrate the Wonder: A Family Christmas Treasury.* New York: Ballantine, 1988.

*The United States Women's Group in Jamaica Present Festivals and Recipes.* Kingston, Jamaica, 1970.

Urlin, Ethel. *Festivals, Holy Days, and Saints' Days: A Study in Origins and Survivals in Church Ceremonies and Secular Customs.* Detroit: Omnigraphics, 1992.

Voth, Norma Jost. *Festive Christmas Cookies.* Scottdale, Pennsylvania: Herald, 1982.

Waldo, Myra. *The Complete Round-the-World Cookbook.* New York: Doubleday, 1954.

Watts, Franklin, ed. *The Complete Christmas Book.* New York: Franklin Watts, 1958.

Waxman, Maron, ed. *Christmas Memories with Recipes.* New York: Farrar, 1988.

Weiser, Franz Xaver. *The Christmas Book.* New York: Harcourt, 1952.

Wernecke, Herbert. *Celebrating Christmas Around the World.* Philadelphia: Westminster, 1962.

*Christmas Customs Around the World.* Philadelphia: Westminster, 1959.

Wilson, Robina Beckles. *Merry Christmas: Children at Christmastime Around the World.* New York: Philomel, 1983.

*Yule Jól in Iceland.* 2 Aug. 2000 <http://www. Simnet.is/gardarj/yule5.htm>

# Correspondence

The following have been arranged alphabetically according to the name of the country.

Embassy of Antigua & Barbuda
Intelsay Building
3400 International Drive, N.W. #2H
Washington, D.C. 20008-3098

Antigua & Barbuda National Archives
Long Street
St. John's
Antigua
Bridget Harris

Embassy of Australia
1601 Massachusetts Avenue, N.W.
Washington, D.C. 20036
F. Rawdon Dalrymple

Embassy of Belgium
3330 Garfield Street, N.W.
Washington, D.C. 20008
Renilde Loeckx, First Secretary
Press and Information

The Committee for Culture
17A Stamboliyski Boulevard
Sofia 1000, Bulgaria

Embassy of the Peoples' Republic of Bulgaria
1621 22nd Street, N.W.
Washington, D.C. 20008

Maria Elena Mendoza
Jefe Depto
Relaciones Públicas
Fundacion
Cema-Chile

Opinion Department
China Daily
2 Jintai Xilu
Beijing
The People's Republic of China

Embassy of the Czechoslovak Socialist Republic
3900 Lennean Avenue, N.W.
Washington, D.C. 20008

Embassy of Cyprus
2211 R Street, N.W.
Washington, D.C. 20008

Ministry of Foreign Affairs
Press and Cultural Relations Department
Christiansborg DK-1218
Copenhagen K.
Denmark

Embassy of Denmark
3200 Whitehaven Street, N.W.
Washington, D.C. 20008
Eigel Jorgensen

Embassy of Finland
3216 New Mexico Avenue, N.W.
Washington, D.C. 20016
Mrs. Pirkko Liisa O'Rourke, Cultural Counselor

L'Ambassade de France
Service Culturel
4101 Reservoir Road, N.W.
Washington, D.C. 20007

Embassy of Greece
Press & Information Office
2211 Massachusetts Avenue, N.W.
Washington, D.C. 20008
Achilles Paparsenos, Press Attaché

Greek Orthodox Church "Holy Trinity"
30 Race Street
Charleston, S.C. 29403
Rosa Paulatos, Secretary

Embassy of Guatemala
2220 R Street, N.W.
Washington, D.C. 20008

Embassy of Iceland
2022 Connecticut Avenue, N.W.
Washington, D.C. 20008
Stefan L. Stefánsson

Embassy of Jamaica
1850 K Street, N.W., Suite 355
Washington, D.C. 20006
Cecile R. Clayton

Office of the Prime Minister
1 Devon Road, P.O. Box 272
Kingston 6, Jamaica

Embassy of Japan
2520 Massachusetts Avenue, N.W.
Washington, D.C. 20008
Nobuo Matsunaga, Ambassador

Jordan Information Bureau
2319 Wyoming Avenue, N.W.
Washington, D.C. 20008

Embassy of Lithuania
2622 16th Street N.W.
Washington, D.C. 20009
Ramune Dainora, Special Assistant to the Ambassador

Conseil General
Direction Generale Des Services Departementaux
Direction Du Developpement
Bureau Du Developpement Culturel Et Sportif
Department De la Martinique

Archbishop's House
25/82 Street
Mandalay 05071
Myanmar
Mgr. Joseph Daniel
Fr. Raphael Kyaw San

Royal Netherlands Embassy
4200 Linnean Avenue, N.W.
Washington, D.C. 20008
Marina Kooren Secretary
Press and Cultural Affairs

Institute of Archeology and Anthropology of the Netherlands Antilles
6-B Johan van Walbeeckplein
Willemstad
Curacao
Netherlands Antilles
Rose Mary Allen, Anthropologist AAINA

Embassy of Peru
1700 Massachusetts Avenue, N.W.
Washington, D.C. 20036
Rosa Maria Wallach, Civil Attaché
Cultural Department

The Roman Catholic Archbishop of Manila
121 Arzobispo Street
P.O. Box 132
Manila, Philippines His Excellency Jaime L. Cardinal Sin

Embassy of the Philippines
1617 Massachusetts Avenue, N.W.
Washington, D.C. 20036

Embaixada de Portugal
2125 Kalorama Road, N.W.
Washington, D.C. 20008

Ambassador of the Republic of Rwanda
1714 New Hampshire Avenue, N.W.
Washington, D.C. 20009
Aloys Uwimana, Ambassador

Saint Vincent and the Grenadines Tourist Office
801 Second Avenue, 21st Floor
New York, New York 10017
Madge Morris

Curia Vescovile
Casella postale 273
Mogadiscio, Somalia
Fr. Georgio Bertin, Diocesan Administrator

Embassy of South Africa
3051 Massachusetts Avenue, N.W.
Washington, D.C. 20008
Anso Rabe, Librarian

Central Office-Embassy of Spain
2600 Virginia Avenue, N.W.
Washington, D.C. 20037

St. Sebastian's Church
Moratuwa
Sri Lanka
Rev. Benedict Jayatilake

Embassy of the Republic of Suriname
4301 Connecticut Avenue, N.W.
Washington, D.C. 20008
Daisy E. Plaat, Cultural Section

Embassy of the Kingdom of Swaziland
3400 International Drive, N.W., Suite 3M
Washington, D.C. 20008
Mrs. L.A. Nhlabatsi, Ambassador

Regina Bendix, PhD
7414 SE 18th
Portland, Oregon 97202
(Switzerland)

Turkish Embassy
1606 23rd Street N.W.
Washington, D.C. 20008
Benki Dibek, Director, Information Center

# Index

9 780738 840376